The Literacy Jigsaw Puzzle
Assembling the Critical Pieces of Literacy Instruction

Beverly Tyner

INTERNATIONAL
Reading Association
800 BARKSDALE ROAD, PO BOX 8139
NEWARK, DE 19714-8139, USA
www.reading.org

The International Reading Association attempts, through its publications, to provide a forum for a wide spectrum of opinions on reading. This policy permits divergent viewpoints without implying the endorsement of the Association.

Executive Editor, Publications   Shannon Fortner
Acquisitions and Developmental Editor   Tori Mello Bachman
Managing Editor   Christina M. Terranova
Editorial Associate   Wendy Logan
Design and Composition Manager   Anette Schuetz
Design and Composition Associate   Lisa Kochel

Cover   Design, Lise Holliker Dykes; Art, yienkeat and Aleksandr Bryliaev at Shutterstock.com

The publisher would appreciate notification where errors occur so that they may be corrected in subsequent printings and/or editions.

Library of Congress Cataloging-in-Publication Data

Tyner, Beverly.
  The literacy jigsaw puzzle: assembling the critical pieces of literacy instruction / Beverly Tyner.
      p. cm.
  Includes bibliographical references and index.
  ISBN 978-0-87207-439-2
  1. Language arts--United States. 2. Reading comprehension--United States. 3. Literacy--United States. I. Title.
  LB1576.T96 2012
  372.6--dc23
                                   2012025335

Suggested APA Reference

Tyner, B. (2012). *The literacy jigsaw puzzle: Assembling the critical pieces of literacy instruction.* Newark, DE: International Reading Association.

CONTENTS

ABOUT THE AUTHOR

Beverly B. Tyner, EdD, is an educator with more than 30 years of experience. Her career includes positions as a teacher, principal, and school district curriculum director. She was also a graduate professor and the director of student teaching at Kennesaw State University in Atlanta, Georgia, USA.

In 2004, Beverly published her first book, *Small-Group Reading Instruction: A Differentiated Teaching Model for Beginning and Struggling Readers*, with the International Reading Association. In 2005, she published a sequel to that book: *Small-Group Reading Instruction: A Differentiated Teaching Model for Intermediate Readers, Grades 3–8*. (Second editions of these texts published in 2009 and 2012, respectively.) Beverly has also produced training DVDs that accompany her books. In addition, she has published research in the *Journal of Educational Psychology* that supports her reading intervention model.

Currently, Beverly is a private literacy consultant. Her work includes presenting at national and international conferences, consulting with schools and school districts, and writing curricular materials. Most recently, she has been assisting school districts with the implementation of reading intervention models and the Common Core State Standards. Beverly is well known for her practical yet research-based models in reading instruction. She feels that her most important work continues to be with students and teachers within the classroom setting.

Beverly resides in Chattanooga, Tennessee, with her husband, Paul, and is the mother of four grown children.

Author Information for Correspondence and Workshops

The author welcomes questions and comments about this book. Beverly can be contacted at beverly@literacylinks.net.

This book has been more than 10 years in the making. I have spent the past 10 years working in the area of small-group differentiated reading instruction. Although this model has been very successful in fostering students in reading, it has become apparent to me that this piece of the literacy jigsaw puzzle, in and of itself, will never be enough to get the results that we want and that our students desperately need. My recent quest has been to examine the vast number of literacy considerations that must be addressed—and be given careful consideration—throughout the school day. I focused on developing ways to strategically plan for and assemble these pieces in such a way as to maximize literacy learning for every student.

My experiences in education have been both deep and wide. During the first part of my teaching career, my classes were made up of students whose abilities mirrored a bell-shaped curve. The majority of students functioned as expected for their grade level, with a few higher and a few lower. This is no longer the case. Now the average classroom more resembles an inverted bell, heavily weighted on each end. This phenomenon presents one of the biggest challenges that we now face in education.

The diversity represented in each classroom presents unique teaching challenges. Whereas before, teachers could successfully deliver the grade-level curriculum consistently in whole-group instruction, this may currently only be appropriate for a handful of students. Many students have already mastered the grade-level skills presented, and many lack the background knowledge necessary to access the curriculum. Mix into this scenario the students who don't speak English and those with special learning needs, and the complex teaching considerations become clear. This clarifies the need to reexamine how the school day is structured and how instruction is delivered to meet the needs of all students. This will require careful examination of each piece of the literacy puzzle and thoughtful planning for delivery.

Perhaps the two most important pieces of the literacy puzzle are the students and the teachers. Without the consideration of the needs of each child, even the most carefully crafted literacy instruction will be ineffective. Without an expert teacher to make critical day-to-day decisions based on the learners in the classroom, the effectiveness of the plan will be all but lost. These two pieces must be tempered with other important literacy pieces that are embedded in district and state mandates, best practices, research, and what is motivating and meaningful to every student.

A Look Ahead

Chapter 1 gives an overview of the driving factors behind good literacy instruction, including standards, curriculum design, and curriculum delivery. Chapter 2 presents a framework for delivering the literacy curriculum. Implications for whole-group, small-group, and independent practice are discussed. Chapter 3 provides planning models as well as concrete examples of appropriate strategies to use in whole-group instruction that are appropriate for all students. Scenarios for the primary and intermediate grades are also presented. Chapter 4 focuses on differentiating literacy instruction to meet the needs of a wide range of learners in any given classroom. Small-group differentiated instruction as well as the power of individual reading and writing conferences are discussed. In Chapter 5, appropriate activities for independent literacy practice as well as research and project-based learning are presented. The types and purposes of various literacy assessments are discussed in Chapter 6. Chapter 7 focuses on assembling the critical literacy pieces in a first-grade classroom. A theme-based approach to integrated instruction is the foundation for the instructional delivery. Chapter 8 focuses on a fourth-grade classroom and the planning and delivery of a comprehensive literacy program that is also thematically based. The Concluding Reflections provides a summary and final conclusions. The Appendix includes reproducibles that are useful in planning for literacy instruction. The names of the teachers and students throughout this book are pseudonyms.

This book is intended to assist teachers in identifying, assembling, and delivering a comprehensive literacy plan. It is also intended to assist teachers in training as they study the teaching of literacy in the primary and elementary grades. Administrators will find this resource valuable as they assist teachers in planning and developing effective literacy instruction that will aid in closing the gap between the most struggling students and the most gifted. Finally, teachers of special-needs students will view this resource as an inclusive model for supporting these learners with a focused team approach.

Although the current literacy challenges may seem daunting for many teachers, these challenges also come with great opportunities. At present, we have the opportunity to develop and provide the meaningful literacy instruction necessary to improve the lives of every student in our classrooms and schools. This will, in fact, be the instruction needed to make possible future education opportunities for many challenged students and expand the talents of our most gifted learners. Delivering the gift of literacy to each and every student is both an honor and a privilege that comes with teaching.

CHAPTER 1

Identifying the Critical Pieces of Literacy Instruction

A great education begins with great literacy skills. Students who are competent readers, thinkers, and communicators will be able to access the education and resources necessary for success both in school and in their future life endeavors. This is indeed the goal of schooling. Our nation has spent an enormous amount of time and money to make this goal a reality for all students, but for the most part, we have been unsuccessful (National Center for Education Statistics, 2011). A literate citizen must be able to read, write, speak, and think with purpose and ease. Therefore, literacy instruction must prepare students to enter adulthood and the world of work able to function as a part of a global economy and successfully as a part of a democratic society. Our common literacy goal must be to improve the literacy achievement of all students, including the gifted, the English learners, and the special-needs students. All children deserve the opportunity to grow into literate, functional adults. Although the levels of achievement will vary based on the capabilities of each child, the goal is still the same: to develop literacy skills in each student to his or her highest potential.

Educators must be keenly aware of the myriad factors that affect literacy instruction and the importance each piece plays in planning, delivering, and assessing literacy learning. First, the school, district, or state must establish standards for language arts that students need to learn or be able to do at each grade level. This requires that teachers have a comprehensive knowledge of the required grade-level language arts standards as well as content area standards as they scaffold and extend instruction based on student needs and established benchmarks. After the standards have been established, the curriculum needed to support these standards must either be developed or purchased. The literacy curriculum provides a scope and sequence, required texts, and suggested activities; the curriculum serves as a road map for teachers as they deliver instruction.

Perhaps the most important piece of the literacy puzzle is the delivery of the curriculum and its effect on teaching and learning. This includes infusing evidence-based best practices and selecting the most effective instructional venues needed to deliver the curriculum. Finally, assessing students to provide the data necessary to guide and adjust instruction to meet the needs of individual students is essential. The success in assembling all of these critical pieces of literacy instruction ultimately rests on the shoulders of teachers who make the critical day-to-day instructional decisions that directly affect the literacy development of their students.

Along with the lofty goal of developing high literacy levels for all students comes the task of addressing the diversity of abilities in every classroom. This is perhaps the most challenging obstacle that teachers currently face. From my observations across the United States, there is typically a three- to four-year grade-level difference in reading levels among students in any given elementary classroom. This requires teachers to be able to adapt instruction to meet these diverse needs on a daily basis. Differentiating literacy instruction to meet the needs of a wide range of learners is most certainly an important piece of the literacy puzzle. Figure 1 outlines the framework for examining the critical pieces of literacy instruction. Although each piece is introduced and briefly discussed in this chapter, the detailed discussion of the planning and implementation of these pieces in the classroom is addressed in the later chapters of this book.

Establishing the Literacy Standards

The first part of planning for effective literacy instruction is to determine what we expect students to know, understand, and produce as it relates to language arts. These are the standards that all students are expected to master at each grade level. Although these standards do not tell us how to teach, they outline what is to be accomplished with students in the language arts areas. Standards can be developed locally or from a common set of standards that have been created on the local, state, or national level. At present, most states have adopted the Common Core State Standards (CCSS). However, the states or local schools that have not adopted these standards have developed similar language arts standards that serve as learning benchmarks. Regardless, these standards hold the same level of importance as the language arts curriculum is developed and delivered to students within those states or local schools.

Before we move further into this discussion of Common Core standards, I want to clarify that this text is not intended to be a road map for the CCSS. Instead, this book addresses the planning and delivery of any high-quality standards-driven literacy program. So discussing each area of the Common Core standards in detail broadens the scope of this book beyond its intended measure. In the following sections, I briefly summarize the implications for curriculum and instruction presented by the CCSS. You can read further details about each standard and see how the standards are structured across grade levels by visiting the website of the Common Core State Standards Initiative (www.corestandards.org). You can also download full PDFs of the standards documents to become more familiar with them.

The Common Core State Standards for English Language Arts provide a clear framework to help teachers prepare students for the successful matriculation from high school to the future world of college and careers, laying out a vision of what it looks like to be literate in the 21st century. The CCSS are designed to provide learning that is both rigorous and relevant to the real world. These grade-specific standards define end-of-year expectations and cumulative progress. Achieving the standards involves shared responsibility among teachers in varying grade levels and subject areas.

An emphasis on these required literacy achievements allows educators to use their professional judgment and experience to decide how to reach these goals. The standards do not mandate such things as a particular writing process or an all-inclusive list of texts

FIGURE 1
Framework for Examining the Critical Literacy Pieces

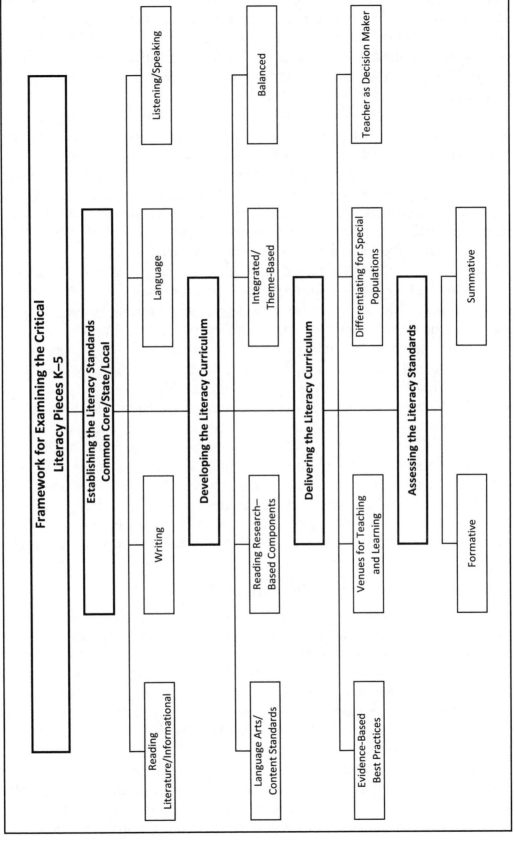

that students need to read; that is best left to individual schools and school districts. The adoption of the CCSS is, however, a critical piece for consistency in an attempt to prepare students for college and their future careers. Further, the standards guide the revision of curricula and state assessments to make learning more uniform across the country. The bottom line is this: Consistent standards provide common benchmarks for all students, regardless of their location.

The Common Core standards present an interdisciplinary approach to literacy that recognizes the need to use these important literacy skills across content areas. For planning purposes, teachers need to look beyond the traditional reading block as they seek to connect reading, writing, listening, and speaking experiences across content areas. This initiative, in my opinion, is long overdue. Over the last two decades, states, school districts, and even individual schools have spent millions of dollars and untold time developing standards only to have them rewritten or sitting on a shelf gathering dust. In the past, many teachers became so confused with the turnover in standards that they had difficulty even identifying the most current standards document. The CCSS bring consistency for teachers as they plan and deliver instructions that support common goals.

Most states have chosen to adopt the Common Core State Standards, with each state adapting up to 15% of the standards for their own state. How then will the standards affect the nature of everyday classroom instruction? The implications for educators are both exciting and daunting. Teachers need to shift what they teach, how they teach, and how they assess students. Although the CCSS do not tell teachers how to teach the standards, they provide an important starting point in identifying the knowledge and skills that all students must be equipped with upon graduation.

Clearly, the standards will not, in and of themselves, guarantee success with students. It takes well-prepared teachers armed with a plethora of powerful strategies to ensure that students reach these lofty goals. However, the standards provide a clear vision of the end product, which makes it easier to design instruction that produces the desired results. The sections that follow summarize the major implications or changes that the Common Core standards will have on both curricula and instructional practices.

Balancing Literature and Informational Text

Obviously, reading literature has always been a high priority in any language arts standards program. Perhaps the biggest shift seen in the CCSS is the inclusion of informational text as a part of the language arts curriculum. This represents a substantial change in the way reading has been taught. Informational text now holds an equal place in text selections used for reading instruction. Teachers need to reconsider their roles because reading will be taught across all content areas. Implications for how the school day is organized are a natural outcome of implementing these new standards across the curriculum.

The need for a curriculum that makes sense with this balance in literary and informational text must be addressed. Theme-based instruction that supports both text types provides the framework needed to address these issues. Teachers need to plan beyond the traditional reading block to integrate instruction. For example, a second-grade class might be studying a unit on animal habitats, and there are numerous informational texts available to support this study. Additionally, poetry, songs, picture books, and fables are appropriate literary text examples to support the theme. Embedding a variety of genres in both literary and informational text provides the necessary balance.

The Importance of Foundational Skills

The foundational skills highlighted in the CCSS have been shown by research, time and again, to be crucial to literacy development (see, e.g., Morrow & Gambrell, 2011; National Institute of Child Health and Human Development [NICHD], 2000). These foundational skills, including print concepts, phonological awareness, phonics and word recognition, and fluency, underpin the necessary knowledge for students to access the other standards. Many teachers have traditionally viewed these foundational skills in isolation, and in recent years, some of these foundational skills have been taught out of the context of reading for comprehension. For example, fluency in some instances has focused solely on speed to the extent that students felt that it was more important to read fast than to read to understand. The CCSS clearly identify these skills as foundational and should be quickly mastered to get to the ultimate goal: using these skills in the real reading process. By placing these foundational skills in their own strand within the Common Core, teachers can gauge the importance of these foundational skills to the reading process.

Writing to Demonstrate Comprehension

Perhaps no other area in literacy will change more because of the Common Core standards than writing instruction. The kinds of writing that students are now expected to produce will change substantially.

Writing in the elementary grades has traditionally focused heavily on personal narratives. Much of the writing now focuses on written comprehension, demonstrating a deep understanding of what the students have read. Writing about reading includes presenting evidence from the text to support an opinion or argument. Here we begin to see the important connections that must be made between reading and writing. Without a skilled reading of the text, students are unable to respond with the appropriate text evidence. Students should be able to write in response to a variety of text types and purposes across the content areas.

By nature, writing takes time, especially well-thought-out pieces. Teachers now need to readjust time allocations to allow for this kind of extensive writing. Workbook pages and ditto sheets will not get the job done. Rather, fewer and more in-depth written assignments that might be completed over a number of days will become the norm. These rigorous writing standards require teachers to begin in the early grades to build the reading and writing processes necessary for success as students matriculate through the grades.

Incorporating Speaking and Listening

The speaking and listening strand encompasses the need for students to be able to use oral communication and interpersonal skills interchangeably. Students must learn to work together and listen carefully to ideas shared by others, a skill that all job holders use on a daily basis. Although this standard at first glance seems to be easily achievable, these opportunities in most classrooms have been lacking. Much of this can be attributed to time limitations in that teachers have felt that they just could not get it all in. Again, we see an opportunity for integrated instruction, with speaking and listening becoming integral parts of the curriculum as students share information. Technology, including digital text features that are embedded in video and audio, is becoming increasingly important for students to acquire and share information.

Embedding the Language Standards

The language standards encompass conventions, effective use, and vocabulary, which means students are expected to adhere to the essential rules of standard written and spoken English. In the past 10 years, the teaching of language skills (grammar) has occurred outside the reading block, which has led to isolated instruction in grammar with little application to the writing process. The CCSS require that this grammar instruction be embedded, as much as possible, in the writing process. Vocabulary instruction needs to grow exponentially, especially across content areas, to increase disciplinary literacy. Without a doubt, this area provides the most important vehicle to access complex text. It is interesting to note that vocabulary and language conventions are presented in a separate category. This was done intentionally to emphasize the need to teach these two elements concurrently in reading, writing, speaking, and listening, not in isolation.

Determining Text Quality and Complexity

Perhaps the most controversial of the Common Core State Standards relates to the requirements for texts. Lack of exposure to high-quality and complex texts has been associated with the failure of some students as they enter college. Two critical keys are needed to address this issue. The first is to identify texts with these attributes: What makes a text high quality or more challenging? The second challenge is to then prepare and support students to navigate this more complex text.

To make these determinations, the text is evaluated in three specific ways: qualitative considerations, quantitative considerations, and reader and task considerations. Each of these three components are equally important. Figure 2 demonstrates the equal importance of each component of text complexity and the need to balance each measure in an appropriate way.

Qualitative measures of text complexity require teachers to examine four factors when making appropriate grade-level text selections: levels of meaning, structure, language conventionality and clarity, and knowledge demands. These factors can only be established through careful examination of the text, beginning with the levels of meaning in literary texts and the purpose in informational texts. The complexity of the text structure is also a consideration. Additionally, teachers must carefully evaluate language conventionality and clarity to determine the appropriateness of the text for a specific group of readers. Finally, teachers must recognize the amount of background knowledge

FIGURE 2
Components of Text Complexity

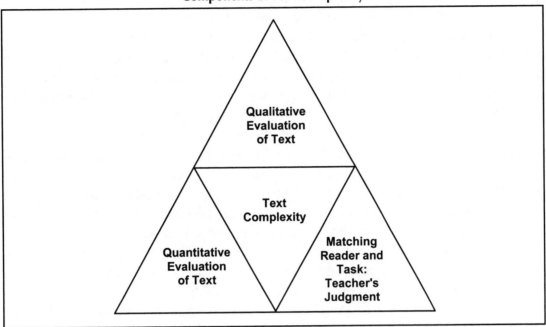

necessary to adequately understand the text's message. These qualitative measures are to be used in addition to the quantitative measures that I describe later in this chapter.

A computerized program that is consistent in measuring the complexity of text best determines quantitative measures. It is important to keep in mind that complexity is not necessarily the same as difficulty. Research is currently being conducted so recommendations for programs that are consistent in predicting text complexity are available to educators. A program that is currently available is the Pearson Reading Maturity Metric (www.readingmaturity.com).

The third component of the complexity triangle requires teachers to apply professional judgment of the reader and task; this measure holds equal weight with the other two components. The teacher must consider, first and foremost, whether the student will be able to read and understand the book with or without the support of the teacher. Reflection by the teacher on the context that the book will be used in is important to this process. As teachers examine a text, they must consider whether the text is worth student and instructor time, attention, and effort. With a variety of text choices available, teachers must determine whether the particular text is the best text available for the instructional purpose. Although the text may address the specific content, is the style and tone appropriate to the age of the student? Along with this, the teacher must consider the alignment between the task and the text so the readers reach the desired learning outcomes.

Along with the overarching standard that requires students to read texts at high complexity levels is the need for teachers to scaffold the support necessary to make the text accessible to a wide range of readers. Striking a balance between providing enough support but not too much is critical. Traditionally, teachers have given too much away as they struggled with this issue. In other words, in some cases, teachers have resorted to spoon-feeding, including reading the text to the students. This is no longer acceptable. Students are not only expected to read the text but also to read the text closely and think critically while reading, including making connections among ideas and between texts. There is no place for spoon-feeding as we address the rigor of the Common Core standards. This requires a comprehensive effort to change the way we teach reading in the early grades so students are capable of reading and understanding complex text in later grades. This also supports the need for teachers in the elementary grades to be grounded in the standards in subsequent grades. If teachers continue to view specific grade-level standards with tunnel vision, we will continue to miss the mark.

The task of moving students through increasingly difficult text complexity is easier said than done, of course. This has significant implications for text selections for whole-group, small-group, and independent practice. Differentiating reading instruction in small groups will be the necessary venue for fostering the most struggling reader and the most advanced. To support students in their growth with more complex text, students need to read text at the appropriate instructional level: the text that a student can read and understand with some support by the teacher. In some cases, we have perhaps set the bar too low when determining this instructional level, usually at 90–95% accuracy (Rasinski, 2010). If we expect students to read text below these levels, teachers must actively instruct and support students. This has special implications for beginning readers who require closely leveled text. As students move out of the decoding phase of reading, there is more leeway in text selections. Make no mistake: If we continually present texts to students at a level that causes frustration, the goal of moving students through increasingly difficult levels of text complexity will be all but lost.

On a personal note, let me share with you my experience with my daughter. As a first grader, Jennifer struggled in reading. The basal story for the week was a stretch, and she was clearly frustrated. When I returned home from work one day, Jennifer called me to her bedroom and announced, "I am reading the best book that I have read in my whole life!" I was thinking, "It's the only book you've read by yourself in your whole life." Imagine my surprise when I looked down and found *Fun With Dick and Jane* neatly tucked in her lap. A lesson learned: Children enjoy reading when they are presented with books that they can read. My fear is that teachers will embrace text complexity and reject the notion that there is an important place for books that can be read successfully, without frustration. These books will not always be the books that are grade-level appropriate. Keep in mind the purpose for each text shared with students.

Developing the Language Arts Curriculum

The responsibility for developing or purchasing a curriculum that supports students in reaching these rigorous standards falls to individual schools, school districts, or states. A large part of this book addresses the ways in which this curriculum is addressed and delivered. We must consider the place that the CCSS, or any state or local standards, hold as the curriculum is addressed. The standards are not the curriculum. The literacy curriculum embraces the standards and allows educators to shape and sequence the topics, appropriate textbooks, and materials needed to address the standards. A strong literacy curriculum brings clarity to our schools' endeavors and brings consistency within and among schools. Curriculum may best be defined as an outline of what will be taught. The literacy curriculum specifies literacy works, periods, genres, themes, and ideas. It should then be up to the teacher to decide how to present the material and how to structure class time to best meet the needs of students. A good literacy curriculum offers both structure and flexibility. Teachers need the flexibility to devote extra time to certain topics or to pursue a topic spontaneously here and there, but it should be done judiciously and sparingly. An established curriculum allows teachers to plan in advance and build their resources over time. Without a defined curriculum, we risk confusion, inconsistency, loss of common knowledge, and loss of integrity.

A comprehensive literacy curriculum requires great thought and time; therefore, curriculum development has mostly been left to textbook companies. It is not enough, however, for a textbook company to say that they have indeed incorporated the standards. The questions that must be answered are How are the standards presented and embedded in integrated literacy instruction? and Are the activities well thought out and rigorous? Most textbook companies tout that their materials are theme based. However, on careful examination, the themes are so loosely contrived that they often have no instructional merit.

If we are to learn from the past, we will view these boxed materials with a fresh set of eyes: wiser in our purchases and wise enough to plow through the sales pitches and free materials that can be distracting. Even with the purchase of a state-of-the-art packaged literacy curriculum, there will always be a need for teachers to pick and choose as well as supplement the curriculum to meet the needs of individual students. Teachers are indeed the critical decision makers who are most capable of adapting and delivering literacy instruction that will ultimately gauge the success of that instruction.

The Importance of an Integrated Literacy Curriculum

The Common Core standards require teachers to go deeper into the content, in contrast to the breadth currently seen in an overcrowded curriculum. Integrated instruction addresses this need. Integrated instruction is not necessarily theme based; there is a subtle difference. For example, the teaching of language arts can be integrated as students read then write about what they have read. The writing assignment might also include focusing on a particular writing style, such as a friendly letter. Here we see an integration of reading, written comprehension, and writing style. For comparison, theme-based instruction goes one step further: It provides the format for addressing a particular theme, usually in a content area that includes reading and writing that supports the theme in a seamless flow of instruction.

Integrated instruction has been shown to increase student achievement (Bean, 1997; Kovalik, 1994). It should, therefore, be given more than lip service in a comprehensive language arts curriculum, especially in light of the interdisciplinary approach to literacy instruction that is necessary to achieve the CCSS. Research on brain-based teaching has explained that the brain learns, and recalls learning, thorough patterns that emphasize coherence rather than fragmentation. The more teachers plan for these connected patterns in explicit and meaningful ways for students, the easier the brain will integrate the new information (Hart, 1983). This supports the need for both an integrated and theme-based curriculum. Students engaged in meaningful learning experiences in an integrated curriculum that includes connections to students' lives are all aspects of brain-compatible teaching and learning (Caine & Caine, 1994). This allows students to connect and assimilate ideas in authentic contexts, taking into consideration their perceptions of real-world problems (Bransford, Brown, & Cocking, 1999; Kovalik, 1994). Using technology to further research and solve problems in real-world settings also enhances student learning (diSessa, 2000).

A truly integrated curriculum gives the glue necessary to hold the curriculum together for both teachers and students. It gives substance to the teaching and relevance to the learning. Furthermore, as teachers strive to address the standards, this theme-based approach creates learning foundations for key concepts to be integrated. The overall goal is to select themes that are engaging and motivating for students that also address the standards in content areas.

The purpose for developing the curriculum is to address the standards in a meaningful and powerful way. Yet, in a knee-jerk reaction to respond to these high-stakes standards, some educators are turning to a curriculum that resembles a checklist of the standards. It is important to keep in mind that this kind of instruction will be a dead end for students who are in desperate need of high levels of integrated literacy experiences. Only when the standards are addressed in an integrated and meaningful way will they be most likely digested by the students.

An integrated curriculum with embedded standards also has implications for how students are assessed. Disconnected, meaningless instruction that can be regurgitated on a closed-response assessment is no longer the norm. Along with major standards revisions, assessments to measure the standards will change to reflect the deeply integrated thinking that the current literacy standards demand.

The Importance of Balance in the Literacy Curriculum

As educators begin to develop or investigate purchased language arts curricula, the goal should be to maintain balance. Balancing the literacy curriculum requires respect for research and responds to the individual needs of students as teachers respond to their developmental levels with the purpose of reading for pleasure, joy, and comprehension.

There are at least three reasons to support the use of a balanced approach to developing and delivering the curriculum. A balanced approach (1) is respectful of a wide range of research findings, (2) supports the wisdom of best practices, and (3) recognizes that no single approach is best for all students. This approach includes research from many areas and also best practices from reading research. This could quite possibly represent the voice of reason to a continuing pendulum swing in views on reading instruction that have characterized much of the 20th century.

Although most people agree that the literacy curriculum should be balanced, there has been no research indicating how time should be allocated among reading, writing, comprehension strategy instruction, vocabulary instruction, oral language development, and phonics instruction. The classroom teacher best makes these critical day-to-day decisions.

Additionally, balance must be respectful of the inclusion of a variety of literacy genres. Much like a well-balanced diet, the literacy diet should include various literary genres, such as fairy tales, myths, folk tales, and novels. This also applies to balance in informational text selections, such as content material, newspaper articles, speeches, and biographies—especially for achieving the Common Core standards.

Perhaps Pressley (n.d.) has best described true balanced literacy instruction:

> It involves explicit, systematic, and completely thorough teaching of the skills required to read and write in a classroom environment where there is much reading of authentic literature—including information books, and much composing by students. Balanced literacy instruction is demanding in every way that literacy instruction can be demanding. Students are expected to learn the skills and learn them well enough to be able to transfer them to reading and writing of texts. Yes, this is done in a strongly supportive environment, with the teacher providing a great deal of direct teaching, explanations and re-explanations, and hinting to students about the appropriateness of applying skills they have learned previously to new texts and tasks. As children learn the skills and use them, the demands in balanced classrooms increase, with the goal of the balanced literacy teacher being to move students ahead, so that every day there is new learning; every day students are working at the edge of their competencies and growing as readers and writers. (p. 2)

This balance must also be respectful of teacher-led versus student-led discussion. Historically, the teacher has been viewed as the dispenser of knowledge as students listen attentively to consume the information. In a balanced classroom, student talk is as important as teacher talk. Rather than have students work independently, they routinely should be working with other students to research, explore, and discuss while learning. In a balanced instructional setting, the teacher also acts as a facilitator.

All aspects of developmental literacy instruction must be viewed with balance in mind. If we are to learn from past mistakes, we recognize that going too far in one direction or another has never proven to be successful in moving student achievement forward. Teachers must remain vigilant and open to establishing and maintaining balance in both developing and delivering instruction.

The Importance of the Essential Components of Reading Instruction

With eyes squarely focused on the new Common Core State Standards movement, it is important that the work completed by the National Reading Panel in researching the essential components of reading instruction not be overlooked (NICHD, 2000). There are five components associated with the process of reading that work together to create the reading experience: phonics, phonemic awareness, vocabulary, reading comprehension, and fluency. As children learn to read, they must develop and orchestrate these skills to become readers who are capable of high levels of literacy learning. It is imperative that we review and reflect on what has been learned about the process of learning to read and how these components intersect with the CCSS.

Fluency

Fluency is the reader's ability to read with enough speed, accuracy, and expressions to understand the text's meaning. Students' abilities to read fluently and automatically in decoding text is linked to higher levels of text comprehension (Bell & Perfetti, 1994). Typically, comprehension breaks down when students are asked to read text that is too difficult for their reading abilities. This has special implications as we address text complexity.

The Common Core language arts standard for fluency is found in the standard for foundational skills. It is important to note that accuracy over speed is the focus in fluency development in the CCSS. This is a welcome change from an emphasis on speed and should bring the voice of reason back to effective fluency instruction. Substantial research has supported multiple rereadings of a text to build fluency (e.g., Meyer & Felton, 1999; Rasinski, 2010).

An important point that must not be overlooked when focusing on fluency is that it must be developed with text that students can read comfortably, so it would not be appropriate to work on fluency with text that students find too difficult. Teachers need a deep understanding not only of the importance that fluency plays in comprehension but also of the level of text complexity appropriate for building fluency.

Phonics

The Common Core standards cite the need for phonics and word analysis in the foundational skills standard, requiring that students "know and apply grade-level phonics and word analysis skills in decoding words" (National Governors Association Center for Best Practices & Council of Chief State School Officers [NGA Center & CCSSO], 2010b, p. 16). Assessment of an individual student's knowledge of phonics features is instrumental in guiding phonics instruction. Small-group instruction may be the best way to differentiate phonics instruction based on student assessment (Ehri, Nunes, Stahl, & Willows, 2001). Without opportunities to apply what they are learning about phonics, students will not become fluent readers or writers. Therefore, they should not be restricted to the teaching of isolated phonics skills. Highly decodable text is often overused in the early grades; teaching phonics as it relates to reading does not mean that students must only use purely phonetically based readers (Allington, Woodside-Jiron, 1998). On the contrary, a variety of texts that includes sight-word–oriented texts should also be incorporated. Again, the word balance can be used to describe the role between phonics and appropriate instructional strategies.

Phonemic Awareness

The National Reading Panel has recognized phonemic awareness as a research-based component in effective reading instruction, and it is addressed in the CCSS in foundational skills. Phonemic awareness is one of the best predictors of success in learning to read, which supports the need for its focus in the early grades (Ehri & Nunes, 2002; NICHD, 2000).

Children enter school with varying degrees of phonemic awareness, and assessment best guides teachers in determining its emphasis in both whole-group and small-group instruction. For struggling readers, the small-group venue provides more support (Cunningham, 2007). Recognition of phonemic awareness in the CCSS is addressed specifically in kindergarten and early first grade. Beyond that point, only the most struggling readers might need additional support in this area.

Vocabulary

Few would argue the importance of vocabulary as it relates to effective reading instruction, and it has been identified as the most critical cause of the lack of reading comprehension (Blachowicz & Fisher, 2004). Therefore, vocabulary knowledge is addressed in the Common Core standards in the language standard. Many children learn to word call and have no knowledge of the meaning of some of the words. A quality literacy curriculum includes multiple opportunities for all students to learn new words. Teachers should build a word-rich environment in which students are immersed in words for both incidental and intentional learning and the development of word awareness (Blachowicz & Fisher, 2009; NICHD, 2000).

Wide reading is the hallmark of word learning (Blachowicz & Fisher, 2006). For many students, especially young or struggling readers, developing an extensive listening vocabulary is the precursor to gleaning new words in their own reading. Reading aloud is essential so students have the opportunity to be introduced to words that may be too difficult for them to read and understand on their own (Beck & McKeown, 2001; Snow, Burns, & Griffith, 1998). Even in the early grades, exposure to complex text through read-alouds is critical for vocabulary development.

Comprehension

One of the most challenging issues in implementing the Common Core standards is the need to require students to read and comprehend complex text. To accomplish this, teachers need to fully understand the comprehension process and how best to assist students in reaching this high standard. Comprehension does not stand alone; it is embedded in decoding, vocabulary, and fluency. Therefore, a lack of comprehension could be the result of fluency deficits, decoding issues, or limited vocabulary knowledge. Additionally, without adequate comprehension skills, students might lack the inability to think while reading or lack the background knowledge to thoroughly understand the text's message. It is important for teachers to understand the integral relationship between comprehension and the other major components of reading (see Figure 3).

Reading texts at high levels of complexity is beneficial if and only if a student is able to read the text with around 98% accuracy (Blachowicz & Fisher, 2004). A teacher's lack of understanding of research in this area can lead to frustration for the teacher and students as text is presented at unattainable levels. Teachers need to adjust instructional

FIGURE 3
Contributors to Poor Comprehension

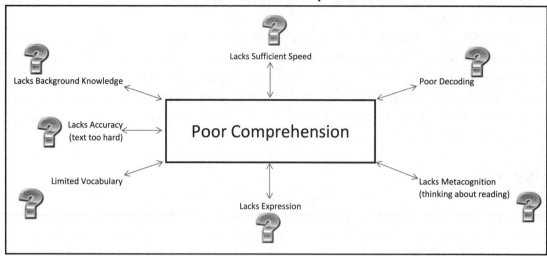

delivery to address this issue. Additionally, the CCSS require students to write to demonstrate deep comprehension, which requires focused instruction and a major shift in how students are assessed on comprehension. Traditional short-response comprehension assessments no longer suffice as the primary means to assess comprehension.

Delivering the Literacy Curriculum

In a truly balanced literacy approach, how you teach is just as important as what you teach. We can be cognizant of literacy standards as well as research-based components and still miss the mark if we fail to consider the how in delivering everyday instruction. Teachers must continue to use research and evidence-based practices to gain an understanding of the strategies that are most effective in delivering instruction. Additionally, teachers must consider the most appropriate venue or format to present that instruction. Maintaining the best teaching practices without ignoring the current research and evidence requires balance. Much too often, education swings too far in one direction or the other.

The Importance of Evidence-Based Best Instructional Practices

Evidence-based best instructional practices are critical considerations as the literacy puzzle is assembled. What is an evidence-based best instructional practice? Simply put, it means that when this practice is used with a specific group of students, improvement is documented. In other words, these instructional practices have a record of success that is both trustworthy and valid (Morrow & Gambrell, 2011). Certainly, there is no one best practice; teachers must be diligent in keeping abreast of the most current research, which allows teachers to pull from a variety of evidence-based practices to best meet the needs of their students. According to Whitehurst (2002), evidence-based instruction involves teachers making decisions using "professional wisdom integrated with the best available empirical evidence" (slide 3). Thus, evidence-based practices must be included in every comprehensive literacy framework.

Currently, there is a plethora of evidence-based best practices and principles to consider, and educators must be diligent in searching for and implementing these practices. There are numerous resources available that detail the latest research and evidence-based practices. The recent edition of Best Practices in Literacy Instruction (Gambrell, Malloy, & Mazzoni, 2011) identifies 10 evidence-based best practices for comprehensive literacy instruction:

1. Classrooms should reflect a culture that fosters literacy motivation. The teacher should foster literacy by creating a community of literacy learners.
2. Students learn best when they read for authentic meaning-making purposes: for pleasure, to be informed, and to perform a task.
3. Teachers should provide appropriate scaffolded instruction in the five core skills (phonemic awareness, phonics, vocabulary, fluency, and comprehension) to promote independent reading.
4. The school day should include time for self-selected reading.
5. Providing students with high-quality literature across a wide range of genres will build a love for reading and address the Common Core standards.
6. As themes or topics are explored, multiple texts should be used to increase background knowledge, connect concepts, and increase vocabulary.
7. The classroom should reflect and encourage community and collaboration.
8. A balance of teacher- and student-led discussions of texts is important to build lifelong learners.
9. Students need ample opportunities to use technologies that connect and expand concepts.
10. Differentiate instruction based on student assessments to accommodate the needs of individual students.

These practices are, in fact, the pieces that most teachers agree on as important to a quality literacy experience. Knowing how to make this happen in the classroom is what becomes overwhelming for many teachers. As this book was developed, I gave careful consideration to addressing these practices in a practical way.

The Importance of Multiple Instructional Venues for Teaching and Learning

A variety of instructional delivery venues provides the vehicles for delivering a strong literacy curriculum. These teaching venues begin in whole-group instruction with modeled and shared literacy experiences. Differentiating literacy instruction in small-group settings provides all students with the opportunity to grow in their literacy endeavors as well as opportunities to navigate more difficult texts. Additionally, students need opportunities to practice and orchestrate their literacy skills individually, with partners, and in small groups with other students. Individual feedback to students provides valuable support for growth. These teaching venues support the gradual release of responsibility model (Pearson & Gallagher, 1983), which supports the theory that the teacher must first model literacy skills while students observe. Then, the teacher and students share the responsibilities needed to complete the literacy tasks. Finally, the students orchestrate these literacy skills with the sideline support of the teacher. The ultimate goal is for students to be able to seamlessly orchestrate their literacy skills without the support of the teacher.

Deciding what to focus on in whole-group versus small-group instruction and what students practice and produce as they work with partners or individually is instrumental in the success of the language arts program. These venues are important pieces of delivering the literacy plan and are addressed in Chapters 2, 3, and 4.

The Importance of Differentiating Literacy Instruction

The diversity in every classroom presents perhaps the biggest challenges for classroom teachers. Providing appropriate instruction for this diverse group of learners requires different instructional strategies. At its core, differentiated instruction provides all students with the appropriate level of challenge and the appropriate supports to help them reach learning goals. Students learn best when they are presented with challenges that are obtainable—not so difficult that the learner feels overwhelmed or so simple that the student is not having to think (Bess, 1997; Tomlinson, 2003). Technology is also an important key to supporting diverse learners by creating avenues for individual access to content and expression.

The CCSS were written so that as many students as possible have access to these rigorous standards, including students with special needs and English learners. This is critically important as the issue of text complexity is addressed and instruction adapted. Teachers need to alter instructional strategies so all students have the opportunity to access increasingly difficult text. This text complexity must be tempered with the needs and unique capabilities of each student. It is important to create instructional opportunities based on what students know and what comes next in the developmental sequence. A differentiated classroom requires a skillful teacher who creates many opportunities for students to access the curriculum.

Although standards are established for grade-level attainment, the instruction necessary for individual learning must not be one size fits all. Differentiation allows for multiple paths to reach the learning goals. Key implications for curriculum instruction require teachers to use varied grouping strategies based on the goals of the lesson. In other words, teachers need to recognize when homogeneous or heterogeneous groupings are the most optimal for learning. Differentiating literacy instruction for special populations, including English learners and students with exceptionalities, is instrumental in addressing their special needs. There is no other choice if educators are sincere about providing a quality education for all students.

The Importance of Teacher as Decision Maker

Research findings and assumed best practices must always be tempered with the fact that a finding may not be a best practice if, for example, instruction is not adapted to fit the strengths and needs of a particular group of learners. All children enter the schoolhouse with unique personalities and background knowledge that must be respected. Individual students will typically respond differently to the same instruction. Simply put, research and best practices must fit the students; teachers must understand their students' strengths and needs and adapt instruction to promote optimal learning and literacy. Effective teachers must be keenly aware of their students' knowledge levels and constantly self-question, reflect, teach, and reevaluate to inform the most powerful instruction. In other words, teachers are literacy designers, equipped with knowledge of literacy instruction and the individual literacy needs of each student. Quality literacy instruction can only be achieved when skillful, knowledgeable, and dedicated teachers are allowed the latitude to use their professional judgment to make instructional decisions that enable students to reach their highest literacy potential.

In the past decade, there has been an unprecedented move to require teachers to use a prescribed, boxed literacy program with fidelity. Unfortunately, trained, knowledgeable teachers have, in some cases, been reduced to mere robotic-like instruction. Effective teachers cautiously guard against the tendency to teach reading and language arts as a series of skills or components to be taught in a prescribed, linear format. They recognize the importance that each literacy piece plays in the overall literacy development of their students.

The teacher is undeniably the most important ingredient in the literacy jigsaw. The pieces are easily identifiable, but the assembly requires a knowledgeable and skilled teacher. What happens between the classroom walls on a daily basis ultimately determines the fate of our students' literacy growth. The teacher must understand literacy learning well enough to adapt the learning environment, materials, and methods to particular situations and students. Others can provide training, require plans, monitor assessments, or dictate the literacy curriculum, but the reality of its success or failure rests squarely on the shoulders of the classroom teacher. The teacher is the cornerstone for building a successful literacy program.

The Importance of Assessing Literacy Achievement

A significant part of the assessment process is the documentation that ensures that students are on track to meet the standards. Therefore, assessments must reflect and support effective instruction and include all students from the outset, including English learners, economically disadvantaged students, and students with disabilities. As a result, students will not only learn from a more rigorous and relevant set of standards but also be introduced to new types of assessment that are significantly different from most current state tests.

Obviously, assessments have always been an integral part of the instructional process, but assessments of the next decade will center on more rigorous requirements. These assessments will focus on more real-world relevance and present interdisciplinary situations.

Students will be asked to perform at the evaluation and synthesis levels of Bloom's taxonomy (Forehand, 2010), which are in the top tier of performance. Assessments that include performance-based tasks rather than closed responses, such as multiple-choice responses, which are typically at a low level of rigor, will be the norm. In a performance-based task, students are asked to create answers or products to demonstrate knowledge and skills.

Without question, assessment will remain at the forefront in evaluating and determining the growth of students in their literacy journeys. It will continue to guide instruction as well as measure the progress that students are making toward established grade-level benchmarks. Many teachers now have their income partially tied to the gains that students make under their direction. Determining the best way to assess and matching the purpose of the assessment are critical pieces of a comprehensive literacy program. Chapter 6 addresses both formative and summative literacy assessments and their value as teachers make critical literacy decisions.

CHAPTER 2

A Framework for Delivering the Literacy Curriculum

After the literacy standards have been established and a curriculum to support the standards has been developed, the focus then becomes the method of delivering the curriculum. In this chapter, we review the instructional venues that are appropriate for presenting and practicing literacy elements in the classroom setting. By necessity, much of the school day is spent in whole-group instruction with students who represent a wide variety of learning needs. Small-group instruction plays an essential role during the school day as the teacher differentiates for specific literacy needs. Additionally, individual conferences that provide feedback to students in the areas of reading and writing play an important role in literacy growth. Finally, students need ample time to practice and orchestrate important literacy skills. Along with this, students are expected to work with others to complete tasks such as research and composing presentations to present to others. Figure 4 shows the framework for delivering the literacy curriculum.

An Optimal Literacy Learning Model

After carefully planning the literacy curriculum, a rationale for delivering it must be established and justified. In other words, for what reasons would the curriculum be delivered in one context or another?

The rationale for the instructional venues that are appropriate for whole-group, small-group, and independent practice incorporates the theory of the optimal learning model (Pearson & Gallagher, 1983). This research-based model recognizes that the responsibility for completing literacy tasks shifts gradually over time from the teacher to the student. This model supports the teacher first modeling the particular literacy strategy in whole-group instruction and then using the strategy again, as the students participate while the teacher gives direction and support. Next, students are expected to use the strategy in a small-group or individual setting, with the teacher stepping back from direct participation to monitor the use of the strategy and give support when necessary. Finally, the teacher expects each student to use the strategy independently while he or she monitors students directly and indirectly by reviewing student work.

Vygotsky's (1978) research and theories of learning form the basis for instructional scaffolding and the gradual release of responsibility that underpin the optimal learning model (Pearson & Gallagher, 1983). He believed that a teacher should help children learn new concepts and skills by interacting with them: explicitly teaching the

FIGURE 4
Literacy Delivery Framework

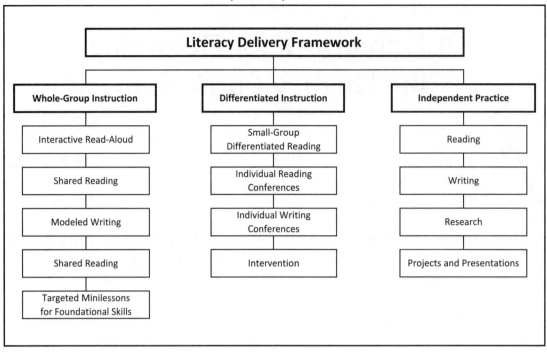

next incremental step, then providing supported practice, and finally providing opportunities for independent practice and application of the skill. He referred to this teaching–learning process as scaffolding. Others, such as Routman (2002), have since adapted this model. Routman has referred to the revised model as the gradual release of responsibility. The "I do" part of Routman's model describes the teacher modeling the literacy strategy or skill, and the "we do" part is the sharing of this experience between the teacher and the students. The "you do" part is when the student takes over the responsibility for practicing the skill or strategy, with the sideline support of the teacher. As teachers strive to scaffold levels of support for students that encourage maximum learning gains, the instructional day calls for differing venues for instructional delivery. In this chapter, we explore the venues that are most powerful in whole-class instruction, differentiated instruction, and independent literacy opportunities. Figure 5 depicts this gradual release of responsibility and the teaching venues that support this theory.

Venues for Delivering Whole-Group Literacy Instruction

The role of teacher as decision maker begins with the daunting task of providing whole-group instruction that is meaningful to all students: the struggling, the gifted, and every

FIGURE 5
Teaching Venues That Support the Gradual Release of Responsibility

Setting	I Do	We Do (I Do/You Help)	We Do (You Do/I Help)	You Do
	Whole Class	Whole Class	Small Group/ Individual	Individual/ Small Group
Instructional Venues	Interactive Read-Aloud Modeled Writing Modeled Minilessons for Foundational Skills	Shared Reading Shared Writing Shared Minilessons for Foundational Skills	Small-Group Differentiated Reading Individual Reading Conferences Individual Writing Conferences Guided Practice of Foundational Skills	Student-Selected Reading and Writing Teacher-Assigned Reading and Writing Practice/Projects/ Presentations
Teacher/Student Responsibility Roles	T T T T	T T T S	S S S T	S S S S
	Teacher Responsibility	→ Collaboration →		Student Responsibility

student in between. Because students spend the majority of their school day in whole-group instruction, there must be careful consideration of how literacy instruction is delivered, especially as it relates to the wide range of literacy learners in any given setting. Rich literary and informational texts provide the centerpiece for whole-group instruction and the foundation for developing background knowledge, vocabulary, rich discussions, and a wide variety of writing opportunities. An integration of presentation venues as well as the integration of subject matter is used to provide depth, rigor, and accessibility to quality literacy texts and instruction for all students. The role of the teacher in the whole-group setting is to provide equal access for all students to the established grade-level standards. Proven strategies for delivering whole-group literacy instruction include interactive read-alouds, shared reading, modeled writing, shared writing, and targeted minilessons; the following sections detail each of these strategies.

Interactive Read-Alouds

Interactive read-alouds promote a love of reading, stimulate the imagination, and provide students an opportunity to develop an ear for the vocabulary and structures of language in print. Just as reading aloud to children by parents is an important activity, read-alouds continue to be a routine literacy venue used by elementary school teachers. The role of reading aloud to students goes far beyond simply reading a book for entertainment. Historically, reading aloud to students in the classroom has been a staple routine for enjoying a great story, calming the students, or even relaxing after lunch. Although there is certainly nothing wrong with these activities, the role of read-alouds has evolved into a foundational instructional delivery venue.

The term interactive read-aloud defines the more instructional focus and inclusion of students in the experience. An interactive read-aloud is best described as a planned oral reading by the teacher of a book or print excerpt, usually related to the current theme or topic of study. Interactive read-alouds include the teacher reading out loud—the "I do" part of the teaching process—but the teacher also verbally interacts with the students throughout the process, encouraging them to contribute to the discussion. This literacy experience engages students as they listen and interact with one another and the teacher. Additionally, these read-alouds can be used to model reading strategies that contribute to comprehension. Planned read-alouds meet grade-level standards with a focus on the integration of literacy activities.

An interactive read-aloud offers rich literacy opportunities for a wide range of learners. Students should sit near the teacher on a rug or at another designated spot. This close proximity allows the teacher to better monitor the interaction of the students and encourages the building of community spirit among classmates. The interactive read-aloud offers all readers the opportunity to build background knowledge, vocabulary in context, and deep comprehension of the text. Because students do not have access to the text and therefore are not reading along with the teacher, students are not burdened with the actual decoding of the text and can focus all of their attention to thinking about the meaning of the text. The teacher integrates strategies before, during, and after reading to increase comprehension and vocabulary development. Students are included in text discussions that are critical to the comprehension process.

Instructional Focuses of Interactive Read-Alouds

Figure 6 shows the instructional focuses of interactive read-alouds based on some of the reading research-based components outlined by the National Reading Panel (NICHD, 2000). As we consider these components herein, interactive read-alouds provide rich opportunities in both vocabulary and comprehension that make this venue an attractive option in whole-group instruction.

The interactive read-aloud presents opportunities to develop listening, speaking, reading, and writing vocabulary. Understanding vocabulary is critical to the comprehension of any text, especially those that are more complex. A major issue for many struggling readers is their lack of vocabulary knowledge. Building listening and speaking vocabulary through read-alouds is instrumental to these students as they access more difficult texts as a reader. For more advanced students, additional reading and writing vocabulary may be acquired. As the teacher reads above the students' grade level, most of them have the opportunity to gain knowledge of new words. There are two main ways that students learn new vocabulary: through reading or listening to someone

FIGURE 6
Instructional Focuses of Interactive Read-Alouds

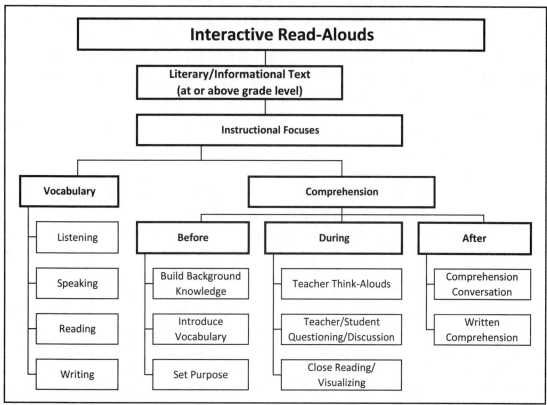

read. Words are the basis for understanding. You can either help students learn these words through their own eyes or through their ears (Trelease, 2006).

Prior to reading, strategically select vocabulary words from the text that are both important to the comprehension of the text and appropriate for the grade level. Good vocabulary choices are not necessarily the most difficult words in the text; instead, the words selected should likely be encountered by students in multiple text formats. Proper nouns, such as names or places that are of little importance outside of the text, should not be selected. Before reading, present the vocabulary words and establish a purpose for reading the text. Further, engage the students in examining context clues to determine the meaning of other unknown words while the text is read.

Interactive read-alouds also provide good opportunities for building listening, speaking, and written comprehension skills. Research-based comprehension strategies are addressed as appropriate before, during, and after reading. Prior to reading, build the students' necessary background knowledge for understanding the text. During reading, use think-aloud strategies to share understandings as the text is read. Teacher and student questioning provide engaging comprehension conversations at strategic points to further explore the text. After reading, a specific comprehension strategy is employed to summarize the text. Use either a comprehension conversation or a written response to support the comprehension focus and model grade-level writing standards.

Text Selections for Interactive Read-Alouds

Text selections for interactive read-alouds should represent a wide range of genres, including both literary and informational selections. The texts should, in some way, support grade-level standards. Another element that should be considered is the quality and interest that the read-aloud will provide. To be confident with the read-aloud selections, read them prior to sharing with the class. Casually pulling a book from the shelf at the last minute will not provide the intensity needed for this critical delivery component.

Benefits of Interactive Read-Alouds

For many of us, interactive read-alouds were first experienced on our parents' laps. Prior to a child's ability to read independently, read-alouds serve an important purpose. Children learn the joy of a great story in this setting while acquiring a strong literacy foundation as they make their way to personal reading success. Children who are read to also get a jump start on listening vocabulary, thinking skills, and listening comprehension. Parents recognize the need to talk about the pictures, words, and characters in a book. For those students who never experience this childhood ritual, teacher read-alouds help fill this gap and provide much needed motivation to become a reader or more competent reader.

Interactive read-alouds level the playing field for those students who struggle with reading grade-level text. When students lack the ability to successfully access the text, reading aloud to them is a good option. Students who find the work of reading too overwhelming will most likely lose motivation. Lack of motivation is often cited as the reason students struggle in reading. The following are additional benefits of interactive read-alouds:

- Builds background knowledge in a variety of content areas
- Allows the teacher the opportunity to model new reading strategies and to demonstrate them by thinking aloud
- Provides models of fluent reading
- Develops a sense of story/text
- Provides opportunities for explicit listening and speaking vocabulary instruction
- Builds a community of readers
- Develops active reading skills
- Allows all students access to high levels of text complexity

With a loaded schedule, many teachers do not view reading aloud as an activity worthy of the instructional time it takes. However, using interactive read-alouds is likely one of the most powerful ways to close the gap between successful and struggling readers, especially in a whole-group setting. Many struggling readers lack the desire, background experiences, or vocabulary knowledge necessary for successful reading. Interactive read-alouds meet all three needs by building a wide range of background experiences, developing an extensive listening and speaking vocabulary, and most of all, learning to love reading and creating lifelong learners. Chapter 3 provides a sample planner as well as concrete examples of interactive read-alouds in primary and intermediate classrooms.

Shared Reading

Perhaps the most misunderstood term in literacy instruction is shared reading. For the purposes of this book, the term simply means that the students have access to the text as the teacher and students read it together. Shared reading is the "we do" element of the gradual release of responsibility model, as the teacher and students share the reading of the text. Shared reading is a whole-group literacy venue that allows all students access to grade-level text. Although the ultimate goal is for all students to be able to read and understand grade-level text independently, it is not always the reality. A wide range of readers must be accommodated as the text is shared during whole-class instruction. Therefore, the teacher must give the support needed to allow each student access to the text. Shared reading typically occurs with text that is appropriate for the grade level and might include poetry, songs, and other literary and informational text pieces.

Perhaps the most daunting task for teachers is deciding how to present the text so it is accessible to all readers, especially those students who are not capable of successfully reading and understanding grade-level text on their own. Figure 7a shows common strategies for sharing grade-level text and points out the limited effectiveness for most of them. For example, allowing students to listen to the text on a CD reduces opportunities to read closely and provides little opportunity for discussion as the story is read. More significant issues arise when students are asked to read the pages of the text in a round-robin fashion. Certainly, listening to 20 different students read a story, some of whom cannot read it fluently, would certainly make it difficult to understand. This strategy, therefore, should be discouraged. Other strategies rely on partner reading as a way to read the text, often pairing more capable readers with struggling readers. This arrangement does little for either partner and takes the teacher out of the equation in terms of guiding comprehension. A more viable option is for the teacher to be the lead reader (reading out loud) while the students whisper read. Requiring students to use a brightly colored bookmark as they read along also helps teachers monitor student engagement. Although struggling students might not read every word perfectly, even limited word calling is a better alternative and requires more student engagement. This also gives the teacher opportunities to invite student discussions at strategic points in the text.

Instructional Focuses of Shared Reading

The instructional focuses of shared reading are fluency, vocabulary, and comprehension (see Figure 7b). Fluency is developed in shared reading as grade-level text selections are read and reread. Research has been clear about the need to develop fluency through practice with text that is instructionally appropriate—that is, text that a student can read with 90–95% accuracy (Rasinski, 2010). For students reading below grade level, this is accomplished with short text selections that are reread multiple times. Preselect grade-level vocabulary from the shared text and introduce the words prior to reading. Unlock additional vocabulary during the reading based on context clues and address research-based comprehension strategies again before, during, and after reading.

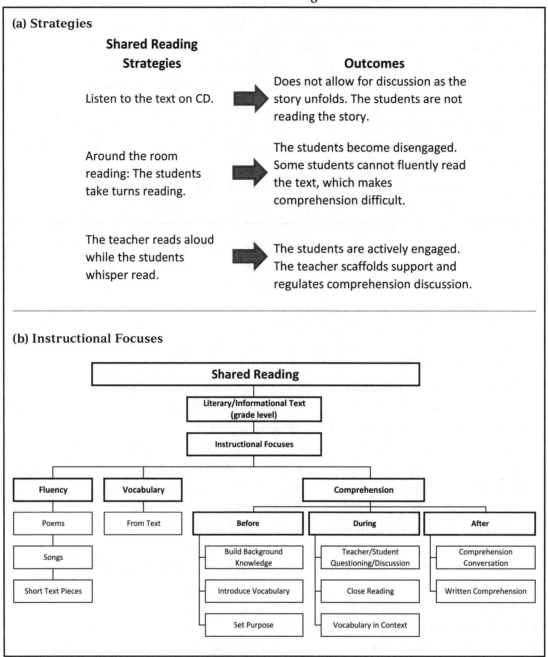

(a) Strategies

Shared Reading Strategies	Outcomes
Listen to the text on CD.	Does not allow for discussion as the story unfolds. The students are not reading the story.
Around the room reading: The students take turns reading.	The students become disengaged. Some students cannot fluently read the text, which makes comprehension difficult.
The teacher reads aloud while the students whisper read.	The students are actively engaged. The teacher scaffolds support and regulates comprehension discussion.

(b) Instructional Focuses

Shared Reading → Literary/Informational Text (grade level) → Instructional Focuses

- Fluency
  - Poems
  - Songs
  - Short Text Pieces
- Vocabulary
  - From Text
- Comprehension
  - Before
    - Build Background Knowledge
    - Introduce Vocabulary
    - Set Purpose
  - During
    - Teacher/Student Questioning/Discussion
    - Close Reading
    - Vocabulary in Context
  - After
    - Comprehension Conversation
    - Written Comprehension

Text Selections for Shared Reading

First and foremost, the text selected for shared reading should be grade-level literary and informational text. The very nature of shared reading calls for shorter rather than longer text pieces. It is difficult at best to engage the entire class in long text pieces that are often difficult for some students to read, even with the support of the teacher. By selecting shorter texts, students can also work on developing fluency as these pieces are read and reread. With the appropriate length of the text and repeated readings, struggling readers also grow in fluency. Poetry or songs are good text choices for this purpose because students love to read or sing beloved poems and songs multiple times. These text pieces are not only engaging but also rich in vocabulary and comprehension opportunities.

Starting the school day with a shared reading activity builds community and sets the stage for a successful day of literacy learning. Maintaining a balance in the genres required with a focus on the grade-level standards should be incorporated in the shared reading venue.

Benefits of Shared Reading

Shared reading is an instructional delivery venue that is appropriate for whole-group instruction with a diverse group of readers. As grade-level texts are presented, shared reading provides the teacher with the necessary support for student access. Shared reading is also appropriate during content area instruction. Additional benefits of shared reading include the following:

- Allows students to see themselves as readers as they are supported in the reading and rereading of familiar texts
- Provides students with a safe, nonthreatening environment in which to practice new and familiar reading strategies
- Provides students with essential demonstrations of how reading works and what readers do to construct meaning from text
- Uses strategies for decoding unknown words and constructing meaning from the text
- Develops fluency, phrasing, and reading strategies
- Increases comprehension of grade-level text

Chapter 3 gives a detailed sample planner for preparing lessons for the shared reading format. Grade-level standards must be presented in such a way as to give all students the access to and background knowledge for these materials. The suggested implementation methods described assist teachers in making this access a reality.

Modeled Writing

Perhaps the area in the language arts standards that has been most neglected in recent years is writing. Writing in the elementary grades has traditionally been grounded in the teaching of writing personal narratives. In many states, there is a mandated fourth-grade writing assessment that emphasizes this genre, so much of the year focuses on writing that addresses this prompt type. Writing informational text pieces has been rare. When students are asked to write responses to texts, it usually involves short responses.

There are several reasons for these phenomena. First, many teachers are uncomfortable with teaching writing. Additionally, writing takes time: time for instruction, modeling, practice, and revision. Providing feedback to students and assessing writing also takes time. Recently, there has been a universal misconception that writing could not be a part of the reading block. The intention was for teachers to understand the difference between teaching the writing processes and writing about reading. In many instances, this caused writing to be addressed in isolation if at all.

Modeled writing provides an opportunity for teachers to demonstrate the writing process for a variety of purposes and for a variety of audiences, and it can be instrumental in developing students as writers. Modeled writing serves as the "I do" part of the gradual release of responsibility model. This teaching venue relies on the teacher to establish the writing purpose and process and to use think-aloud strategies as the text piece is developed. It is important to note that in modeled writing, student participation is limited. It is difficult for some teachers to refrain from allowing student input as a part of this writing process; however, this is the venue needed to model writing strategies for the students. There is a place for both modeled and shared writing venues in the process of supporting students.

Generally, modeled writing begins with an interactive read-aloud that is used as the basis for the written response, which demonstrates students' comprehension of the text. After the reading, the teacher begins talking about what he or she intends to write and the purpose for the writing. As the teacher writes, he or she thinks aloud as the piece is orchestrated.

The planning process not only involves the specific comprehension purpose for the written response but also identifies the writing process or trait that is the focus in the text development. Figure 8 shows the instructional focuses of modeled writing, which are discussed next.

Instructional Focuses of Modeled Writing

In many instances, the writing demonstrates written comprehension based on a text that provides the format for the modeled writing process. Modeled writing should focus on one or more of the research-based comprehension strategies identified by the National Reading Panel (NICHD, 2000), such as examining cause-and-effect relationships or character traits. Additionally, select a specific writing process or trait, such as word choice or sentence fluency, as a focus to incorporate as the text is developed. These two focuses offer an integrated way to provide real writing with a process focus.

Although in recent years, writing has been viewed as a subject disconnected from reading or the content areas, the Common Core State Standards include writing as a critical component in all subject areas, specifically responding to reading through writing with text-supported evidence. This means there is now a greater need for teachers to model writing. When they enter school, most students do not know how to write, in much the same way that they do not know how to read. Quality writing comes with many modeled demonstrations by teachers. Although modeled writing can be time-consuming, it is a necessity as students develop their own writing expertise because

FIGURE 8
Instructional Focuses of Modeled Writing

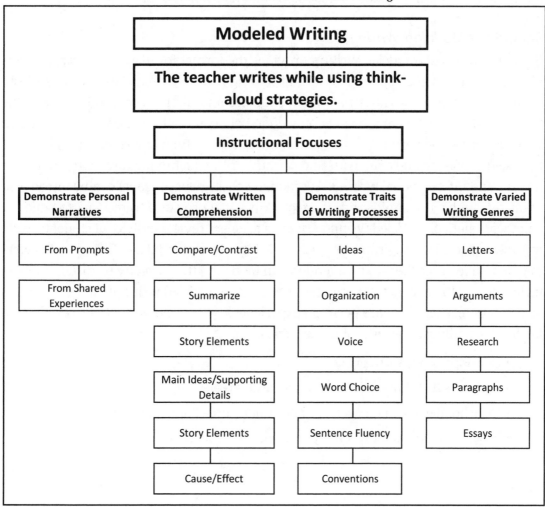

writing is a process. The writing process or writing traits should also be included in modeled writing, including a focus on ideas, organization, voice, word choice, sentence fluency, and conventions. Integrating grammar instruction in a real writing venue makes good sense, too.

Whereas personal narratives have been the primary form of writing introduced and practiced in the elementary grades, the CCSS require an extended focus on demonstrating comprehension through writing—in other words, writing a response that demonstrates deep understanding of a text. This is a major shift in how writing has been viewed and taught in the elementary curriculum. Personal narrative writing should not be overlooked, of course, as it is an important form of writing and often engaging for students. Again, the word *balance* comes to mind: Maintain a balance of writing types for a variety of audiences and for a variety of purposes.

Modeled writing should be included routinely in any primary or intermediate classroom. A rule of thumb is to include at least one modeled writing for literary text and one for an informational piece each week. Chapter 4 details the planning process as well as the classroom implementation of this important instructional venue.

Benefits of Modeled Writing

First and foremost, modeled writing provides the format for teachers to create a real piece of writing while applying important writing processes and skills as students observe. This often occurs after reading a text piece and furthers comprehension of the text. This illustrates the important connection between reading and writing. Modeled writing is also a powerful venue when a new concept or type of written response is introduced. Applying and demonstrating various writing techniques are modeled in both literary and informational writing. Additionally, these new concepts can be introduced in tandem with more familiar writing techniques that provide a framework to build on. Another benefit of modeled writing arises as teachers review individual students' writing and notice common problems, such as lack of vivid vocabulary. This modeled writing venue allows teachers to be intentional in modeling this strategy by discussing and including vocabulary that is more descriptive in the modeled writing. Modeled writing also allows teachers to share personal experiences, which motivates students. The following are additional benefits of modeled writing:

- Develops concepts of print
- Produces text that students can read and reread
- Incorporates writing processes and traits with a connected purpose
- Provides a format for teaching grammar in context

Shared Writing

Shared writing is the "we do" part of learning to write. Shared writing provides an interactive setting as students move toward independence in writing. In shared writing, the teacher still does the actual writing but does so with input from and conversations with students. In most instances, the teacher has modeled the particular technique or activity with another text piece prior to engaging students in a shared writing with a similar focus.

The differences between modeled and shared writing are subtle. Whereas modeled writing is directed and modeled by the teacher, shared writing provides the stepping-stone for students to move to the next step in becoming competent writers as they contribute to the writing process. This process involves the students as they share ideas and thoughts with the class as the teacher gives feedback and incorporates their input into the writing. The essence of shared writing is the collaborative writing process, with the teacher serving as scribe and supporter, and the students freely contributing to the process. Students need multiple shared writing experiences prior to transferring these writing skills to the independent writing level.

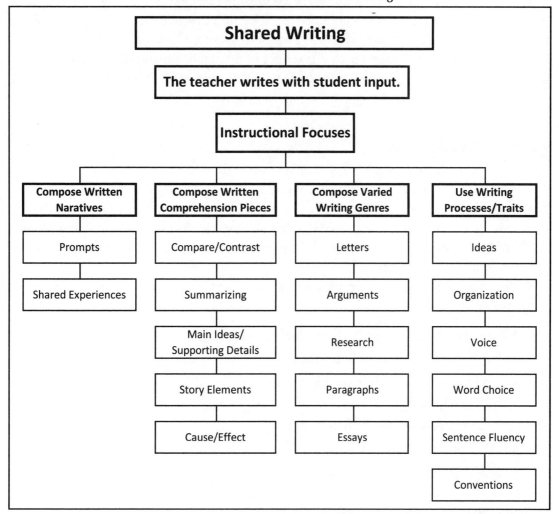

Instructional Focuses of Shared Writing

The instructional focuses of shared writing are similar to modeled writing (see Figure 9). Shared writing is an appropriate venue to use after providing ample modeling. The purposes for the writing activity should be specific rather than random. Plan for the shared writing intentionally so corresponding standards are addressed and students are engaged in the process. Both literary and informational text responses, as well as personal narratives, must be equally addressed in modeled and shared writing. These writing venues provide opportunities to connect reading and writing across the curriculum in meaningful ways for students.

Benefits of Shared Writing

This venue allows students to do what was demonstrated by the teacher in modeled writing via a think-aloud. As students build confidence with these written response activities, they are more likely to be successful in independent writing. Another benefit of shared writing is that these jointly written example pieces can be posted and used as references for students in independent writing. It is important to preserve the text pieces created during shared writing to use as anchor charts for students to review as models for their own writing. A mistake that teachers often make is using the dry-erase board for shared writing and then erasing these valuable examples at the end of the lesson. Chapter 3 presents a model for planning and implementing shared writing.

Targeted Minilessons

There are times during whole-group instruction when the teacher needs to present a minilesson that focuses on a particular foundational skill. Targeted minilessons should last no longer than 10–15 minutes and could be as short as a minute or two. An effective minilesson includes the teacher modeling the skill, students practicing with the teacher, and then students performing the skill independently. Again, the "I do, we do, you do" process provides the structure.

When considering appropriate content for these minilessons, consider the following questions:

- Does the content support grade-level standards?
- Can I present the material in a meaningful way to all of my students?
- Can I connect the skill to the bigger literacy picture?
- Am I teaching the lesson because it is in the teacher's guide or because most of my students need instruction in this skill?
- Is the lesson best taught in the context of other lessons?
- How will I assess the effectiveness of the minilesson?

Instructional Focuses of Targeted Minilessons

Figure 10 displays categories of specific skills that lend themselves to the targeted minilesson venue. The first category falls under the area of language, which is an identified strand in the Common Core State Standards. Within the language component are the subcategories of vocabulary and conventions of standard English. Vocabulary includes the areas of word meanings, word parts, and word relationships. Students must be able to determine or clarify the meanings of grade-appropriate words encountered through listening, reading, and media use. The conventions of English include those skills that are needed to accurately express oneself in both writing and speaking, commonly referred to as grammar. Although these language standards sometimes present opportunities for minilessons, they are more purposefully transferred and taught in the context of real reading, writing, speaking, and listening.

The components in the foundational skills category of the CCSS also lend themselves to some focused minilessons. These skills include knowledge of concepts of print, the alphabetic principle, and other conventions of the English writing system. The areas of phonics, word analysis, fluency, and phonemic awareness may also fall within this

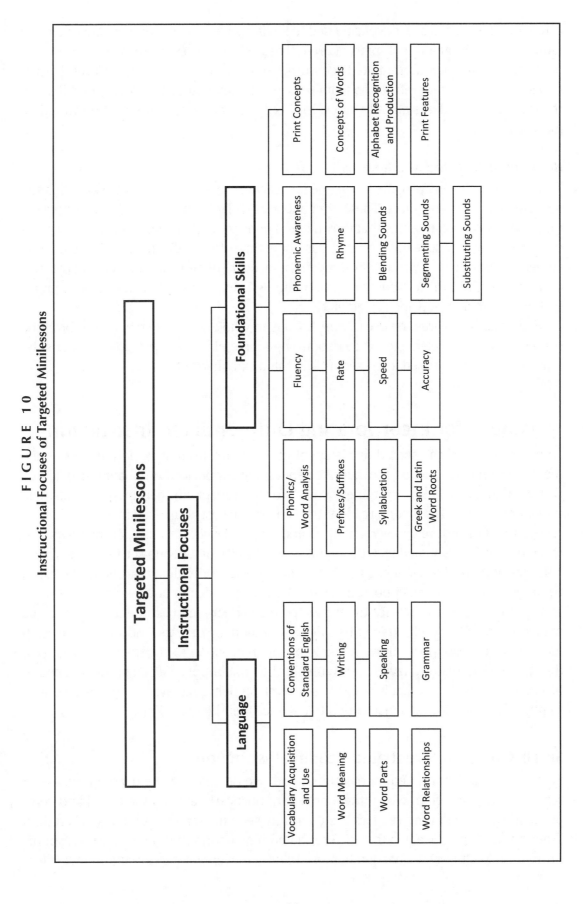

FIGURE 10
Instructional Focuses of Targeted Minilessons

category. These skills are inexplicitly tied to all literacy endeavors and a comprehensive literacy plan. The amount of instruction in these skills varies with the needs of the students and should be differentiated according to the needs of the group. Careful attention should be given to refraining from presenting minilessons that focus on skills that the majority of students already know. In this case, small-group instruction would be more appropriate.

Benefits of Targeted Minilessons

Targeted minilessons provide the venue for teachers to address specific skills that the majority of the class requires. These brief but powerful teaching interludes give students directed instruction in areas that they need to hone to further their literacy competencies. Minilessons reduce the extended classroom time often dedicated to skills that many students have already mastered. As students engage in guided and independent practice of the focus skills, those students who remain deficient in this skill can be brought together in a small group and remediated.

Chapter 3 explores the use of minilessons in whole-group instruction in both the primary and upper elementary classroom. A sample planner is provided to focus the purpose and activity used to present this isolated skill instruction.

Venues for Incorporating Differentiated Instruction

Although much of the school day is spent in whole-group instruction, it is essential that a portion of the day be dedicated to venues that support differentiated instruction. Differentiated instruction promotes growth for all students in their literacy skills. The developmental needs of young readers and writers are best addressed in venues that are respectful of their developmental reading and writing levels. Because of time restraints, much of this differentiated instruction takes place in a small-group setting, assembling students with like literacy needs. Additionally, shorter individual reading and writing conferences offer unique opportunities to focus on specific literacy needs.

Without opportunities for differentiated instruction, many students will continue to miss the mark of reaching their true literacy potential. Students who struggle in reading will have few opportunities in whole-group instruction to engage in text that is at the appropriate reading level, even with significant support. Gifted students need to be challenged with text that is above grade level. Students achieving at grade level also require additional focused instruction to enhance their literacy skills.

Small-Group Differentiated Reading Instruction

Small-group differentiated instruction is the "we do" part of the gradual release of responsibility model, in which the teacher supports students as they read and comprehend text. Struggling readers are generally seen in small group more often than other students because it is this differentiated instruction that gives them an opportunity to make the gains needed to close their achievement gap. Struggling readers, in particular, need ample appropriately leveled text choices to provide growth opportunities. Currently, most basal readers generally advocate for small-group instruction but provide only one book selection below grade level each week that may or may not be at an appropriate level for a particular struggling student. Additional small-group instruction during the week generally focuses on isolated comprehension or word work skills. During small-group differentiated instruction, it is important to address each essential reading component, including fluency, word analysis, vocabulary, and comprehension.

Those students who successfully read grade-level text are not exempt from small-group instruction because they need additional text selections and instruction at the appropriate literacy level to hone their literacy skills and continue to flourish. The opportunity to reflect and share in the small-group setting allows students to think more deeply about their reading, too. Although these grade-level readers may not need to work in small group daily, a sensible goal would be for them to do so every other day.

Advanced students require support to navigate more complex text usually written above grade level. If these students are limited by the text complexity presented in whole-group instruction, it is difficult at best to grow them to their full potential. A wide variety of genres in both literary and informational texts are included to address the needs of these more accomplished readers. Another mistake we often make with these students is to leave them on their own for independent reading. Growth requires text that is challenging enough to require the teacher's support with comprehension strategies before, during, or after reading. Even students who read at the highest levels need to be guided with in-depth comprehension conversations and discussions. Although these advanced readers require much less time in small group, the classroom teacher should meet with them in small groups routinely.

Instructional Focuses of Small-Group Differentiated Reading Instruction

Figure 11 displays the instructional focuses of small-group differentiated reading instruction This instruction centers around a text selection that is at an appropriate reading level for the group—that is, text that the students can read with 90–95% accuracy and successfully read and understand with the support of the teacher (Rasinski, 2010). The small-group differentiated reading models include the research-based components of fluency, phonemic awareness, phonics and word analysis, vocabulary, and comprehension, as they are appropriate for the specific group of readers. Each of these components is carefully weighted at the appropriate developmental level to address the needs of the specific group of readers. For example, whereas the recipe for struggling readers includes fluency practice in each lesson, more advanced readers who already read fluently do not require this ingredient. Assess and address developmental phonics or word analysis needs as part of the lesson. Center vocabulary instruction on words selected from the text. Incorporate comprehension strategies that are needed to understand the text into each lesson. Chapter 4 discusses various small-group differentiated lesson-planning models that address the developmental needs of all readers.

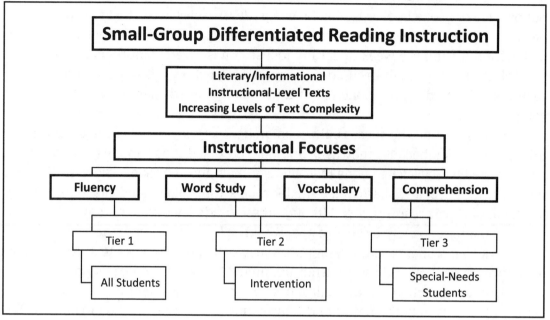

Additionally, small-group differentiated reading groups are the delivery venue for those students who require additional intervention, including students with special needs, students in the Response to Intervention (RTI) process, and English learners. The implications of small-group differentiated reading instruction with these special populations is addressed in Chapter 4.

Text Selections for Small-Group Differentiated Reading Instruction

The most essential component in small-group reading instruction is teaching from texts that best match the students' developmental reading needs. This is no small task. Clearly, we have come a long way in leveling books according to difficulty level. Most schools, however, have insufficient resources to meet the needs of all of their readers. In addressing the need for increasing text complexity put forth by the Common Core standards, leveled text holds an important place in curriculum development. Teachers need to provide sufficient leveled text to address literacy and content standards that progress in difficulty levels. It is unrealistic to think that a fourth-grade student reading two grade levels below could be expected to read and understand a fourth-grade level text. Even with strong teacher support and scaffolding, the text would be so challenging that the student would become frustrated along with the teacher. Although teachers can present these higher text levels in the context of interactive read-alouds and shared reading, these venues in and of themselves are insufficient for assisting these students in literacy growth.

Another concern is the misnomer that all leveled texts are created equally—that is, all leveled using the same guidelines. Teachers are the best decision makers in choosing appropriate text selections. Preview the text structure, vocabulary, and appropriateness of text content prior to introducing a book in small-group setting. Be sure to consider the text complexity measures described in Chapter 1 with respect to qualitative, quantitative, and reader and task.

Texts selected for small-group instruction must represent the same wide range of genres in both literary and informational text. Many times, teachers continually present thick chapter books as ways to address the needs of advanced readers, but thicker books do not necessarily produce better readers.

Historically, especially when small group was used as an intervention, the text selections had very little connection to the classroom curriculum. Take every opportunity to extend the curriculum's grade-level focuses in small group with texts selected at the appropriate levels of difficulty.

Although I am a strong proponent of the important place that leveled text plays with more struggling readers, I believe that we may need to more carefully consider the difficulty levels. In many instances, text selections have been too easy for students, which has inhibited growth. As we begin to more fully address the CCSS, we must be vigilant in making sure that text selections hold the appropriate mix of quality and text complexity.

Benefits of Small-Group Differentiated Reading Instruction

Differentiated reading instruction in small groups gives every student the opportunity for literacy growth. Think of this differentiated instruction as the stair steps necessary for students to reach the next highest level of literacy. If we select appropriate instructional-level texts, students will need the support of the teacher to read and understand the text deeply. Small-group differentiated reading instruction also gives students the opportunity to access text levels that would not be appropriate in independent reading assignments. Currently, most struggling readers rely on listening comprehension to access content material in whole group because the text is too difficult for them to read. In small-group instruction, however, all students can read to gain information. The following are additional benefits of small-group differentiated reading:

- Promotes reading strategies and offers students the opportunity to practice their reading skills

- Increases reading comprehension

- Allows the teacher to monitor individual students' progress (The teacher may need to prompt students to apply their knowledge of reading strategies when difficulties arise, provide further support, or regroup students according to their needs.)

- Expands students' beliefs in their own abilities as readers and consolidates and extends their understanding of a text

Differentiating Through Individual Writing Conferences

Individual writing conferences allow students to share and reflect on their own writing with feedback from the teacher. This is the "you do" with teacher support part of the gradual release of responsibility model. It is virtually impossible for students to grow as writers without specific instruction and feedback from the teacher. The writing conference generally takes place in the revision stage of the writing process and can take different forms. Graves has identified six characteristics of successful writing conferences: (1) have a predictable structure, (2) focus on a few points, (3) demonstrate solutions to students' problems, (4) permit role reversals, (5) encourage use of an appropriate vocabulary for writing, and (6) stimulate pleasure in writing (as cited in Culham, 2003). Most teachers use some variance of these characteristics in their classrooms.

Students should become familiar with the structure of the writing conference so they are well prepared to meet with the teacher. Rather than focus on all aspects of the writing process, each conference should be narrow in focus and address only a few points. The teacher supports students with the knowledge that the teacher will assist in solving problems related to their writing. The writing conference allows the students to share with the teacher, which is a role reversal from the regular classroom setting. Finally, the writing conference encourages and motivates students in their own writing capabilities.

Instructional Focuses of an Individual Writing Conference

Although the instructional focuses vary from student to student and from one conference to the next, the ultimate goal is to provide instruction that assists students in becoming competent writers, capable of clearly communicating in a variety of ways for a variety of purposes. The primary focuses relate to the writing processes themselves, including ideas, voice, organization, word choice, sentence fluency, and conventions. Additionally, as students write to demonstrate deep understanding of a text piece, the thinking behind the writing is a point of focus. Figure 12 shows the instructional focuses of individual literacy conferences that focus on writing and reading (as discussed in the following pages).

Benefits of Individual Writing Conferences

The writing conference differentiates instruction for each individual student. Motivation is perhaps the biggest benefit gleaned from the conferences because the teacher serves as encourager and problem solver, supporting the idea that students are capable writers with an important message to share. The importance of building a trust relationship between student and teacher cannot be underestimated as a benefit. As students begin to trust the teacher as an encourager rather than a criticizer, this opens the door for an increase in writing abilities. The social benefits in writing conferences occur indirectly when students are encouraged to share their completed pieces with the class. This in turn creates a community of writers who mutually respect and attend to the work of others. Students respond positively to the immediate feedback given by the teacher. This venue allows the teacher to be keenly aware of what each student can do as a writer and

FIGURE 12
Instructional Focuses of Individual Literacy Conferences

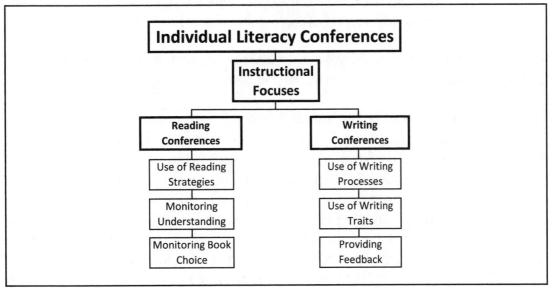

to guide them based on this information. In many cases, students write with little or no feedback from the teacher. Writing conferences provide an opportunity for this much needed feedback in a nonthreatening environment.

I would be remiss if I did not discuss the inherent difficulties with establishing routine writing conferences. They require time. According to the CCSS mandates for writing, we must schedule time for this individual instruction and feedback. By establishing a routine for conferencing a few students daily, the task does not seem so overwhelming.

Differentiating Through Individual Reading Conferences

The reading conference serves much the same purpose as the writing conference. Reading conferences provide teachers with the opportunity to meet individually with students to assess progress, provide guidance as needed, and assist in goal setting for self-selected reading (see Figure 12).

Individual reading conferences usually take place during independent reading time, with the teacher touching base with each reader on a weekly or biweekly basis. Teachers should establish a schedule to meet with students that is flexible enough to accommodate unforeseen problems and teachable moments as they arise. As the teacher poses guiding questions, students verbalize the reading strategies being used. The following are examples of these types of questions:

- Is this book too easy or too hard for you?
- Did you make any personal connections in your reading?
- Did any questions come up while you were reading?

- How are you enjoying the book so far?
- What strategies are you working on in your reading?
- Is there anything that I can help you with?

Additionally, the teacher might ask the student to read part of the text aloud to determine the appropriateness of the text's level and content.

Instructional Focuses of an Individual Reading Conference

The primary instructional focuses of the reading conference are comprehension and the students' ability to use strategies interchangeably to understand the text message. Although the text's topic is briefly discussed, the discussion focuses more on the reading strategies that the student is using rather than the text's content. Probe to discern the strategies that the student is currently using and determine whether these strategies are working appropriately. In other words, teach the reader not the reading! The instructional goal is to guide students in developing strategies that will transfer to many different texts. It is important to not focus on more than one or two strategies at a time. Additionally, ask the student to briefly read from the text to determine whether the accuracy, rate, and expression are sufficient for understanding the text message.

Benefits of an Individual Reading Conference

Reading conferences provide a personal format for the teacher and the students to confer about reading strategies. Again, this is the "you do" part of the gradual release of responsibility model. Most students value this special time discussing the text with their teacher. If students are left to self-select books and read independently, the teacher has no knowledge about the proper fit of the text or the level of the student's engagement. This one-on-one time provides motivation for students as the teacher engages them in personal conversations based on student-selected texts.

It is helpful to keep notes about what is discussed in the conferences both for the teacher and the students. These observations serve a part in the ongoing assessment used to guide instruction. As the teacher reviews individual reading logs kept by the students, the teacher is better able to guide the students in terms of reading varied genres or addressing appropriate text levels that are either too high or too low. As each reading conference is completed, the teacher and the student agree on goals to work on before the next scheduled reading conference.

Independent Practice, Projects, and Presentations

Perhaps the most daunting challenge as teachers strive to deliver a comprehensive literacy curriculum is engaging students in meaningful independent literacy activities. Rather than view these activities as time fillers or busy work, these should be considered as the culminating activities that teachers have carefully trained students to be able to do on their own. A dilemma that many teachers face when they try to implement small-group instruction is the inability to manage independent practice. However, this is indeed an important time for students to orchestrate their literacy learning. Another way to think about this time is its importance for students to practice and hone their literacy skills without teacher support. It is the "you do" part of the gradual release process, which is the ultimate goal of effective literacy instruction. In other words, this is the time to push the birds out of the nest, allowing students the time needed to grow in their own literacy learning.

Independent activities can be completed individually, but students often work with partners and small groups. Independent simply means that students are working without the direct guidance of the teacher. Assignments include time for research, extensive reading and writing, and preparing presentations to share with others. Perhaps the most difficult part of independent practice is monitoring the activities. This time is not meant for busy work unworthy of teacher feedback. This literacy work is in all probability the most important work of the day because these are the activities that the teacher has carefully prepared for students to capably complete without the teacher, which leads to literacy independence. Chapter 4 discusses activities and concrete examples of meaningful independent activities for a diverse group of students.

Instructional Focuses of Independent Practice, Projects, and Presentations

If we agree that there must be time for independent practice, what should the students actually be doing? First and foremost, they are engaged in reading and writing tasks that they are capable of successfully completing without teacher support. In essence, students spend much of their independent time working in diverse assignments with texts and activities that are appropriate for a wide range of readers and writers. That said, it makes sense to assign students extended work with texts currently being read in their small-group instruction to promote further reading, discussions, and writing about the text or topic. This allows students to engage in reading and writing activities that are appropriate for their particular literacy levels. Although most of the activities that students engage in independently are differentiated, there are times when it is appropriate for all students to complete the same assignment. For example, as a follow-up to a whole-group minilesson, all students might be asked to complete an assignment for independent practice. Figure 13 shows the instructional focuses of independent literacy practice, projects, and presentations.

The instructional focuses of independent learning include bringing together and orchestrating reading, writing, speaking, and listening skills. Students continue to develop fluency as they read independent-level text. Independent time is also spent exploring vocabulary more extensively and for students to engage in research to further understand a topic. Another focus includes time to work cooperatively to develop presentations to present to an audience.

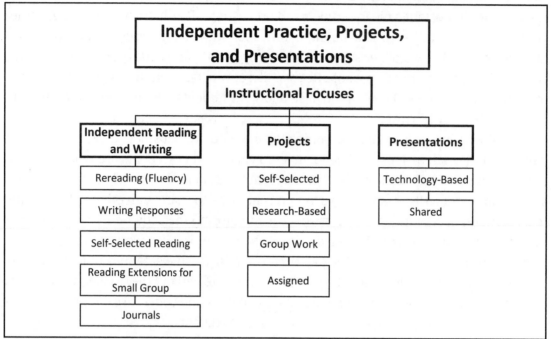

Benefits of Independent Practice, Projects, and Presentations

Independent activities set the stage as students orchestrate their literacy learning. It gives students the time needed to develop as readers and writers as well as the time to work collaboratively as they build a literacy learning community. This also gives students access to extended time and opportunities to work at their individually appropriate developmental reading and writing levels.

For teachers, there is an additional instructional benefit. Independent literacy time should extend beyond the time that teachers spend in small-group instruction. As students are engaged in extended independent literacy activities, consider using some of this time for individual reading and writing conferences.

Planning for and Implementing Whole-Group Literacy Instruction

With the majority of the school day spent in the whole-group setting, carefully planned instruction that benefits a wide range of literacy learners is essential. Whole-group literacy instruction includes opportunities for the teacher to model reading and writing and share these literacy experiences with students. Whole-group instruction also includes specific targeted skill lessons that are instrumental in developing the foundational skills that underpin both reading and writing. Much of the reading and writing processes are interrelated and flow seamlessly in language arts instruction that includes both literary and informational texts as the centerpiece. In this chapter, we focus on the specific venues of whole-group instruction: the interactive read-aloud, shared reading, modeled and shared writing, and targeted skill lessons. The provided vignettes show whole-group lessons in action in primary- and intermediate-grade classrooms.

The Interactive Read-Aloud

The interactive read-aloud is an instructional venue in which the teacher reads a text piece out loud while the students listen and actively engage in conversations to further their comprehension. This read-aloud is carefully planned and begins by establishing the learning goals that the students should know or be able to do as a result of the lesson. Next, the teacher carefully selects the text to read aloud that supports the learning goals. Selecting appropriate strategies that will aid students in reaching these goals is also a critical part of the planning process. Instruction primarily focuses on vocabulary acquisition and comprehension. Strategically identifying the key comprehension and vocabulary strategies for before, during, and after reading gives each interactive read-aloud the structure needed for in-depth comprehension of the text.

Establishing Learning Goals and Assessments

The learning goals for the lesson are what you expect students to know or be able to do as a result of this interactive read-aloud experience and should be established early in the planning process. Closely align learning goals to the grade-level standards in language arts. Additional standards in the content areas are also appropriate when selecting informational text. Along with establishing these learning goals, choose the appropriate assessments for determining whether the learning goals have been met.

Always begin planning with the end in mind. Establish the culminating comprehension focuses and activities in the planning process that will guide the instructional sequence.

Text Selections

The next step in the planning process is the selection of the text to be used for the interactive read-aloud. This cannot be left to chance. The text selections should represent a wide variety of genres and generally be written above the instructional reading levels of most students in the classroom. In addition to the traditional literary genres, informational text must also be considered. The Common Core State Standards require that informational and literary texts receive equal instructional time and be considered in balancing the text choices. By selecting quality, well-written informational text pieces, teachers provide students with materials that are engaging and supportive of grade-level content standards. Content-based read-alouds enhance the curriculum and provide students with support, especially those who lack background knowledge about the specific subject area addressed in the text. Text selections should be for specific instructional purposes. As text quality and text complexity issues move to the forefront in literacy instruction, the interactive read-aloud provides equal access for all students to these text types, which is especially critical for those students who are unable to successfully read these texts independently.

Obviously, teachers have numerous choices for read-alouds: library books, books from personal collections, classroom books, magazine articles, newspaper articles, poetry, and so forth. The selection process should not be done without a great deal of thought about the purpose for the text. While selecting texts for this interactive reading, pay careful attention to the grade-level standards. Intentional decisions concerning vocabulary and comprehension focuses are an important part of the planning process because these texts will provide important foundations for comprehension conversations as well as opportunities for written comprehension responses. As students reach the upper elementary grades, these texts might also serve as mentor texts in reading and writing, offering examples of particular writing or reading strategies.

Preread the texts in their entirety before making selection decisions. A good rule of thumb is that if the book appeals to you, it will most likely appeal to students. Here are some questions to guide text selection for an interactive read-aloud:

- Does the text support your language arts learning goals (i.e., the building blocks to the standards)?
- Does the text support your unit of study?
- Does the text meet the guidelines of appropriate quality and text complexity for your grade level?
- Is the text written above the reading level of most students in your classroom?
- Does the text provide diversity in genres?
- Is the length of the text appropriate for the students?

• Which grade-level standards will the read-aloud support in language arts and in related content areas, if appropriate?

The instructional purposes for interactive read-alouds were discussed in Chapter 2. Developing listening and speaking vocabulary for all students is an accomplishable goal. Students reading above grade level may also expand their reading and writing vocabulary with exposure to this high-quality text. In much the same way, listening and speaking comprehension is an inclusive focus for all students. Reading and writing comprehension is also addressed as written responses are modeled by the teacher and shared with the students.

Addressing Vocabulary and Comprehension Focuses

Prior to reading the text, prepare students with strategies that will enhance text comprehension as well as vocabulary acquisition. First, set a specific purpose for reading the text so students focus on a particular aspect of it during reading. The purpose should relate to the learning goals. Next, provide the background knowledge that students will need to adequately comprehend the text. This is especially true for informational text or any subject matter that may be unfamiliar to the students. Encourage them to make connections to the text topic as a way to access their background knowledge. Additionally, introduce preselected vocabulary from the text that will be important for students to know and understand at the particular grade level. The selection of vocabulary should be limited and related to the comprehension of the text. This does not mean that the vocabulary selections will necessarily be the most difficult words in the text or proper names. Think in terms of the words that students will come in contact with in multiple settings or important content-specific vocabulary connected to grade-level standards. It is also important for students to have opportunities to determine word meanings from context clues during reading. Modeling this strategy assists students in their own reading as they encounter unknown words. Finally, when using an informational text, preview the text features prior to reading to discuss their importance in understanding the text.

During the reading, employ varied strategies that provide both modeling opportunities and interaction opportunities for the students. Think-alouds communicate the teacher's thinking as it applies to understanding the text. Think-pair-share strategies initiate discussions between students as the text is explored. Predictions are made and confirmed, and questioning by both the teacher and the students provides opportunities for student interactions. When a pictureless text is read, visualizing is also an option. In the preplanning process, make note of strategic points in the text for intentional questioning or discussion.

When the read-aloud is completed, summarize the text with a primary comprehension focus. In literary text, this focus might be to summarize the story elements or concentrate more deeply on a particular one. The activity for addressing this comprehension focus could be whole-class comprehension conversations, modeled or shared written responses, or independent written responses. Additionally, revisit the story vocabulary that was presented before reading. In informational text, the culminating comprehension focuses might include sequencing, main ideas and supporting details, cause-and-effect relationships, or comparing and contrasting.

Quality instruction begins with a quality plan. (See the Appendix for a reproducible planner that is helpful for orchestrating lessons for interactive read-alouds.) The success of the read-aloud is directly related to the lesson plan. Concrete examples of both literary and informational interactive read-alouds are presented in the following vignettes.

Interactive Read-Alouds in the Primary-Grade Classroom: Literary Text

Ms. Davis, a kindergarten teacher, selects the book *Wolf!* by Becky Bloom (1999) for a variety of reasons. First, the book supports the current classroom theme of friends: real and imaginary. The book is highly entertaining, and Ms. Davis feels that the students can relate to the wolf and his problem in learning to read. The book can be easily read in one sitting, which is important for these young students. Finally, the text provides foundations for addressing important standards in literary text and offers an opportunity for all students to participate regardless of their reading abilities. Figure 14 shows a sample lesson plan for a primary-grade interactive read-aloud for this text. A blank template can be found in the Appendix.

This kindergarten class of 22 students includes two English learners and two students who have been identified as having special needs. Ms. Davis begins the lesson by calling students to the carpet.

FIGURE 14
Sample Lesson Plan for a Primary-Grade Interactive Read-Aloud

Planner for Interactive Read-Alouds and Shared Reading

Text: "Wolf!" by Becky Bloom   Type: Literary

Learning Goals: Language Arts (LA) or Content Area (CA)
- LA: Identify the main problem and solutions in the story.
- LA: Ask and answer questions about key ideas and supporting details to confirm understanding.
- LA: Summarize the story using key vocabulary words.

Before Reading

Build Background Knowledge: Theme: making new friends; make connections

Introduce Story Vocabulary: educated, emergency, ignore, peered, emergency, wandered

Set the Purpose: To find out how the wolf solves his problem

During Reading: Teaching Points
- Page 6: I wonder why the other animals aren't afraid of the wolf.
- Page 7: How has the setting changed?
- Page 11: What new problem is the wolf facing?
- Page 15: What do you think the wolf will do next? What evidence do you have based on what has happened so far?

After Reading

Comprehension Focus: Problem and solutions

Vocabulary Review: Use each vocabulary word in a sentence that tells something about the story.

Written Response: Shared writing; complete a problem/solution T-chart

Assessment: Teacher observation

Before Reading

Ms. Davis: We have been talking about friends this week, and today we are going to read a book about a wolf who wants to make friends. Have you ever had problems making new friends?

Kate: Yeah, when I moved here, nobody would be my friend.

Ms. Davis: Why do you think it is hard to make new friends when you are the new student in the class?

Tarah: Well, we don't know you yet, and you might not be nice.

Ms. Davis: I think you are right. When you already have friends, sometimes we think that we don't need new friends. Today we are going to read a story about a wolf who is having problems making new friends. Take a look at the front cover of the book. Does this remind you of another story we read about some pigs and a wolf?

46

Maria:	Oh yeah, we read the Three Little Pigs, but the wolf was mean in that story. This wolf doesn't look mean.
Lauren:	Yeah, and this book only has one pig on the cover.
Ms. Davis:	Good observation! Do you think this will be a true story or an imaginary story? Turn to your talking partner.

Ms. Davis previously assigned Peanut Butter and Jelly talking partners and established this think-pair-share routine with her students. Students are assigned weekly talking partners and are designated as either Peanut Butter or Jelly. Ms. Davis observes as students discuss.

Ms. Davis:	Laura and John, can you share your ideas?
Laura:	Well, we both think that the book will be make-believe because a real wolf doesn't wear glasses.
John:	Yeah, and a wolf wouldn't make friends like we do.
Ms. Davis:	Thumbs up if you agree with Laura and John.

[All of the students give thumbs up.]

Ms. Davis:	It looks like we all agree. If we look at the cover of the book, we can get some more clues.

[She and the students continue the discussion.]

Ms. Davis:	I want to show you some words that we will read in the story today. I have some pictures in this pocket chart. We will try to find a picture that matches each word. The first word is *emergency*. [She shows the word written on an index card.] I think you know what an emergency is. This morning we had an emergency when the hamster got out of the cage. I am going to point at each of the pictures. Give me thumbs up or thumbs down if you think it is a picture of an emergency.

It is important to give all students a chance to respond. Ms. Davis printed appropriate pictures from the Internet to support the vocabulary in the story. Visual supports increase the acquisition of vocabulary for all students, especially English learners. She continues the process until each vocabulary word has been appropriately matched with a corresponding picture.

Ms. Davis:	When I read one of these words in the story, I want you to help me by making a sound or movement to remind us about what the word means. For the first word, *emergency*, let's all make a siren sound and pretend that our fist is the siren and hold it in the air. Let's practice that together.

[Ms. Davis continues describing actions that dramatize each of the vocabulary words.]

Ms. Davis:	As we read the story, I want you to think about all the problems the wolf has in the story and how he solves his problems.

It is important to establish a purpose for reading the story to further engage students in the comprehension process.

During Reading
Ms. Davis begins reading the book aloud. At appropriate, preselected stopping points, she demonstrates her thinking about the story and engages students in answering questions, posing questions, and making predictions based on evidence from the story.

Ms. Davis:	[after reading page 6] I wonder why the other animals aren't afraid of the wolf. I think they should be afraid. What do you think?

Paul: Maybe the other animals know he isn't dangerous.

Ms. Davis: Why do you think that?

Paul: The other animals don't even look up at him, and their faces don't look scared.

Ms. Davis: I'm glad that you looked at the illustrations to give you clues about what is going on in the story. Now, on page 8, we are going to see the word *ignored*. When I read that word, I want everyone to show me what the animals look like when they ignore the wolf.

[She continues reading aloud.]

Ms. Davis: [after page 9] How has the setting changed on this page? Turn to your partner. Jellies, you go first.

[She monitors as the students discuss and then continues reading aloud.]

Ms. Davis: [after page 11] What new problem does the wolf face on this page?

Trinity: Now the wolf can read, but he is reading too slow, and the other animals still don't pay any attention to him.

Ms. Davis: What do you predict he might do to solve the problem?

Lauren: I think he wants to make friends so much that they he'll go back to school again.

Ms. Davis: I'm going to continue reading the story to see if Lauren's prediction is right.

[She continues reading the story aloud.]

Lauren: No, I was wrong. He doesn't go back to school. He goes to the library to get his own book.

Ms. Davis: Yes, but you made a good prediction, and it made sense with where we were in the story.

[She continues reading the story aloud.]

Ms. Davis: [after page 15] Based on what has happened so far in the story, what do you think the wolf will do next?

Kate: I think the wolf won't give up because he didn't give up the other times when the animals didn't like the way he read.

It is important that students justify their predictions based on text evidence so wild guessing is discouraged. Ms. Davis finishes reading the story aloud, stopping at predetermined points to use think-alouds that demonstrate a variety of comprehension strategies.

After Reading

Ms. Davis: First, let's go back to the question that I asked before we read the story. How does the wolf finally solve his problem about making new friends? Talk it over with your partner.

[She monitors as students share. Then she conducts a shared writing activity.]

Ms. Davis: I am going to write the problems that the wolf had on the left side of my paper. What was his main problem?

Trinity: His big problem was that he didn't know how to make friends.

[Ms. Davis writes that on the chart paper.]

Ms. Davis: What are some of the ways that he solves his problem? Grace and Perry, what do you think?

Perry: He's a lot nicer, and he doesn't growl or try to scare the other animals.

Grace:	Yes, and he has better manners. He knocks at the gate instead of just jumping over it.

[The discussion continues. Ms. Davis records the students' responses on the chart paper.]

In this story, there are several solutions to the main problem. See Figure 15 for the completed chart.

FIGURE 15
Sample Problem–Solution Chart

Problems	Solutions
Animals ignore him. →	He learns to read.
He reads too slow. →	He practices.
He reads too fast. →	He practices.
He has no friend. →	He learns to read to the animals.

Ms. Davis:	Let's take another look at our vocabulary words. Let's see how the word *emergency* was used in the story and create our own sentence. I'll do the first one. The wolf only had some money for emergencies. Now, you do one. What about the word *peered*?
LaDonna:	I forgot what that is.
Ms. Davis:	That's OK. Let's get a friend to help, and then I'll come back to you.
Maria:	The wolf peered over the fence at the other animals. That means he looked.
Ms. Davis:	Great job, Maria. Now, LaDonna, can you show me the action we did for the word *peered*? Everyone do it with her.

It is important to go back to students who answer incorrectly so they know that you are not ignoring their incomplete responses. Ms. Davis continues the activity with each vocabulary word.

Assessment

Ms. Davis assesses the learning goals through her observations of students' responses.

Lesson Summary

This interactive read-aloud is both educational and entertaining. Students are actively involved in the story through questioning and discussion opportunities. The summary of the story takes the form of a shared writing experience that easily connects these two important whole-group instructional venues and addresses the learning goals.

Interactive Read-Alouds in the Intermediate-Grade Classroom: Historical Fiction

Mr. Fyock, a fifth-grade teacher, selects the historical fiction text *They Came From the Bronx: How the Buffalo Were Saved From Extinction* by Neil Waldman (2001) to share with his class for several reasons. The book supports the current social studies unit of study on the westward expansion. Through this story, point of view can be explored by the class through the eyes of an American Indian grandmother as she recounts the impact that the westward expansion had on the American Indians. Additionally, the author's use of two settings is engaging and provides an example of a writing style rarely used in books at this grade level. Mr. Fyock feels that this text will provide rich discussion and the opportunity for students to apply their background knowledge of the subject to another situation.

The class of 25 students includes three special education students and an English learner. Using a document camera, Mr. Fyock shares the exceptional illustrations in the text with the entire class. Figure 16 shows a sample lesson plan for the book.

FIGURE 16
Sample Lesson Plan for an Intermediate-Grade Interactive Read-Aloud

Planner for Interactive Read-Alouds and Shared Reading

Text: "They Came From the Bronx: How the Buffalo Were Saved From Extinction" by Neil Waldman   **Type:** Historical fiction

Learning Goals: Language Arts (LA) or Content Area (CA)
- Identify examples where the narrator's point of view influences how the events are described.
- Compare and contrast two settings in the story.
- Determine the author's purpose for writing the story.
- Compare and contrast first-person and third-person accounts of facts from various resources.

Before Reading

Build Background Knowledge: Recall historical facts from social studies textbook.

Introduce Story Vocabulary: reservation, trading post, extinct, slaughter, sustain (use predict-o-gram)

Set the Purpose: To determine whether the narrator's account of the westward expansion is factual or tainted by her own experiences

During Reading: Teaching Points
- After the introduction: What clues do we have about the author's purpose for writing this book?
- Page 2: Predict the purpose for the two settings.
- Page 4: Find clues about the point of view of the grandmother and identify specific language as support.
- Page 8: Is this quotation factual: "but the white leaders had decided to force us to give up our ancient way of life"?

After Reading

Comprehension Focus: Compare and contrast the grandmother's point of view and historical facts.

Vocabulary Review: Review the predict-o-gram and justify your answers.

Written Response: Present an argument: Was the grandmother's point of view factual? Give evidence to support your argument.

Assessment: Rubric for written response

Before Reading

Mr. Fyock: Today's story is about an Indian grandmother who tells her grandson about the impact that whites had on the American Indian way of life. We just completed our unit of study on the westward expansion. First, let's think about what we already read about this in Social Studies. Talk with your partner about what you remember.

This serves the purpose of building background knowledge and making connections to the text.

Mr. Fyock: Alex, why don't you and Laura share some things that you remember?

Alex: Well, when the whites went west, it really changed the American Indian way of life like when they took over the Indians' land.

[The discussion continues as students contribute their thoughts.]

Mr. Fyock: Before I begin reading, let's look at some words from the story. [He displays the preselected vocabulary: *reservation, trading post, extinct, destination, slaughter, sustain.*] Now I want you to make some quick predictions about how these words will play out in the story. With your partner, make some predictions about each word and how it might relate to the characters, settings, problems, or solutions in the story that we will read today. You have three minutes to make your lists.

[The students quickly record each vocabulary word and discuss with their partners.]

This exercise gives students the opportunity to make predictions based on evidence from their previous study of the subject.

Mr. Fyock: As we read today, the main character, the American Indian grandmother, tells the story in first person, from her point of view. As I read, think about what you already know about the subject and how her viewpoint affects the story. Are her thoughts in line with what you already learned, or is she tainted by her own experiences?

During Reading

Mr. Fyock: I want to begin by reading the book's introduction. This introduction will give us a chance to examine the author more closely and some of his purposes for writing the book.

[He reads the introduction as students listen.]

Mr. Fyock: Now, with your partner, identify one purpose that you think the author had for writing this book.

[Partners complete a quick think-pair-share activity.]

Mr. Fyock: Joshua and Leon, tell us what you came up with.

Joshua: Well, we really aren't sure if we're right. We think that he wrote the story because it was part of his life when he was a child. Does that count?

Mr. Fyock: Certainly, it does. Most authors are personally connected to their stories in some way.

[He reads the book aloud and uses a document camera to allow students to view the illustrations more closely, stopping at predetermined points to delve deeper into the text to support the main learning goals.]

Mr. Fyock: [after reading page 2] What do you notice about the story and the author's use of settings? Turn and talk with your partner. You have 30 seconds.

[The students discuss as Mr. Fyock monitors.]

Mr. Fyock: Emma, can you and Dillon share with us?

Emma: It's really weird. We think there are two stories taking place at the same time.

Mr. Fyock: Everyone, thumbs up if you agree with Emma.

[All students agree. Mr. Fyock continues reading the story and stops at critical points for further discussion by the students.]

Mr. Fyock: [before page 4] As I read page 4, I want you to think about the words that the grandmother uses to describe the events. What clues do we get from the words about her point of view?

[He reads the page aloud while students listen.]

Mr. Fyock: Does anyone remember something that she says that gives us a hint about her point of view?

Sam: She talks about how the white men tried to trick the Indians into buying guns. I'm not sure that's what really happened.

[Mr. Fyock and the students continue the discussion and read on.]

Mr. Fyock: [after page 8] I want to read a quote from this page: "but the white leaders had decided to force us to give up our ancient way of life." Based on what you know already, do you think this is a fair statement? Talk this over with your partner.

[He monitors as the students discuss. Then, Mr. Fyock completes the read-aloud as students engage in discussions.]

After Reading

Mr. Fyock: First, I want you to look at the predictions you made with your partner using the vocabulary words. You have three minutes to discuss the words and change the categories of any words that you want to change.

[The students work in think-pair-share.]

Mr. Fyock: Let's start with the term *trading post*. Thumbs up if you listed it as the problem.

[Most of the students agree.]

Mr. Fyock: OK, what about the solution? Did anyone change the category after reading the story?

Derrick: Yeah, we did. We thought that a trading post would be a setting, but now we know that it was a problem. The grandmother in the story said that the problems with the white people were at the trading post.

Mr. Fyock: That was a good observation.

[He continues leading the discussion of each vocabulary word and asks students to justify their answers.]

Mr. Fyock: As we think about the story, begin to look at some evidence about the grandmother's point of view. Form groups of four from two sets of partners and compare the grandmother's point of view with the information we read in our Social Studies textbook. Use your textbooks to help you. Find evidence in the book that either supports her views or shows a conflict in how she portrays the events. You need to record what you find and be ready to report to the group. You will present an argument: Is the grandmother's point of view factual or not? Give evidence from your Social Studies textbook to support your argument. Include at least one quotation that supports your viewpoint. You will have time this afternoon to work on this project. Your group needs to be ready to present to the class on Friday.

Assessment

Mr. Fyock assesses the learning goals through his observations of students' responses during the reading as well as his observations of the completed written documents.

Lesson Summary

Interactive read-alouds are excellent venues for addressing language arts standards as well as content standards. This fifth-grade example provides a text that connects content area study and rich opportunities for writing. This type of theme-based instruction helps students make important connections in their literacy learning.

Shared Reading

Unlike the interactive read-aloud, the shared reading venue allows for all students to have access to the text that is read. Whereas the teacher was the sole reader in the interactive read-aloud, the students read with the teacher in this venue.

The focus of shared reading revolves around grade-level text and understanding it. Although the planning model for shared reading is the same as for the interactive read-aloud, these two venues support different text types. Whereas the interactive read-aloud uses text written above grade level, the shared reading selections are appropriate for the grade level. Therefore, for students reading at or above grade level, shared reading is a suitable venue for developing fluency and is therefore included in the student learning goals. For students who struggle to read grade-level text, strategically plan for opportunities that will support these readers in alternative settings. Also include instructional focuses that are appropriate for the grade level and relevant for the text piece in comprehension and vocabulary development. Careful thought in planning will pay great dividends in student learning.

Establishing Learning Goals and Assessments

First and foremost, the learning goals should serve as stepping-stones to the established language arts standards for the specific grade level. The learning goals provide the backbone needed to effectively structure the shared reading lesson. Along with the learning goals comes the need to determine when these goals have been reached. Therefore, choosing the assessment procedures for the lesson should be a part of the planning process.

Text Support for Shared Reading

Shared reading is based on grade-level text; therefore, careful selection of the text is instrumental for a successful lesson. The wide range of reading abilities among students in any given classroom makes shorter reading pieces more desirable. Shared reading in the early primary grades could also be implemented with a Big Book rather than a standard-sized text so students can participate in the reading. Using a document camera to enlarge a book is also an option. (A word of caution: All Big Books are not appropriate for shared reading because many are written above grade level and therefore should be used in an interactive reading format. Check the text carefully to determine whether it is readable for most of the students.)

Poetry and songs make excellent shared reading texts and are generally enjoyed by all students. Choose from a variety of poems and songs: seasonal, humorous, content related, and so on. Students enjoy rereading these genres, which provide much-needed motivation and opportunities for building fluency. Short literary texts as well as informational pieces are also good choices for shared reading.

In many classrooms, the basal story for the week and the science or social studies textbook can be a good centerpiece for shared reading. Remember that most content textbooks are generally written above grade level. Regardless, all students must have access to the text; therefore, the teacher must be responsible for leading the reading of the text.

Instructional Focuses of Shared Reading

Shared reading focuses on reading and understanding grade-level text. As stated previously, to understand the text, it must be read at an appropriate rate with accuracy and expression. Fluency only comes with practice, therefore rereading the text or part of it should be a part of the plan. At the beginning of the lesson, present the vocabulary words that were preselected from the text and then revisit them numerous times during the lesson. Additionally, guide the students in determining new word meanings using context clues. All research-based comprehension skills are addressed as they relate to the specific text piece, including strategies employed before, during, and after reading. In many instances, use this shared text as a springboard for modeled or shared writing experiences. Clearly, this is the most critical venue for the focus of grade-level language arts skills that are applied to grade-level text.

The following vignettes show both a primary-grade and an intermediate-grade example of shared reading. The primary-grade scenario focuses on a poem, and the intermediate-grade scenario focuses on a short fable.

Shared Reading in the Primary-Grade Classroom: Poem

This second-grade class has been studying the life cycles of insects; therefore, Mrs. Todd selects a poem called "Caterpillars" by Brod Bagert (1993) for the class as a shared reading. This class is made up of 22 students, four of whom are English learners. The poem has great rhythm and rhyme to explore as well as a very prominent point of view. "Caterpillars" is written at the second-grade level and is used for rereading throughout the week to provide opportunities for students to develop fluency, which is especially beneficial for the English learners. On day 3 of the rereading of the poem, Mrs. Todd models writing that addresses the change in the author's point of view from the beginning of the poem to the end. At the end of the week, each student audiorecords a reading of the poem, and Mrs. Todd uses these recordings for assessment purposes. Figure 17 shows a sample lesson plan for this primary-grade shared reading.

Before Reading

Mrs. Todd: We've been studying the life cycle of the butterfly, so I thought you would enjoy reading this poem, "Caterpillars." Let's think about what we've learned about caterpillars. Turn to your talking partner and share one thing that you know about caterpillars.

FIGURE 17
Sample Lesson Plan for a Primary-Grade Shared Reading

Planner for Interactive Read-Alouds and Shared Reading

Text: "Caterpillars" by Brod Bagert   Type: Poem

Learning Goals: Language Arts (LA) or Content Area (CA)
• Read the poem with appropriate rate, accuracy, and expression.
• Recognize rhythm and rhyme in the poem.
• Determine the theme of the poem.
• Determine the meaning of words from context clues and by using word parts.

Before Reading
Build Background Knowledge: What do you know about caterpillars?

Introduce Story Vocabulary: unsuspecting

Set the Purpose: How does the author's point of view change during the poem?

During Reading: Teaching Points
• How does the author's point of view change during the poem?
• Who is unsuspecting? Why?
• What is the disguise?
• What is the theme of the poem? What does the author want us to learn?

After Reading
Comprehension Focus: Identify the theme of the poem.

Vocabulary Review: How is "unsuspecting" used in the poem?

Written Response: (Modeled) First, then, next, last, summary

Assessment: Teacher observation

She previously assigned talking partners and uses this think-pair-share format routinely.

Mrs. Todd: Troy, can you and Jamie each share one thing that you've learned about caterpillars?

Troy: We know that a caterpillar comes from a cocoon.

Jamie: And we know that it turns into a butterfly.

Mrs. Todd: I wonder if the caterpillar in the poem today will turn into a butterfly.

[She takes the opportunity to think aloud to demonstrate her thinking to the students.]

Mrs. Todd: The poem is really kind of funny, but it has an important message for all of us. The author of this poem is Brod Bagert. We read some other poems that he wrote. What do all of his poems have in common?

Ashley: All of his poems are really funny. I hope this one will be, too.

Mrs. Todd: I want to show you one word from the poem before we read. [She writes *unsuspecting* on the board.] Does anyone know what this word means?

Antwon:	I don't know that word, but I do know what a suspect is. If the police think that someone did a crime, he is a suspect.
Mrs. Todd:	You're right, Antwon. That is one kind of suspect. What if I said, "I suspect we won't go out for recess today because it is raining."
Rachel:	It's like you think we won't go out for recess.
Mrs. Todd:	So if we are suspecting something, we are thinking that it will happen. Now, let's put the prefix *un-* in front of the word. Turn and talk to your partner about what you know about the prefix *un-*. Remember to listen to what your partner has to say and then respond.

[She monitors as students share.]

| Mrs. Todd: | Let's get ready to read. Use your reading bookmark as I read the poem first while you follow along. As I read the poem, notice how the author changes his mind about caterpillars from the beginning of the poem to the end. |

During Reading

Because the poem is short, and Mrs. Todd does not want to interrupt the rhythm of the poem, she chooses to read it straight through the first time without stopping. Teaching points will be reviewed after this reading. All students are required to follow along using a reading bookmark. This increases the probability that they will actually follow the text while she is reading.

After Reading

Mrs. Todd:	Let's go back to the question I asked before I read. How does the author change his view of caterpillars from the beginning of the poem to the end? Turn and talk to your partner to see if you can answer the question.

[She monitors as students share.]

| Mrs. Todd: | Everyone, give me a thumbs up if you think you know the answer to the question. |

[She observes the students' responses.]

Mrs. Todd:	Wes, can you and LeBron tell us what you came up with?
LeBron:	At first, he thinks caterpillars are nasty and hurt people.
Wes:	But then, at the end, he likes them because he knows they'll become butterflies.
Mrs. Todd:	Yes, I think he realizes that they are going to grow and change into something beautiful. In the poem, the author says, "I see past their disguise" [line 9]. What is the disguise?
James:	It's like the butterfly is disguised as a caterpillar…kind of like when we dress up for Halloween.
Mrs. Todd:	Who is unsuspecting in the poem?
Anna:	The animals that the caterpillar might sting are unsuspecting. It's like they don't think the caterpillar might sting them.
Mrs. Todd:	So, what do you think the author wants us to learn from this poem?
Liam:	I think the caterpillar can turn into something beautiful.
Mrs. Todd:	I think you're exactly right. Just because something doesn't look too good, it can still have something beautiful inside. You really did a good job of explaining that. We're going to practice this poem all week so we can get really good at reading it. Let's read it one more time together before we put it away. I'll be the lead reader this time, and you whisper read along with me.

FIGURE 18
A Second-Grade Teacher's Modeled Writing Response to a Poem

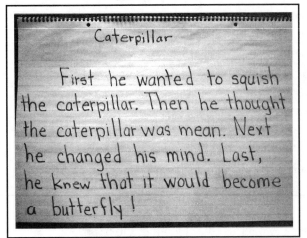

Caterpillar

First he wanted to squish the caterpillar. Then he thought the caterpillar was mean. Next he changed his mind. Last, he knew that it would become a butterfly!

As the lead reader, Mrs. Todd reads out loud while the students whisper read along with her. This provides necessary support for struggling readers. As the week progresses, the students chorally read the poem. Additionally, the poem goes into individual poetry folders so the students can practice reading it outside of group. On subsequent days, Mrs. Todd focuses more on the author's point of view as well as the specific rhythm and rhyme of the poem. As a culminating activity, she conducts a modeled writing that summarizes the poem using a "first, then, next, last" format (see Figure 18). This writing focuses on sequencing the important events in the poem.

Assessment
Mrs. Todd observes the students' responses to assess most of the learning goals. Additionally, she reviews the audiorecordings made by each student at the end of the week to monitor accuracy, rate, and expression.

Lesson Summary
The grade-level poem provides a short shared reading selection that also supports the current unit study in science. This vignette points out the value of poetry in the development of fluency, vocabulary, and comprehension. Poetry selections build a community of learners as students are supported in developing their literacy skills.

Shared Reading in the Intermediate-Grade Classroom: Fable

Ms. Lawrence selects a fable as a shared reading for her fourth graders. She finds that her students struggle in recognizing the theme and the author's purpose in a story and feels that this fable provides a concrete example of each. "The Bad Kangaroo" is from the book *Fables*, which is a collection written by Arnold Lobel (1980) that was a Caldecott Medal winner in 1980. This short, one-page fable has an important message. The readability is at the upper fourth-grade level, and because it is the last quarter of the school year, Ms. Lawrence feels that the tale is appropriate for the majority of her students. Figure 19 shows the lesson plan for this intermediate-grade shared reading.

Before Reading

Ms. Lawrence: Today we are going to read a fable. The author is Arnold Lobel, who wrote stories called fables. We read another fable earlier this year. Turn to your talking partner and discuss what you know about fables.

[The students discuss while she monitors.]

Ms. Lawrence: The fables in this book are similar to the famous fables that were originally told by a man named Aesop. He made up most of the fables to teach people a lesson. Arnold Lobel also wrote some fables. His fables are like Aesop's in that they have animals in them, and they have morals that tell us about life. There is one word that I want you to pay particular attention to in the text: *lavatory*.

Some of you may not be familiar with this word, but you should be able to figure it out by clues in the story.

Rather than discuss the meaning of the word prior to reading, Ms. Lawrence decides to have students apply context clues to determine meaning.

Ms. Lawrence: Today we are going to read a fable called "The Bad Kangaroo." I am going to be the lead reader and read out loud, and I want you to whisper read along with me. As we read this story, think about the lesson that the author is trying to teach.

The lead reading supports the struggling readers while engaging all students in the reading process.

During Reading

Because the selection is only one page long, Ms. Lawrence decides not to stop during the reading. She feels that her fourth-grade students are proficient enough to think about the story during reading.

After Reading

Ms. Lawrence: So, what was the author's purpose for writing this fable? What lesson is he trying to teach? Turn and talk to your partner.

[The students discuss while she monitors.]

Ms. Lawrence: Who would like to tell us about your partner conversation? OK, Aime and Keenon.

Aime: The author is trying to tell people that their children act just like they do, so they should use better manners at home.

Keenon: So, is the author's purpose the same as the moral of the story?

Ms. Lawrence: Good observation. The author uses the moral to give his point of view. What other parts of the story make it a fable?

Aime: The animals act like humans.

Ms. Lawrence: Yes, they do. I'm sure you can think of situations like this that happen with real people. Today I want you to write your own story using humans as the characters in a situation that could really happen. It can be something that you have actually seen. At the end of the story, include your own moral for the story. Before you begin writing, I would like for you to reread the story.

Ms. Lawrence tells students to reread the story to build fluency. Figure 20 shows a student writing example modeled on "The Bad Kangaroo."

FIGURE 19
Sample Lesson Plan for an Intermediate-Grade Shared Reading

Planner for Interactive Read-Alouds and Shared Reading

Text: "The Bad Kangaroo" by Arnold Lobel   Type: Fable

Learning Goals: Language Arts (LA) or Content Area (CA)
- Identify the attributes of a fable.
- Understand and identify the moral of a story.
- Write a story with a moral in a situation that could really happen.
- Read the fable with appropriate accuracy, rate, and expression.

Before Reading

Build Background Knowledge: What are the characteristics of a fable?

Introduce Story Vocabulary: lavatory

Set the Purpose: Identify the author's purpose for writing the fable. What lesson is he trying to teach?

During Reading: Teaching Points
- Identify the parts of a fable in the story.
- What is the author's purpose?
- How does this apply to real life?

After Reading

Comprehension Focus: Explain the moral of the story.

Vocabulary Review: How is the word "lavatory" used in the fable?

Written Response: Write a story that could happen today and has the same moral.

The Spoiled Child

Once there was a little girl in the grocery store. She was with her mother in line at the grocery store. The little girl started crying that she wanted some candy. The mother screamed at her at the top of her voice that she couldn't have it. The little girl screamed louder and the mother screamed even louder. Finally, the store manager came to calm them down.

Moral: Children act just like their mothers.

Assessment

Ms. Lawrence observes the students' responses to determine whether the learning goals have been reached. Along with her observations, Ms. Lawrence reviews the written works completed by the students.

Lesson Summary

This fable provides an appropriate shared reading text for this group of fourth-grade students. Its short length makes it more accessible for students who struggle in reading grade-level text. The text also provides students with an opportunity to apply their knowledge to a new situation in the form of an independent writing assignment. This shared reading experience provides grade-level text for the focus of reading and writing comprehension.

Modeled and Shared Writing

Modeled and shared writing are venues that support a variety of purposes and learning goals. The modeled writing process is controlled entirely by the teacher. The teacher thinks aloud as the text is constructed. Shared writing, however, provides students with scaffolded support as they move toward independence in applying the skill. Although the teacher acts as the scribe in both writing venues, the students contribute ideas and make decisions as the text piece is constructed during shared writing. The modeled writing process provides the initial exposure to a new skill either in the process of writing or in the written comprehension strategy used to respond to the text.

The planning process for both modeled and shared writing is similar: Establish the learning goals and assessments first. Also, identify text selections, if necessary, and lesson strategies. (See the Appendix for a reproducible planner for both modeled and shared writing.)

Establishing the Learning Goals and Assessments

To plan the lesson, begin by identifying the student learning goals and the assessments needed to gauge the students' progress toward meeting these goals. Become familiar not only with the grade-level writing standards but also with all of the language arts standards that might be included in this writing activity. These goals could relate to the writing standards, language standards, or reading comprehension standards. Next, identify the writing format, which can be as simple as a list, a graphic organizer, a letter, or a well-written paragraph. Writing assessments are best documented through teacher observations as students contribute to the shared writing, or by using writing rubrics as students complete an independent writing piece that addresses the same standards as the modeled or shared writing.

Many of the modeled and shared writing pieces are responses to the read-aloud or shared text, which is identified on the lesson plan. Determining appropriate strategies to use before, during, and after the writing completes the planning process.

Text Support for Modeled and Shared Writing

Writing in response to a commonly shared text piece provides equal access to the background knowledge needed to respond to the text appropriately. Many times, students struggle with writing because they think have nothing to write about. The common text gives all students the background knowledge that supports the writing process. Again, these text selections should represent a wide variety of text genres, and the writings should cover a variety of writing genres.

Modeled and shared writing that are supported by text provide a unique opportunity to integrate standards from a variety of areas in an authentic way. For example, after reading Arnold Lobel's (1970) *Frog and Toad Are Friends*, the teacher might decide to complete a Venn diagram as a shared writing piece. The learning goals include comparing and contrasting Frog and Toad. Not only is the language arts standard addressed, but the teacher also focuses on word choice in selecting adjectives to describe Frog and Toad. In informational text, content area standards could also be a focus. In most instances, a writing process or trait is addressed as well as a writing comprehension focus. Of course, it is also important to apply correct English standards.

Instructional Focuses of Modeled and Shared Writing

Written comprehension is an important focus as students respond to text. This might include writing about main ideas and supporting details, comparing and contrasting concepts, presenting an opinion with supporting evidence, and any number of other ways that text comprehension can be expressed. Additionally, it makes good sense and is a good use of instructional time to also include important writing processes and traits as the text pieces are constructed. Therefore, the planning process provides the inclusion of both important writing processes and traits as they relate to the written comprehension piece. The inclusion of critical language skills such as grammar gives students an authentic venue to apply these skills.

Including Personal Narratives and Writing Prompts

Although many of the written pieces are text based, writing personal narratives and responses to prompts should not be ignored. These writing types are easily incorporated into the modeled and shared writing venues. These writing types can be very challenging for students who have limited experiences or little imagination. In modeled writing, share personal experiences, which is highly motivating to most students. As students are asked to respond to a specific writing prompt, both shared and modeled writing are important. Balancing the writing formats in the same way that you balance the reading genres provides a wide range of practical and meaningful writing experiences. The following classroom vignettes in a primary-grade and an intermediate-grade setting show lessons for both modeled and shared writing.

Modeled Writing in the Primary-Grade Classroom: Informational Text (Science)

Mrs. Holt follows a previous day's reading of the book *Insect Families* by Lisa Trumbauer (2003) with a modeled writing lesson. She has several purposes for the modeled writing. First, she wants to revisit the ways in which all insects are alike, which is a grade-level science standard. The lesson goals also include identifying a main idea and supporting details. Additionally, she will introduce these first graders to organizing and writing a paragraph. The main idea, three supporting details, and a summary sentence is the basis for writing the paragraph. Mrs. Holt is also focusing on correct punctuation and formatting for a paragraph. The modeled writing venue allows her to think out loud as she constructs the paragraph. Figure 21 shows a sample lesson plan for this modeled writing lesson.

Before Writing

Mrs. Holt: Yesterday we read the book *Insect Families* and learned ways that all insects are alike. Turn and talk with your partner to see if you can remember some of those ways.

[Mrs. Holt monitors as students discuss.]

Mrs. Holt: Who would like to share first? OK, Juan, can you tell us one way that all insects are alike?

Juan: Yeah, all insects have six legs. I think that's the easiest one to remember.

Mrs. Holt: Good, that's right. Who can give us another one?

[The discussion continues.]

Mrs. Holt: Let's take another look at the diagram of an insect and review those three body parts again. [She displays the insect picture with the three body parts labeled.] Does anyone remember one more way that insects are all alike? It has something to do with when they are born and turn into adults.

[No one responds.]

Mrs. Holt: All insects have a life cycle. That means that they grow and change from when they are born to when they grow up. Today I am going to show you a way to write down our information about how insects are alike in a paragraph. Listen carefully because this is my time to share.

[She posts chart paper onto the board.]

FIGURE 21
Sample Lesson Plan for a Primary-Grade Modeled Writing

Planner for Modeled and Shared Writing

Text: "Insect Families" by Lisa Trumbauer   **Type:** Informational Text (Science)

Learning Goals: Language Arts (LA) or Content Area (CA)
• Tell three ways that insects are all alike.
• Recognize the structure of a paragraph.

Written Comprehension Focus (if applicable): Main idea and supporting details

Writing Format: Paragraph

Writing Process/Traits: Conventions of print: paragraph indent, capitalization, punctuation

Before Writing
• Yesterday we read a book about insects. We learned the ways that all insects are the same.
• Today I want to show you how to write a paragraph about what we learned.

During Writing: Teaching Points
• Paragraph indent
• Topic sentence
• Detail sentences
• Closing sentence

After Writing
• Read the paragraph together.
• Discuss how this paragraph helps organize our thinking.

Assessment: Teacher observation

Mrs. Holt: I need to think of a first sentence that will tell about what I am writing about, so I will write, "All insects are alike in some ways." I need to indent the first line of my paragraph, which means that I need to move my writing over to start the first line. Oh, I also need to remember to use a capital letter for the first word.

[She completes writing the first sentence and then reads it aloud.]

FIGURE 22
Sample Modeled Writing of a Five-Sentence Paragraph for First Graders

Insects
All insects are alike in some ways. They all have six legs. They all have three body parts. They do not have any bones. That is how they are all the same.

Mrs. Holt: That is my topic sentence. It tells what I am going to write about. The next thing I need is a detail about the first sentence, so I need to tell one thing about how insects are all alike in the next sentence. I will talk about the six legs first. So, I'll write, "They all have six legs."

[She continues the think-aloud process until she completes the five-sentence paragraph.]

Figure 22 shows the completed writing sample. Remember, it's important to keep these writing samples around the classroom to serve as references for the students to refer to when completing their own writing.

After Writing

Mrs. Holt: Let's go back and read the paragraph together.

[She and the students read the paragraph together.]

Mrs. Holt: When we are writing a paragraph, we must always begin with the main idea. Then, we write about that idea. The last thing we write is an ending, or a sum-it-up sentence. By the end of the year, you will write your own paragraphs.

Lesson Summary

This modeled writing serves several important purposes. First, it summarizes an important science concept that is appropriate for the grade level. Next, it provides an opportunity to demonstrate how to construct a short paragraph. As an added bonus, the modeled writing can now be used as a shared reading piece for the class as they read and reread it together.

It can be difficult to complete a modeled writing without involving the students, but there is a very important reason for not including their input: The next step is to use a shared writing experience to reinforce the skills as the students participate.

Assessment

By nature, a modeled writing does not require student participation. The teacher can, however, observe students' responses in a summary after the paragraph is completed. The most appropriate assessment comes later as the students write their own paragraphs using the skills that were demonstrated.

_____

Shared Writing in the Intermediate-Grade Classroom: Friendly Letter (Persuasion)

Mrs. Shook wants to introduce her third-grade students to persuasive writing. Additionally, she wants to review the format for writing a friendly letter. As the letter is constructed, an in-depth look at the characters in the story and their traits is explored. Figure 23 shows the lesson plan for this shared writing activity.

FIGURE 23
Sample Lesson Plan for an Intermediate-Grade Shared Writing

Planner for Modeled and Shared Writing

Text: "Click, Clack, Moo: Cows That Type" Type: Narrative Text
  by Doreen Cronin

Learning Goals: Language Arts (LA) or Content Area (CA)
• Write a friendly letter using the correct format.
• Persuade the audience with at least two arguments.

Written Comprehension Focus (if applicable): Main idea and
                                        supporting details

Writing Format: Friendly letter

Writing Process/Traits: Voice, organization

Before Writing
• Watch the YouTube video of "Click, Clack, Moo: Cows
  That Type."
• Discuss the reasons for the duck's success in getting
  the diving board.

During Writing: Teaching Points
• Review the friendly letter format.
• Organization: State opinion first.
• Provide two arguments to persuade the farmer.

After Writing
• Write a friendly letter from the hens that gives two
  arguments to the farmer.

Assessment: Use a rubric to score the students' letters.

Before Writing

Mrs. Shook first shows her students a YouTube video based on the book *Click, Clack, Moo: Cows That Type* by Doreen Cronin (2000). This is the hilarious story of the cows on Farmer Brown's farm that want him to provide electric blankets.

After watching the video, Mrs. Shook focuses on the letters written to the farmer.

Mrs. Shook: I wonder why the ducks are more persuasive than the cows in getting what they want. I wonder why the farmer builds the diving board for the ducks, but he won't give the cows electric blankets. Turn and talk to your partner about your thoughts about this situation.

[She monitors as students discuss.]

Mrs. Shook: Do you have any thoughts about that?

Sue-Lin: The only thing we could think of is that the ducks told the farmer why they want the diving board.

Mrs. Shook: That's a good observation. When you are trying to persuade someone to do something, you need to convince that person with reasons why he or she should do it. Let's see if we can rewrite the cows' letter so Farmer Brown might give them electric blankets.

[She posts chart paper onto the board.]

During Writing

Mrs. Shook: What do we do first when we write a friendly letter?

Chandra: We need to start with a heading, so maybe we should say, "Dearest Farmer." That would make him feel more appreciated.

[Mrs. Shook writes the heading on the chart paper.]

Mrs. Shook: I think the first sentence that the cows started with is good because it tells what they want, so I'll write that.

[Mrs. Shook writes the first sentence.]

Mrs. Shook: Now, the cows need to justify why they need the blankets. It's good to give some creative reasons because we really don't know what the cows are thinking. When you are trying to persuade someone, you need to make your argument important to the person you're writing to.

Seth: Why don't we write that if they are warmer, they'll give more milk? That would make the farmer happy.

Mrs. Shook: I think you're right. The farmer will really pay attention to that. Everyone, thumbs up if you agree.

[She observes the positive responses and writes the next sentence.]

62

Mrs. Shook:	Help me think. How could we make it easy for the farmer to do this?
Nadia:	Maybe we could tell him that the electric blankets don't have to be new.
Tommy:	That would save him some money.
Mrs. Shook:	If I were the farmer, that would help persuade me.
Seth:	So, can we put that in the letter?
Mrs. Shook:	Thumbs up or thumbs down...what do you all think?

[The students all agree, and she writes the next sentence. The discussion continues until the letter is complete with three reasons the farmer should give the cows electric blankets. Then, Mrs. Shook guides the students through the format for closing the friendly letter.]

After Writing

| Mrs. Shook: | I think Farmer Brown would definitely reconsider giving the cows electric blankets if he read this letter. Now, I want you to write a letter to help the hens. Make sure that you follow the friendly letter format. Also, make sure that you include at least two arguments to persuade the farmer. |

See Figure 24 for a struggling writer's student sample.

Assessment

Mrs. Shook observes the students' comments while the text is written. The friendly letter assigned as an independent writing serves as a primary means of assessing the learning goals. A rubric that assesses the friendly letter format as well as the two arguments required make this assessment easy.

Lesson Summary

Shared writing is a good way to get students excited about the writing process. By viewing the video of the book, the students are motivated to write because they enjoy the story. The CCSS present argument as an important format in writing. It is, therefore, important to introduce this concept at an early grade level. Using the friendly letter format, which is familiar to the students at this stage, the presentation of the argument is easily relatable.

FIGURE 24
A Third Grader's Friendly Letter to Persuade

Dear Farmer Brown,
We would like blankets so we can stay warm. Then we will give more eggs.
Thanks,
The HENS

Targeted Skill Lessons

Planning Targeted Skill Lessons

Although teaching literacy skills is best accomplished through integrated instruction, there is, by necessity, a place for the isolated teaching of foundational skills. These skills are those that need more explicit instruction or more focus that cannot be addressed in other instructional venues. The frequency of using whole-class time for targeted skill lessons should be decided by the teacher based on observations and assessments of the students. Due to the intensive, isolated focus of these lessons, text support is not appropriate.

Establishing Learning Goals and Assessments

As with any effective lesson, the planning of the targeted skill lesson is essential (see the Appendix for a reproducible for planning targeted skill lessons). Begin by identifying the learning goal or goals: the purposes for the lesson and what the learner should know or be able to do as a result of the lesson. Next, establish the students' knowledge of the skill and help them make connections to previous learning, if applicable. Perhaps the most important planning decision is determining how to model the skill. Most certainly, demonstration and think-aloud strategies are important.

After the modeling is completed, decide how to provide an opportunity for students to practice the skill with support. At this point, pinpoint students who still fail to understand or apply the skill. In this case, another model might be called for. Finally, the students apply this skill in some form of independent practice. This is appropriate only if the teacher feels that the majority of students are proficient enough for this type of independent practice. Keep in mind that the independent practice and assessment might come several days after the targeted skill lesson. Again, the "I do, we do, you do" gradual release of responsibility model is used.

Instructional Focuses of Targeted Skill Lessons

Targeted skill lessons are appropriate for the foundational skills associated with phonics, phonemic awareness, vocabulary, grammar, and so forth. Chapter 2 discusses the specific foundational and language skills that are appropriate for this venue.

For example, a second-grade standard is for students to decode words with common prefixes. Although the teacher includes discussion of these prefixes as they relate to words that are encountered with this feature in modeled or shared reading, this skill calls for systematic instruction for most students in the meaning of each prefix. In other words, this important skill cannot be left to chance. If the teacher reviews assessments that show this as a deficit for the majority of the class, a targeted skill lesson would be appropriate. However, if there are only a few students in the room who lack this skill, the skill might best be taught in a small-group setting. Whole-group instruction should be reserved for instruction that is valuable for the majority of the class.

The following classroom scenarios give examples of both a primary-grade and an intermediate-grade targeted skill lesson. In the primary-grade classroom, the lesson focuses on digraphs, and the intermediate-grade minilesson focuses on similes and metaphors. A blank lesson plan can be found in the Appendix.

Targeted Skill Lesson in the Primary Grades: Digraphs

In Mrs. Yetter's first-grade class, students continue to confuse and misuse digraphs in their reading and writing. Therefore, she decides to use a targeted skill lesson to provide additional support in the use of digraphs so the students can fluently apply the skill in their decoding and writing. Figure 25 shows a sample lesson plan for this lesson.

Teacher Modeling

Mrs. Yetter: We've talked about digraphs some this year, and today we're going to look at four digraphs that we see in our reading and writing all the time. Who remembers what a digraph is?

Sally: A digraph is when two letters are together, and they only make one sound.

Mrs. Yetter: Thumbs up if you agree with Sally.

[She observes the students' responses.]

Mrs. Yetter: Let's look at the four digraph cards on the board. We have /ch/, /sh/, /th/, and /wh/. Now, I want to put a picture under each digraph that represents that sound. Let's see, this is a picture of a sheep, and *sheep* sounds like /sh/ at the beginning, so I'm going to put it under the digraph /sh/.

[She continues using think-alouds as she posts an appropriate example picture under each digraph.]

Guided Practice

Mrs. Yetter: Please take out your dry-erase boards and markers. As soon as you have the board on your desk and the top off your marker, show me the ready position.

She established the ready position routine previously to help students focus on the task at hand.

Mrs. Yetter: Now I am going to show you a picture. The first picture is a chair. Everyone, say *chair*.

It is important for students to hear themselves say the word.

Mrs. Yetter: Let's see where we would sort that card. Look at the first card: *sheep/chair*. Do they sound the same at the beginning of each word? Thumbs up or thumbs down. Right, they don't sound the same. What about the next picture of cherries? Say *cherries/chair*. Do they sound the same at the beginning? Thumbs up or thumbs down. Yes, they sound the same. Now it's your turn. Let's look at the next picture. Say *thumb*.

[Students say the word.]

Mrs. Yetter: Now say each of the pictures to yourself to see which picture sounds the same at the beginning. Then, write the digraph that you hear at the beginning of *thumb*.

The process continues as the students write the appropriate digraph for each picture card. Mrs. Yetter reinforces and assists as needed.

Independent Practice (Assessment)

Based on the students' responses during guided practice, Mrs. Yetter wants to assess students independently on this skill.

FIGURE 25
Sample Lesson Plan for a Primary-Grade Targeted Skill Lesson: Digraphs

Planner for a Targeted Skill Minilesson

Learning Goals
- Recognize and produce the beginning digraphs /ch/, /sh/, /th/, and /wh/.

Build/Access Background Knowledge
- Review and define digraphs.

Model: Teaching Points
- Use letter cards and picture cards to sort pictures under the correct digraph.

Guided Practice
- Write the correct digraph on a dry-erase board as picture cards are displayed.

Independent Practice
- Complete a sheet with eight pictures and correctly write the beginning digraph for each picture.

Assessment
Assess the students' worksheets with this rubric
- 7–8 correct: Established
- 5–6 correct: Developing
- Less than 5 correct: Struggling

Mrs. Yetter: I'm going to give you a sheet of paper with eight pictures on it. Please say the name of each picture to yourself. Next, write the digraph that you hear at the beginning of the word on the line beside each picture.

[She gives the students five minutes to complete the assessment and then collects the papers for review.]

Lesson Summary

Mrs. Yetter identifies a specific phonics need and decides to address it in a targeted skill lesson. She provides both modeled and guided practice to support the students. To assess the students' mastery of this skill, she has them complete a quick assessment independently that guides her next instructional decisions.

Targeted Skill Minilesson in an Intermediate-Grade Classroom: Similes and Metaphors

Mr. Bernard, a fourth-grade language arts teacher, is planning a targeted skill minilesson that focuses on similes and metaphors. Although these figures of speech have been introduced informally in literature read by the class, he feels that recognizing and understanding these important elements of both reading and writing should be the focus of a separate lesson. Additionally, Mr. Bernard wants to assess his students' knowledge at the end of the minilesson to see if there is a need for follow-up instruction. Figure 26 shows the lesson plan used for this minilesson.

Teacher Modeling

Mr. Bernard: Sometimes I feel like this class is a three-ring circus! Turn to your talking partner. What do you think I mean by this statement?

[He monitors as students discuss.]

Mr. Bernard: Do we have any volunteers who would like to share?

Andrew: Well, I've been to a circus with three rings, and a whole lot was going on. I guess you're saying that there's a lot going on in our class.

Mr. Bernard: Let me show you a short video clip of a three-ring circus so everyone sees what one looks like.

[While the class watches the video clip, he realizes that many of his students have never had the opportunity to go to a circus and that this video is critical to their understanding.]

Mr. Bernard: After watching the video, do you have some other observations? Why did I compare our class to a three-ring circus?

FIGURE 26
Sample Lesson Plan for an Intermediate-Grade Targeted Skill Minilesson: Similes and Metaphors

---

Planner for a Targeted Skill Minilesson

Learning Goals
• Recognize the differences between similes and metaphors.
• Know the purpose for using similes and metaphors in writing.
• Write a poem using similes and metaphors correctly.

Build/Access Background Knowledge
• Discuss figures of speech.
• Recall the use of similes and metaphors in writing.

Model: Teaching Points
• "This class is like a three-ring circus!"
• View a YouTube video of a three-ring circus.
• Read and discuss poem written entirely of similes or metaphors.

Guided Practice
• With a partner, label each phrase in a list of 10 as either a simile or a metaphor.
• Next, change two similes into metaphors.
• Then, change two metaphors into similes.

Independent Practice
• Write a short poem using either all similes or all metaphors.

Assessment
Review the students' poems to determine whether similes and metaphors have been used correctly.

Roderick:	Well, it was really noisy and kind of crazy. Sometimes we can get kind of loud and crazy.
Mr. Bernard:	Actually, I had all of those things in mind when I made that comparison. Let me write that in a sentence on the board.

[He writes, "Sometimes our class is like a three-ring circus."]

Mr. Bernard:	When we compare two things and use the words *like* or *as*, we call it a simile. Why do you think we use similes when we talk or write? Gina, why don't you share your thoughts?
Gina:	Well, it's like you can see it in your mind, so it makes it a lot more interesting.
Liza:	Yeah, and you can make things sound really funny.
Mr. Bernard:	Let's look at a short poem that I wrote using only similes.

[He shares his poem "Comparisons," then leads a discussion on identifying the similes and how they should be interpreted in the poem.]

Mr. Bernard:	"This classroom is Mr. Bernard's kingdom." Turn to your partner and discuss what I mean by this line in the poem.

[He monitors while students discuss.]

Mr. Bernard:	Luke, what do you and Sadie think?
Luke:	This is your kingdom because you rule the classroom. It's not really a kingdom, though. You're just comparing our classroom to a kingdom.
Mr. Bernard:	How is that comparison different from the first one I used about the three-ring circus?
Sadie:	This time you said that this classroom *is* a kingdom, not *like* a kingdom.
Mr. Bernard:	Right. That is exactly the difference. When we compare two things without using the words *like* or *as*, we call that a metaphor. Let's look at another poem that I wrote that is made up entirely of metaphors.

[He shares the poem "An Animal Is…" and discusses the use of metaphors.]

Mr. Bernard:	Let's look at this metaphor from the poem: "Elephant is a large gray mountain." How could we change that into a simile?
Marta:	Could we say, "The elephant is like a large gray mountain"?

[The class discussion continues.]

Guided Practice

Mr. Bernard:	These sheets are a list of 10 similes and metaphors. Work with your partner to decide whether each one is a simile or a metaphor and label each one on your paper. Then, choose two similes and turn them into metaphors. After that, I want you to choose two metaphors and turn them into similes. I'm available to assist you if you need help.

Independent Practice

Technically, this activity falls somewhere between guided and independent practice because Mr. Bernard is available to guide when necessary. After the students complete the activity, they meet back in whole group to share their work.

The next day, Mr. Bernard asks the students to write a short poem that includes either all similes or all metaphors. He uses the poem as an assessment of the skill. Figure 27 provides an example of a poem written with metaphors as an independent activity.

FIGURE 27
A Fourth Grader's Metaphor Poem

Winter Is...

*A white wonderland where everywhere you
turn is covered with snow.*

*Children and their family drinking hot chocolate
in front of a warm fireplace.*

Wind gusting in your face on a freezing, winter day.

Owls hooting nosily in the dark, cold night.

*Snowflakes falling down from the sky
and gently falling all over me.*

*Being bundled up in snowsuits and boots having
a snowball fight with friends on a cold, snowy day.*

*The aroma of hot chocolate being drank by my family
in front of a crackling fire on a cold, misty night.*

*My grandpa's yummy fudge as I bite into it on
a cold, brisk day.*

*The gooey marshmallow inside a yummy smore
on a cold, dark night.*

Lesson Summary

Targeted skill lessons serve an important purpose. In this minilesson, the students were able to focus on the concepts of similes and metaphors. Mr. Bernard presents the minilesson in a very entertaining format that helps the students make connections to the concept in the future. The two sample poems are great models that directly address the use of similes and metaphors. Mr. Bernard decides to let partners work together on the guided practice to provide peer support for learning the targeted skill. The true assessment of the learning goals comes when the students write their poems independently.

CHAPTER 4

Planning for and Delivering Differentiated Literacy Instruction

To differentiate simply means to see differences between things. As we see differences among readers and writers, we provide the appropriate instruction to meet their needs. In the case of literacy instruction, these differences are recognized and addressed as they relate to the developmental learning levels of students. In any given classroom, it is all but impossible to sufficiently address the needs of a wide range of literacy learners in the whole-class setting. Providing instruction in a smaller group or individual setting provides venues to meet the diverse needs of all students.

The power of small-group differentiated reading instruction cannot be underestimated in addressing student needs. It is, in every sense, the most efficient way to grow every reader in the classroom, whether struggling or gifted. It provides the venue for teachers to deliver instruction that supports growth as well as success. In other words, it is the instruction in which teachers carefully scaffold the necessary support for students to reach the next literacy level.

For a student to experience growth, the student must be in the zone of proximal development (Vygotsky, 1978). This zone is the distance between the most difficult task that a student can do alone and the most difficult task that the student can do with help. Therefore, the role of the teacher is to give students literacy experiences within their zones that encourage and advance individual literacy learning. This is the formula for literacy growth for all students. When teachers are knowledgeable of each student's zone of proximal development, they are armed with the knowledge to grow each student in literacy. As we acknowledge the individual differences among students and adjust instruction accordingly, the process of differentiating instruction is employed.

Another way to differentiate instruction in a more focused way is through individual reading and writing conferences. Although these instructional venues are powerful, the time constraints associated with facilitating individual conferences makes them somewhat more difficult to manage. Regardless, the feedback that these conferences provide is powerful as students hone their literacy skills.

Planning for Small-Group Differentiated Reading Instruction

As with any quality instruction, small-group differentiated reading instruction begins with a sound plan. Evaluate the strengths and weaknesses of each reader to make important instructional decisions. Using assessment data, determine appropriate student groupings based on similar attributes of the readers. Also, use the data to create differentiated lesson plans to support each group.

The overall goal for this small-group venue is to grow students in each essential area of reading, as outlined in the National Reading Panel's report (NICHD, 2000), including fluency, phonemic awareness, word study, vocabulary, and comprehension. Whereas whole-group instruction focuses on grade-level standards as they relate to these components, small-group differentiated instruction focuses on the developmental levels of students in each of these critical areas. In this way, each student receives reading instruction that is in his or her zone of proximal development.

Reproducible lesson planners for both primary- and intermediate-grade small-group differentiated instruction appear in the Appendix. The primary-grade lesson plan accommodates fluency practice and word study in basic alphabetic principles, initial consonant sounds, and common and less common phonics patterns that are appropriate in the primary grades. The intermediate-grade lesson plan addresses the more advanced study of words and word analysis, including sophisticated word features, syllabication, and Greek and Latin word roots. Again, assess each student to determine the correct level of instruction. Both lesson plans address the appropriate comprehension strategies for before, during, and after reading that are needed to understand the text's message. Although primary-grade readers read texts at a lower instructional level, simple comprehension is still a focus. In the intermediate grades, students read more closely and critically as the text is explored.

More specific lesson planning templates that address the specific developmental stages of reading as well as assessments and word study materials can be found in the following books: *Small-Group Reading Instruction: A Differentiated Teaching Model for Beginning and Struggling Readers*, second edition (Tyner, 2009) and *Small-Group Reading Instruction: Differentiated Teaching Models for Intermediate Readers, Grades 3–8*, second edition (Tyner & Green, 2012).

Assessing for Small-Group Differentiated Reading Instruction

To plan for effective differentiated instruction, begin with the assessment of each student's literacy knowledge. In the primary grades, focus on the instructional reading level, vocabulary (sight word) knowledge, and word study skills of each student. Intermediate-grade readers are also assessed in these areas except for sight word knowledge. Use all available information to assemble students with the most similar needs. Then, plan instruction around the developmental reading needs of the students in each research-based component.

Instructional Reading Levels

The instructional reading level is the level that a student can read with the support of the teacher with 90–95% accuracy and with understanding (Rasinski, 2010). Although traditional running records are appropriate to determine appropriate instruction levels for most primary- and intermediate-grade students, they can be problematic with very

TABLE 1
Sight Word Correlation to Reading Levels

Number of Sight Words	Fountas and Pinnell Levels	Early Intervention Levels
0–15	A/B	1–2
16–35	C	3–4
36–60	D	5–6
61–85	E	7–8
86–100	F	9–10

early readers. For example, students who are just learning to track print are not actually expected to read the words, just to memorize the repetitive sentence pattern and correctly point to each word. This can provide some frustration when assessing students at these low levels. Even more concerning, students can get stuck in levels that do not allow for progression. Based on my experiences with thousands of students, I see a stronger correlation between sight word knowledge and instructional reading level in these beginning reading stages. Table 1 gives the correlation between sight word knowledge and early instructional reading levels.

Vocabulary (Sight Word) Knowledge

Students in the early primary grades need to be assessed in sight word knowledge. Figure 28 provides a list of the 100 most frequently seen words in books for beginning readers. Whereas some word lists group words in alphabetical order, this list is organized in order of the frequency that each word appears in text. This listing seems more appropriately aligned to the real reading process. Assess each student on sight word knowledge of the first 100 words. Again, as more advanced readers, intermediate-grade students do not require this assessment.

Word Study

Simple spelling assessments are the best way to assess word study skills. These assessments can either be teacher constructed or found in other reference materials (see, e.g., Tyner, 2009; Tyner & Green, 2012). These short spelling assessments are time efficient and give the teacher the knowledge to address the developmental needs of each student. Word study is often overlooked when differentiating instruction. However, it is an important piece for both remediating struggling readers and advancing more adept readers.

Texts for Small-Group Instruction

The selection of appropriate texts is instrumental in the effectiveness of the instruction. Selecting and previewing the text beforehand is absolutely essential. All leveled books and text pieces are leveled by a variety of sources. Therefore, make selections based not only on the text but also on the readers in the group. As the guidelines for appropriate text complexity and quality that are outlined in the CCSS become more prominent, the process of appropriate text selection will become more important. Along with the need

FIGURE 28
100 Most Frequent Words in Books for Beginning Readers

1. the	26. he	51. be	76. cat
2. a	27. out	52. now	77. them
3. and	28. that	53. when	78. tree
4. to	29. one	54. there	79. where
5. I	30. big	55. into	80. away
6. in	31. go	56. day	81. time
7. is	32. was	57. look	82. as
8. on	33. like	58. eat	83. water
9. you	34. what	59. make	84. home
10. it	35. not	60. his	85. made
11. of	36. do	61. here	86. long
12. said	37. then	62. your	87. has
13. can	38. this	63. an	88. help
14. for	39. no	64. back	89. good
15. my	40. too	65. mom	90. going
16. but	41. she	66. dog	91. by
17. all	42. went	67. very	92. how
18. we	43. see	68. did	93. house
19. are	44. will	69. her	94. dad
20. up	45. so	70. from	95. or
21. at	46. some	71. had	96. two
22. with	47. down	72. got	97. red
23. me	48. little	73. put	98. am
24. they	49. come	74. came	99. over
25. have	50. get	75. just	100. saw

Note. From "100 Most Frequent Words in Books for Beginning Readers," by E. Bodrova, D.J. Leong, and D. Semenov, 1998, Denver, CO: McREL, available at: www.mcrel.org/PDF/Literacy/4006CM_100words.pdf.

to select text at the appropriate level of difficulty, selections in a variety of text genres must be considered, including a mix of literary and informational text, poetry, biographies, and folktales and myths. Teachers at all grade levels must, therefore, be experts in teaching the variety of text genres as well as determining appropriate text levels.

The two vignettes that follow demonstrate small-group lessons using an informational text in a primary-grade setting and a literary text in an intermediate grade.

Small-Group Differentiated Reading Instruction in a Primary-Grade Classroom: Informational Text

Six second-grade students make up this small group in Ms. Cook's class. These students read slightly below grade level and are currently reading a level H book. They are working on recognizing common vowel patterns in both their reading and writing. Ms. Cook chooses an informational book titled *How Do Animals Stay Alive?* by Margie Burton, Cathy French, and Tammy Jones (2011) to support the current science unit on living things. She preselects vocabulary from the text that she feels is important for these second graders to recognize and understand. Figure 29 shows the plan for this lesson.

Fluency

The students in this small group need to practice fluency through rereading. Because the books at this level are longer, the rereading will take place the next day, or Ms. Cook may assign the students to reread the book with a partner when they leave group. She will make this decision based on how well the students do with the new reading today.

Word Study

In today's lesson, the students are focusing on three of the most common *o* patterns. Ms. Cook presents the lesson in a compare-and-contrast format to assist the students in discriminating the patterns in both reading and writing.

Ms. Cook: Today we are going to look at some common patterns for the vowel *o*. Look at the first word: *hot*. [She places a small card with the word written on it in a tabletop sorting board.] What vowel sound do you hear in this word?

Andy: It's the short *o* sound, /o/.

Ms. Cook: Yes. When the vowel has a consonant on both sides of it, the vowel is the short sound. The vowel pattern is consonant-vowel-consonant.

Rebecca: That's just like the *a* and *i* patterns.

Ms. Cook: That's right. It also applies to *u* and *e*. Now let's look at the next word: *boat*. What vowel sound do you hear in *boat*?

Carl: It sounds like /o/, a long *o*. But *boat* also has an *a*, but you can't hear it.

Ms. Cook: Can anyone tell us what is happening with those two vowels?

Wayne: It's just like the other ones where the two vowels are together, but the first one is the only sound you can hear.

[The lesson continues with the third pattern introduced with the word *for*, the *r*-controlled vowel pattern.]

Ms. Cook: Now let's do a spelling sort. Put each header word at the top of your papers. Circle the vowel pattern in each word

[The students write as she monitors.]

Ms. Cook: Now I'm going to call out a word. Decide what the vowel pattern is in each word and write it under the correct category.

FIGURE 29
Sample Lesson Plan for Primary-Grade Small-Group Differentiated Reading: Informational Text

Lesson Planner for Primary-Grade Small-Group Differentiated Instruction

Group: Rockets

Fluency (Rereading)
Text: NA   Level:

Learning Goals
• Recognize, sort, and write common "o" pattern words.
• Recognize and use text features.
• Determine main ideas and supporting details.
Word Study
• Common "o" patterns: "oa," "o–C–e," "or"
• Complete a spelling sort.
Vocabulary: protect, confuse (Preview before reading the text.)

Comprehension
Text: How Do Animals Stay Alive?" by Margie Level: H
    Burton, Cathy French, and Tammy Jones
Before Reading: Background Knowledge, Vocabulary, Purpose
• Text feature preview
• What do animals do to stay alive?
During Reading: Teaching Points
• Why do animals try to make themselves bigger?
• Summarize: What have we learned so far?
After Reading: Comprehension Focus Activity
• Shared writing: Main idea and supporting details

Outside-of-Group Extensions
• Reread the book with a partner.
• Write a five-sentence paragraph about how animals stay alive. Include a topic sentence, three supporting details, and a closing sentence.
Assessments
• Observations
• Rubric for writing a paragraph

FIGURE 30
A Second Grader's Completed Spelling Sort

Spelling Sort

oa	or	o-e
boat	fort	code
float	sport	hole

Dictated Sentence(s):

1) There was a hole in my old coat.

2)

Small-Group Reading Instruction: A Differentiated Teaching Model for Beginning and Struggling Readers (second edition) by Beverly Tyner. © 2009 International Reading Association.

[She calls out two words for each pattern as the students write the words under the correct categories.]

Figure 30 shows a student's completed spelling sort.

New Reading: Comprehension

Before Reading

These students are focusing on both the decoding and comprehension of the text. Ms. Cook includes research-based comprehension strategies before, during, and after reading the text.

Although the readers no longer need a complete picture walk in literary texts, a text feature walk is appropriate for this informational book. This allows Ms. Cook to point out important text features that assist students' comprehension of the book. Also, setting a purpose for reading means the students are more likely to engage in the text message during reading.

Ms. Cook: I think you are really going to enjoy our book today. Let's look at the front cover. The name of the book is *How Do Animals Stay Alive?* This is an informational book, so let's see if there are any text features that will help us understand it. [She opens to the Table of Contents.] How can the Table of Contents help us understand the book?

LaToyia: Well, it tells us the chapters that we're going to read, and it tells us what order they're going to be in.

Karolina: Yeah, it looks like the whole book is about how animals hide so they can stay alive.

[The discussion continues as the picture captions are pointed out.]

Ms. Cook: Let's look at some words that we will see in the book today. The first word is *protect*. How do you think this word will be used in the book? [She displays an index card with the vocabulary word written on it.]

Alphonse: Well, the book is about how animals stay safe, so I think this is how they protect themselves so other animals can't hurt them.

[The word *confuse* is also introduced and discussed.]

Ms. Cook: As we read the book today, let's think about what animals do to stay alive. When we finish reading, we'll see how many ways we can remember.

During Reading

Ms. Cook: Let's look at the first page and read the chapter title together.

[They all read together.]

Ms. Cook: Take a look at the illustration. Based on that picture, we can already guess what this chapter is about.

Raul: It looks like it's showing animals hiding from other animals that might hurt them. That's a real good reason to hide. If the animal doesn't hide, that lion is going to eat it.

Ms. Cook: Very good! Now, I'm going to be the lead reader on this page. That means I'm going to read out loud, and I want you to all whisper read with me.

Ms. Cook wants to use strategies that will allow each student to have the opportunity to read every page.

Ms. Cook: Let's turn to page 8. I want everyone to whisper read to find out why animals try to look bigger than they are.

Each student is required to whisper read so the Ms. Cook can observe each student's fluency.

Ms. Cook: Turn to your partner and tell why animals try to look bigger.

This strategy allows each student a chance to respond.

Ms. Cook: Jason, what do you think?

Jason: The animals try to make themselves look bigger so it will scare other animals, and they will leave the little animals alone.

The process continues as the book is completed.

After Reading

Ms. Cook: So, let's see if we can list the ways that animals protect themselves so they won't be killed. First, I need to write the title. This is the main idea of what we are going to be talking about. [She writes the title on a dry-erase board.] Can someone tell me one way that animals try to protect themselves?

Raul: They hide.

Ms. Cook: Great! Let me write that down.

[The process continues, and the main points are recorded. After the task is completed, Ms. Cook and the students read the list together.]

Extensions

Ms. Cook asks her students to reread the book with a partner after leaving the group. Then she has them write a five-sentence paragraph about how animals stay alive. She reminds them to start with a main idea sentence, follow with three supporting details about the topic, and end with a final sentence that summarizes the ideas to signal the end of the paragraph for the reader.

Assessment

Ms. Cook observes the students as they sort words by correct pattern and then write the words correctly. She also assesses the written extension to determine the success of the additional learning goal.

Lesson Summary

These second graders address all the important reading components in this lesson plan format. Although the rereading takes place the next day, the students are also rereading outside of the group. The focus on decoding skills improves both their speed and their accuracy in reading. Finally, the extensions provide opportunities for the students to write to demonstrate their understanding of the text.

Small-Group Differentiated Reading Instruction in an Intermediate-Grade Classroom: Literary Text

In his fourth-grade classroom, Mr. Harrison works with four small groups in reading. Although he sees the low group four days a week, he rotates meeting with the other three groups, who are reading at or above grade level. The small group that he is working with for this lesson is composed of six students reading on grade level. Therefore, the focus of instruction centers on comprehending the text at deeper levels. Additionally, the study of word features continues to support these fourth-grade students in both their reading and writing.

Word Study

Mr. Harrison: Today we're going to look at two common word roots: *dict* and *scribe*. Let's look at three words with the word root *dict*. [He displays the words *dictation*, *dictate*, and *prediction*.] I think you know most of these words. Can you figure out what all these words have in common with their meanings?

Clint: They all have something to do with talking, like if we have sentence dictation, you tell us what the sentence is.

Joan: Well, I don't know about *dictate*. It means one person ruling, but I guess he could be speaking.

Mr. Harrison: What about *prediction*?

Steven: That's when someone tells what will happen, so that's talking.

Mr. Harrison: So, you've connected all of those words. The word root *dict* means to speak. If we know the meaning of *dict*, it will help us figure out words that we may not know.

[He continues the discussion with the word root *scribe*.]

Comprehension

Mr. Harrison selects the narrative poem "Little Red Riding Hood and the Wolf" by Roald Dahl (1982) to read with the group today. (This poem is included in Appendix B of the CCSS as an example text for fourth- and fifth-grade students; see www.corestandards.org/assets/Appendix_B.pdf, p. 69.) After Mr. Harrison's preview of the poem, he feels that it is a great example of a common theme in literature: overcoming fear. Mr. Harrison follows up this selection with another that also focuses on the same theme.

Before Reading

Mr. Harrison: I think you're really going to enjoy the poem that we're going to read today. It's written by one of our favorite authors, Roald Dahl. This is a narrative poem. Do you remember what that is?

Joe: That's like a poem that tells a story.

Mr. Harrison: Yes, that's exactly right. The story that this narrative poem is going to tell is one that you all know. This poem is called "Little Red Riding Hood and the Wolf."

Joanna: That's like a kindergarten story. Why do we have to read this?

Mr. Harrison: Well, this version of the story is not really appropriate for young children. Roald Dahl rewrote parts of the story that make it better suited for older students. Knowing Dahl as an author, we know that he had a great sense of humor. When he wrote this poem, I don't think he wanted anyone to take it very seriously. However, the poem has an important lesson that we can learn from. I want to discuss three words that we'll see in the story today: *knickers*, *caviar*, and *decent*.

Mr. Harrison recognizes that these particular words cannot be determined through context clues in the poem and feels that it would assist the students' understanding of the poem if the words are defined prior to reading.

Before/During Reading

Mr. Harrison: This is a short poem, so I want everyone to whisper read it first. I want you to find out how Little Red Riding Hood faces her fear of the Wolf.

Mr. Harrison requires all students to whisper read at their own rate so he can monitor the reading and assist any student who might be struggling.

After Reading

Mr. Harrison: Turn and talk to your partner about how Little Red Riding Hood faces her fear of the Wolf.

[He monitors as students share.]

Mr. Harrison: Anita, what do you and Steven think?

Anita: We think she gets smart and starts carrying a gun!

Steven: I think the Wolf finally gets what he deserves.

Mr. Harrison: I want everyone to find the sentence that starts the turning point in the story. Put your finger under that sentence. Joan, can you read that for us?

Joan: "Then Little Red Riding Hood said, 'But Grandma, what a lovely great big furry coat you have on.'" That's where the story changes from the real story. Little Red Riding Hood never asks about the furry coat in the real story.

Mr. Harrison: Right. Do you all agree? Thumbs up or down.

[The students all give thumbs up.]

Mr. Harrison: So we see the conflict develop in the story. How does it begin to escalate?

Clint: I think the conflict starts to develop when Little Red Riding Hood first sees her grandmother. She knows immediately that something is wrong.

Joe: Well, in the real story, she's the victim. She's afraid of the Wolf and runs away for help.

Anita: But in another version, the Wolf eats Little Red Riding Hood.

Mr. Harrison: So back to the question, how does she change in this poem?

Joanna: She isn't afraid of the Wolf anymore.

Steven: Right. She isn't the victim in this poem. She decides to defend herself with the gun.

Mr. Harrison: We've talked about the themes of stories before. This poem also has a theme. I'll give you a clue: It has something to do with the changes in Little Red Riding Hood. Turn to your partner and share your ideas.

[The students discuss while he monitors and listens in for discussion points.]

Mr. Harrison: Joe, why don't you and Clint share what you discussed?

Joe: We think the theme is not to be afraid of things.

Mr. Harrison: Good. Another way to say that is Little Red Riding Hood overcomes her fear of the Wolf. Overcoming fear is a theme that we see frequently in stories. We're going to read a story next week that has the same theme, and we'll compare and contrast the way the themes are presented in both text types. Tomorrow we'll look at the structure of this poem more in depth.

Extensions

Mr. Harrison asks the students to prepare to share the poem, much like a Readers Theatre presentation. He knows that the practice will continue to build the students' fluency.

Additionally, he has the students write an essay that discusses the theme of the poem and provides supporting evidence from the poem that supports the theme.

Assessment
Mr. Harrison assesses through observations and using a writing rubric for the essays.

Lesson Summary
The focus for revisiting the poem tomorrow is to establish the rhyme, meter, and verses in the poem. Additionally, the students practice reading the poem outside of group with assigned parts. The students then present the poem in a reading to the class. This allows the students to continue practicing their fluency even though it is not a focus of the small-group instruction.

Individual Writing Conferences

Just as students go through developmental stages in reading, they also go through these stages in writing. Individual writing conferences allow teachers to gear feedback to individual students based on need. Most teachers find it difficult to find the time for individual writing conferences, but it is time well spent. To get better at writing, students need both feedback and accountability in completing writing pieces. Clearly, there will not be time to take all written pieces through the editing process. In some cases, make decisions about which text piece will be the focus of a writing conference. At other times, the student may choose which written piece to perfect.

A writing notebook or portfolio is important to the writing and conference process. The notebook should contain established writing rubrics, writing ideas, spelling demons, and personal writing goals established in the writing conferences. The writing pieces in the portfolios are a combination of assigned writings and student-selected writings and responses.

Strive to meet weekly with each student to provide feedback and set goals for either a specific piece of writing or overall writing goals. Record these goals and revisit them at the next conference. Writing conferences typically last five to eight minutes. Create a schedule that allows for a group of students to conference daily. Look for short times during the day that are usually down times. For example, although the morning bell rings at 8:00, there are always students who straggle in late. This might be the perfect time to meet with a student or two who are always on time. Or, take advantage of the last 15 minutes of the day, which is often devoted to packing up. If you have a definite weekly schedule, it soon becomes a class routine. Record important conference points on the writing conference record (see the Appendix for the reproducible). This form is kept with each student's writing portfolio so the teacher and student can review previous conferences and goals.

Both primary- and intermediate-grade students benefit from individual writing conferences. This teaching venue provides an opportunity for individual feedback that students need to become better writers. The feedback, especially in the writing process and traits, can be applied to other writing completed by the student. The following vignette shows an example of a teacher–student dialogue about the first grader's writing.

A Primary-Grade Writing Conference

Mrs. Eggleston's first-grade class has been working on writing about the beginning, middle, and end of a story. This week, she read the book *We're Going on a Bear Hunt* by Michael Rosen (2009) as an interactive read-aloud in whole group. After the reading, the students were asked to write one sentence about the beginning, middle, and end of the story.

For today's writing conference, Gloria brings her independent written response to the book *We're Going on a Bear Hunt* (see Figure 31a).

Teacher: Let's take a look at what you wrote about the story. Why don't you read it to me?

[Gloria reads her writing to the teacher.]

Teacher: Wow, you really did a great job writing the beginning, middle, and end of the story. I think you're ready to add some more details to your stories. When we write, it helps the reader if we use some special words to tell how things happened in order. Let's look at the words *first*, *then*, *next*, and *last*. I want you to reread the story to me, but this time include these words in what you've already written.

Gloria: First, the family went on a bear hunt. Then, they had to go through the tall grass and through the mud. Next, they had to go through the river. Last, they saw a bear so they ran back.

Teacher: That was a wonderful story. You're getting so good at your writing that you can now write what you just said. I want you to rewrite your story, but this time I want you to write it using the words *first*, *then*, *next*, and *last*. I don't want you to draw a line for each part. Just write it all together like a real story.

The teacher records important conference points on the feedback form so Gloria will remember what to do, and to provide a record of previous writing conferences (see Figure 31b).

Teacher: When we meet next week, I want you to bring your new story. I can't wait to read it!

FIGURE 31
Sample Primary-Grade Writing Conference

(a) A First Grader's Written Response to a Book

B The family went on a bear hunt and then they had to go throung hight grass.

M And then they went through the mud and they had to go throughnh the river.

E They had seen a bear!!! So they ran back.

(b) The Student's Completed Conference Form

Writing Conference Record Sheet

Name: Gloria.

Date: April 5, 2012

Writing Piece for Conference:

"Going on a Bear Hunt"

Focuses for Conference:
- Review beginning, middle, end.
- Work on transitions- First, then, next, last.

Goals for Next Conference:
Revise "Going on a Bear Hunt" with a First, then, next, last format.

FIGURE 32
Sample Intermediate-Grade Writing Conference

(a) A Third Grader's First Draft of Her Research Report

<u>Bengal Tiger</u>

Did you know that a tiger is one of the four who can roar? The other three are the tigers, the leopards, and the jaguars. The baby's roar sounds like a purr. but when it is big the roar is big. The baby tiger weights 2 pounds when it is born but when it is big it weights a lot more. The father does not help. The mom has to do every thing like feed and protect the babies from danger. I wish I can see a baby tiger one day. BY GRACE @ 1-17-12

(b) The Student's Completed Conference Form

Writing Conference Record Sheet

Name: Grace

Date: May 2, 2012

Writing Piece for Conference:

Research — Bengal Tiger

Focuses for Conference:

Putting information into categories — (Graphic organizer)

Goals for Next Conference:

General Information — Bengal Tigers — Babies — Find more facts about bengal tigers. Create a three paragraph paper using the graphic organizer.

Same and Different — other tigers

An Intermediate-Grade Writing Conference

Mrs. Swanson's third-grade class has been conducting research on a jungle animal of their choice. Today Grace brings the first draft of her research report to her writing conference (see Figure 32a).

Mrs. Swanson: So, Grace, let's talk about what you've learned about the Bengal tiger. Go ahead and read your report to me.

[Grace reads her research report to Mrs. Swanson.]

Mrs. Swanson: You've really found some interesting facts about the Bengal tiger. I especially like what you wrote about the tiger's roar. Now I want to help you organize your writing so readers will be able to understand it better. First, let's come up with some categories for the information that you have about the tiger.

[She sketches a graphic organizer as the information is discussed.]

Mrs. Swanson: One category that I see is about baby tigers. You have a lot of facts about this. Let's put it as one category.

Grace: What about the different tigers that roar?

Mrs. Swanson: Yes, maybe you could add some more details to that part to tell how the Bengal tiger is like and different from other tigers. That would make a good category. Let's call it "How Bengal tigers are the same and different than other tigers."

Grace: So far, I just have stuff about their roars. I need some more information.

Mrs. Swanson: You do have a great interesting fact to start with. I didn't know about the roars.

Grace: I don't think I have any other categories.

Mrs. Swanson:	No, I think we included all the facts in those two categories. Can you think of another category?
Grace:	I'm not really sure.
Mrs. Swanson:	I like the part about the baby tigers. Maybe you could do a category that just talks about the Bengal tigers, like where they live and what they eat.
Grace:	That would be great. I know where to find that information.

Mrs. Swanson draws the graphic organizer on the conference sheet and places it in Grace's portfolio (see Figure 32b). When she meets with Grace next week, she can refer back to the graphic organizer to review Grace's writing.

Individual Reading Conferences

The individual reading conference serves several important purposes. First, it allows the student to share a self-selected book with the teacher. The teacher asks questions, such as Why did you choose this book? and What is currently happening in the story? Another important part of the conference is having the student read a page or two of the book aloud. This allows the teacher to evaluate the appropriate level of difficulty. The teacher also guides the student in text selections that include a wide variety of genres.

In many classrooms, the students are expected to read self-selected books and then take computerized tests for accountability purposes. This type of reading must be tempered with the teacher's knowledge of the texts selected and the students' comprehension of the text that goes well beyond a computerized test. Including a written response along with the computerized test is a valid option.

Maintain a reading conference log for each student in a notebook (see the Appendix for a reproducible). In this log, track the student-selected genres being read to help guide the student's future book choices. Also, use the log to track the amount of time it takes for the student to read the text. For example, if a student is reading numerous books in record time, ask the student whether he or she did not complete some of the books. Alternately, if a student is spending a great deal of time on the same book, this might be a focus issue in the reading conference.

Reading conferences give students the time to make personal connections with the teacher to the reading. Sharing personal reading experiences is highly motivating to most students. It also allows the teacher to share the intrinsic joy of a great story. In the following vignettes, notice how the teachers make personal connections about the reading with each student and how the students respond positively.

A Primary-Grade Reading Conference

It is Laurie's day for her individual reading conference with her first-grade teacher, Miss Chen. Laurie arrives at the table with her self-selected book in hand.

| Miss Chen: | I see that you are reading a new Junie B. Jones book by Barbara Park [1993]. What adventure is Junie having in this book? |

Laurie:	Well, her parents tell her that she's getting a present, but it's really a new baby brother.
Miss Chen:	Why is the book called *Junie B. Jones and a Little Monkey Business*?
Laurie:	Her grandmother calls the baby a cute little monkey, and then Junie goes to school and says that her brother is a monkey. Then, she asks if she can bring him to pet day.
Miss Chen:	Junie always manages to have some great adventures.

Miss Chen decides that she does not need to listen to Laurie read because she has heard Laurie read other Junie B. Jones books fluently. Miss Chen wants to try to convince Laurie to read some other book genres.

Miss Chen:	Laurie, don't you ride horses?
Laurie:	Yeah. I'm going to be in a horse show next weekend.
Miss Chen:	My daughter used to be in horse shows. I have one of her books at home that tells about getting ready for horse shows. What if I bring it to you tomorrow to read?
Laurie:	That would be great. Maybe it'll help me win the show.

Miss Chen records her observations and makes a note to bring the book to school. This will encourage Laurie to broaden her reading with informational text.

An Intermediate-Grade Reading Conference

During the last conference, Hailey, a fourth grader, had just started the book *Bridge to Terabithia* by Katherine Paterson (1977). Mr. Perez is anxious to check in with Hailey about how she is enjoying the story.

Mr. Perez:	So, how far have you gotten in the book?
Hailey:	I just finished Chapter 5, "The Giant Killers."
Mr. Perez:	Why do you think the author used that as a title for the chapter?
Hailey:	In this chapter, Jess and Leslie try to get back at Janice, the school bully. They say she's the giant in school, just like the giants they face in Terabithia. They get her back, all right. They write a pretend note to her that looks like it's from a boy she likes. It's really funny to see them get back at her, and she doesn't even know they wrote it.
Mr. Perez:	I told you last time that this has always been a favorite book of mine. Let's take a look at the next chapter, "The Coming of Prince Terrien." Based on the story so far, what do you think this chapter title might mean?
Hailey:	I don't know, but Terrien sounds a little like Terabithia. Maybe there will be a new friend joining them.
Mr. Perez:	You're going to be really surprised. We'll talk about that next week when we meet.

Differentiating Literacy Instruction
for Special Populations

One of the most difficult issues for many teachers to address is the needs of special populations. These students have many faces: the child with disabilities, the struggling reader, the English learner, the unmotivated student, and the gifted student. Differentiated instruction offers a way to address the diversity in any mixed-ability classroom (Tomlinson, 2001). To meet the needs of all students, we must acknowledge their strengths and accommodate for their literacy learning differences throughout the school day.

Differentiating for Students With Disabilities

Students identified under the Individuals with Disabilities Education Act (IDEA) "are a heterogeneous group with one common characteristic: the presence of disabling conditions that significantly hinder their abilities to benefit from general education" (NGA Center & CCSSO, 2010a, para. 3). The Common Core State Standards provide a historic opportunity to improve access to rigorous standards for students with disabilities and clearly outline the inclusion of these students. The widespread adoption of the CCSS is expected to accelerate a growing movement to link individualized education plans (IEPs) for students with disabilities directly to grade-level standards. The IEPs are written in such a way as to help these students move toward meeting the standards. Further, the CCSS state that these students "must be challenged to excel within the general curriculum and be prepared for success in their post-school lives" (NGA Center & CCSSO, 2010a, para. 2). Common Core assessments for students with severe disabilities are currently being developed.

Teachers need to create levels of support and instructional accommodations that are necessary to meet the unique needs of these students and to enable their access to the general education curriculum. Sometimes this means presenting ideas in multiple ways, changing materials, or altering procedures to allow students with disabilities to learn within the framework of the CCSS.

Just as there is a wide range of learners in the mainstream of regular education students, that same range exists with students with disabilities. Students with more significant cognitive development issues require substantial support and accommodations to have meaningful access to certain standards in both instruction and assessment, based on their communication and academic needs. In either case, the supports and accommodations should ensure that the students receive access to multiple means of learning and opportunities to demonstrate knowledge, but retain the rigor and high expectations of the CCSS.

Many special-needs students can be accommodated in the regular classroom with appropriately planned instruction. As discussed in Chapter 3, whole-group instruction can be structured to meet the needs of a wide range of learners. Small-group instruction in the regular classroom will, in most cases, provide appropriate developmental reading instruction. Special accommodations are most powerfully incorporated as students are grouped by their developmental literacy needs in a setting of no more than three students. As teachers become more adept in constructing and delivering inclusive lessons in the regular classroom, students with disabilities will have a better opportunity to participate in the regular classroom setting. Additional literacy instruction focused on specific needs is addressed with the support of special education services.

There has been an understanding among many educators that special education students need something different in their instruction: a different program, model, or materials. I strongly believe that with experiences with vast numbers of students with disabilities, these students do not need something different if they are receiving quality, research-based reading instruction at the appropriate developmental levels. These students simply need *more* of this kind of instruction. They need more time in each of the essential reading components with appropriate development-leveled materials in a smaller group setting. Therefore, classroom teachers should be diligent in delivering whole-group instruction that is appropriate for students with disabilities and create a small-group schedule that allows students to receive focused, intensive literacy instruction based on their developmental needs. Teachers should present grade-level skills that students can comfortably accomplish with teacher support. The models outlined for small-group differentiated instruction in this book are appropriate for additional intervention for all struggling students.

Differentiating for Struggling Students

The practice of providing intervention for struggling readers has certainly been in place for decades. In an effort to support students at the earliest point of struggle, RTI is a recent model that establishes tiers of support for struggling readers beginning in the regular classroom setting (Batsche et al., 2005). This initiative has resulted in a dramatic drop in the identification of students for special education services. Along with RTI, it is necessary to address these needs beginning in the regular classroom. With the wide range of readers in any given classroom, differentiating for students is becoming the norm.

There has been a plethora of curricular materials offered to "fix" these students. Again, it is not in the materials themselves that we will find the answers but in the teachers' knowledge of how to address the development reading needs of each student that will begin to close the learning gaps. One of the most stressful parts of this RTI process is the need to monitor these students' progress. Clearly, it is important to monitor students' progress toward established goals. However, the nature of the reading process does not lend itself to showing massive amounts of growth in a relatively short amount of time. For example, it is unreasonable to expect that a student reading a year below grade level would catch up in two or three months. When the monitored intervention does not show results, many districts quickly move to an alternative option.

Progress monitoring of students in the RTI process should be administered in time increments that are reasonable for monitoring comprehensive reading growth. In reality, the change should not be in the instructional model itself if it is appropriate and comprehensive but in the intensity, both in time and in a smaller group setting.

Some teachers are left to segment one part of reading, such as sight words, in hopes that a student can show growth each week. Students who are deficient in reading are generally deficient in most of the important components: fluency, vocabulary, phonics, and comprehension. Differentiating reading instruction using a research-based model is the most appropriate way to meet these readers' needs. Further, student intervention should include all components of literacy relative to the student's reading difficulty. Additionally, there should be coordination in instruction between regular classroom instruction and intervention models.

Differentiating for English Learners

The National Center for Education Statistics reports that while the general population as a whole rose 9% from 1993 to 2003, the English learner population grew by 40.7% (McKeon, 2005). This has special implications for educators because the English learner population now comprises 10% of all students. English learners bring with them many resources that enhance their education and can serve as resources for schools and societies. Many of these students have strong first-language and literary skills and bring talents and cultural perspectives that enrich our schools and society.

The clear vision of the Common Core standards for English learners is that they be held to the same high expectations outlined for all students. However, these students may require additional time, appropriate instructional support, and aligned assessments as they acquire both English-language proficiency and content area knowledge. English learners are a highly heterogeneous group. They vary with differences in ethnic background, first language (including regional dialects), socioeconomic status, quality of prior schooling, and level of English proficiency. Each student needs to be diagnosed individually, with instruction adjusted accordingly and progress closely monitored. Students who enter school with limited or interrupted schooling need to acquire background knowledge and skills that have not been developed in their native language. The basic literacy skills can be addressed with students with similar developmental levels. However, there are English learners who enter our schools with high levels of proficiency in their native language. These students most often use their knowledge and quickly apply it once the new language is acquired.

Teachers must be armed with a range of research-based strategies, pedagogy, and instruction to support English learners in building English-language proficiency. Supports such as technology, visual aids, conversation, and respect for their home cultures contribute to these students' success. The use of technology is instrumental in supporting these students across content areas. Technology is particularly useful because it can transcend language differences and provide the content in the native language as a bridge to English.

Teachers must build on the talents of each student and provide additional and appropriate instructional support to those students who need it. This includes adherence to the standards and expectations that are essential to academic achievement. English learners, like English-speaking students, require regular access to teaching practices that are most effective for improving student achievement.

Just as literacy is the key to a good education for general education students, it is no different for English learners. The central foundational education focus should be literacy development. This needs to be supported in their native language when appropriate support is available. When this is not possible, these students need the intense literacy instruction already in place for other struggling readers. In my experience, these students thrive in intervention that is grounded in developmental reading and writing.

Using an integrated curriculum in which students are exposed to words, stories, and related concepts can assist these students in developing understandings. For example, in a second-grade classroom, the teacher presents a unit on animals, and stories about real and imaginary animals are shared. The students write about animals and research a particular one. The teacher asks the English learner to make a poster about an animal from her country and present it to the class. This unit of study is universally understood and therefore allows this student to connect to her own background knowledge.

Researchers are hopeful that future technology will greatly advance opportunities for English learners. Recent research has suggested that the potential for hypertext, hypermedia, and computer-mediated text will support these students' reading development, although the specifics about how this technology will relate to varying language characteristics is presently unknown (Proctor, Dalton, & Grisham, 2007). In one study, fourth-grade English learners were able to use technology to promote learning and effectively apply comprehension strategies. As stated previously, the strategies that prove effective for struggling English-speaking students appear to be effective with English learners as well. Technology is instrumental in differentiating instruction that addresses the explosive number of home languages that students now bring to the classroom.

When English learners were asked how teachers can best support their needs, they made several comments that have been supported by research (Maxwell, 2011). First, the students stated that working in small groups or with a partner was helpful. They also identified characteristics of the most effective teachers: those who were patient and didn't give up on them, teachers who slowed down their speech, and those who explained vocabulary words in the context of the book being read.

To differentiate instruction to meet the needs of English learners, provide literacy-rich environments where students are immersed in a wide variety of language experiences. Also, focus language arts instruction on foundational skills in English that enable English learners to participate fully in grade-level coursework. Provide opportunities for classroom discussion that encourages interaction to develop communicative skills in language arts, and ongoing assessment and feedback to guide learning. Include all reading components at appropriate levels of difficulty to increase literacy learning. Finally, use the grade-level standards, as much as possible, to guide the instruction.

As we review the guidelines of best practices for English learners, we find them not inconsistent with those that we advocate for all English-speaking students. In some cases, teachers feel ill prepared to provide for the needs of these students, but the strategies needed are, for the most part, the same instructional strategies that teachers use for all students.

Differentiating for Unmotivated Students

Lack of student motivation is often a deterrent to the learning process. Many teachers have voiced that unmotivated students are indeed the most challenging. To differentiate instruction to meet the needs of these students, we must look deeper at their motivation issues. Examining students' interests is a good place to start. Students enjoy reading when they are presented with texts that support their interests. Simply talking informally with a student shows that you are interested and want to know more about the student and his or her likes and dislikes. This emotional support has been shown to increase motivation (Wentzel & Wigfield, 2009). Teachers can then differentiate for unmotivated readers by providing texts that are interesting, and therefore motivating, based on these informal conversations.

Much of the lack of motivation that students experience is grounded in an inability to successfully read and understand what is read. This happens most often when students are assigned text that is too difficult to read without the support of the teacher. Therefore, be keenly aware of each student's reading abilities. Differentiating instruction requires finding books that are not only of interest to the students but also readable either independently or with support. Confidence can only be built through previous successful experiences in reading. This confidence continues to build as the teacher encourages autonomy in reading by providing more challenging yet interesting reading material (Zhou, Ma, & Deci, 2009).

Another characteristic of motivated readers is a purpose for reading. These students see reading as an important process, which leads to perseverance when the assignment requires much effort. This is referred to as behavioral engagement (Skinner, Kindermann, Furrer, & Marchand, 2008). The skilled teacher provides meaningful instruction for the unmotivated learner based on all available information and provides authentic purposes for reading and writing. In many cases, this requires going beyond the planned curriculum, but it is well worth the effort if the student can be taught to love to learn.

Differentiating for Gifted Students

Perhaps no other special population has been more ignored than gifted learners. Generally, teachers are so overwhelmed with the needs of the other students that the gifted more often than not are left to their own devices. Teachers often make assignments for these students to complete on their own with little interaction with the teacher or other classmates. This can no longer be the norm. Gifted students need instruction that is differentiated to meet their special needs and provide fertile ground for growth. Differentiating instruction for this special population requires supplementing the curriculum with more complex texts, more in-depth research and writing, and most important, more time spent with a skilled teacher to guide the students in thinking more deeply about their reading and writing. If gifted students are expected to make literacy gains, they need careful guidance and meaningful interactions with the teacher.

CHAPTER 5

Independent Practice, Projects, and Presentations

The adage that practice makes perfect is especially applicable to students as they hone their literacy skills. It epitomizes the role of independent literacy practice. Perhaps no other venue has been used less effectively than independent practice. Historically, this was the time for students to complete workbook pages or basic busy work so the teacher could work with small reading groups. These types of assigned tasks are less than motivating and miss the mark for truly practicing and orchestrating important literacy skills.

Many teachers fear that when students are left to their own devices, chaos will break out. One second-grade teacher once told me, "If I let my students try to work independently, they would be hanging from the light fixtures!" She was probably right if her students did not have the benefit of a teacher who understood the underpinnings for creating an environment that supports effective independent practice. It takes careful preparation, practice, and routines for monitoring and assessing the students' learning to make this time most productive.

Addressing more rigorous literacy standards requires an increase rather than a decrease in the amount of time devoted to independent practice. Students need significant amounts of time to read, write, and complete research as well as time to complete projects and prepare presentations. Additionally, teachers need this time to conference with students, both in small groups and individually, to assist and give feedback. Whereas this independent time was once viewed as insignificant and stuffed with busy work, the effective classroom teacher now views it as perhaps the most important part of the instructional day.

That said, students are only able to effectively practice and orchestrate literacy skills that they have mastered or can do comfortably on their own, with a partner, or with the support of a small group of peers. If any given task is too difficult, it can quickly turn into a downward spiral, not only for the students but also for the teacher. When the teacher is distracted by student behaviors, the teacher loses critical time needed to work with either small groups or individual students.

Independent assignments might extend from whole-group or small-group instruction. Planning for independent time should include the use of extended, integrated assignments with a reduced emphasis on disconnected, shorter tasks. Carefully planned and integrated activities that extend across several content areas are preferable. Consider the value of extending a given assignment over several days or even weeks.

Also, include both individual and small-group research and project-based learning activities during this independent work time. These assignments might connect to the

FIGURE 33
Instructional Focuses of Independent Literacy Practice, Projects, and Presentations

Independent Literacy Practice, Projects, and Presentations

Instructional Focuses

Extensions From Whole Group	Self-Selected Independent Reading/Writing	Extensions From Small Group	Research, Projects, and Presentations
Targeted Minilesson Practice	Monitored Through Individual Reading/ Writing Conferences	Fluency	Teacher-Assigned
Responses for Interactive Read-Alouds		Word Study	Student-Selected
Responses for Shared Reading		Vocabulary	Theme-Based
		Comprehension	Real-World

current theme and be assigned by the teacher, or students might make choices within certain parameters. This does not mean that there should be wide choices, but rather managed choices. Choices lead to student ownership of the work and a greater engagement in the task (Turner, 1995). Additionally, students should use some of this time for self-selected reading and discussions with peers and in individual reading conferences with the teacher. Figure 33 presents a variety of opportunities for independent literacy practice. Detailed explanations as well as concrete examples are presented in this chapter.

Extensions From Whole-Group Instruction

There are any number of independent activities that could be developed in response to lessons completed in whole-group instruction. Varying these assignments keeps independent work fresh and motivating.

Written responses to interactive read-alouds and shared reading completed in whole group are good options for independent activities. These responses could focus on either vocabulary in the text or comprehension of the text. The following are examples of these kinds of extensions:

- After reading *Gregory, the Terrible Eater* by Mitchell Sharmat (1980) as an interactive read-aloud, students are asked to use each vocabulary word in a sentence that tells something that happens in the story. Then, the first graders draw an illustration for each sentence (see Figure 34a).

- After the interactive read-aloud of the book *Liberty Street* by Candice Ransom (2003), a fifth-grade teacher asks her students to complete an acrostic using the word *liberty*. With each letter, the students write about what liberty means to the slaves in the story (see Figure 34b).

- The poem "Winter Night" is used as a shared reading in whole group in a second-grade classroom. Students are asked to write a response to the meaning of the phrase "feet of winter" after completing a shared reading of the poem (see Figure 34c).

There are instances when this independent time is used for practicing isolated foundational skills, such as grammar, word analysis, and phonics. This kind of activity has traditionally dominated much of the time that students spend in independent practice but should be used sparingly and only when needed for additional practice. Most often, this practice follows the targeted minilesson presented in the whole-group setting. It is critical that the modeling ("I do") and guided practice ("we do") are completed in whole group prior to making assignments for independent practice. If not, the students could potentially be practicing incorrectly. Practice in phonics and word study naturally extends from small-group instruction at the appropriate developmental level. There are, however, occasions for students to practice grade-level word analysis skills. Isolated practice in grade-level grammar skills, such as using quotation marks correctly, is appropriate for independent practice.

Examples of foundational skills practice include:

- Correct sentences by inserting quotation marks in the appropriate places.
- Identify the nouns in sentences.
- Use correct verb tenses in sentences.

Whereas the practice of foundational skills traditionally monopolized independent time, the shift toward more integrated practice of essential literacy skills is crucial. The goal is to quickly move students from isolated practice to authentic reading and writing experiences.

The success of the independent activity directly relates to the appropriate modeling demonstrated by the teacher. For example, in the previous activity with the book, *Gregory, the Terrible Eater,* the teacher models the response activity with another text beforehand. Additionally, developing and practicing routines during independent time is essential, such as developing a routine for keeping a journal to track self-selected reading. Establishing designated places to house materials and areas to keep ongoing assignments is beneficial to managing the independent work. Again, make sure that the independent assignment is appropriate for the learners or adjust expectations.

FIGURE 34
Students' Written Responses for Extensions From Whole-Group Instruction

(a) Sentences and Illustrations Demonstrating a First Grader's Vocabulary Acquisition

(b) A Fifth Grader's Acrostic

L   Liberty was valued by the slaves.
I   It was hard to live like a slave.
B   Being able to go downtown was important to the slaves.
E   Everyone helped the girl escape.
R   Rarely did they get a day off.
T   Trying again and again, they were finally free.
Y   You could never understand how hard it was to be a slave.

(c) A Second Grader's Response to a Phrase in a Poem

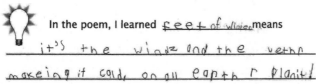

Extensions From Small-Group Differentiated Reading Groups

The best gauge for assigning appropriate independent practice comes from teacher observations in small-group instruction. Careful attention to instructional reading level as well as the vocabulary and comprehension that accompanies it are of utmost importance. Phonics and other foundational skill practice must also be taken into consideration. Practice as it relates to the research-based components is an important starting point when planning independent practice. It makes good sense to plan for a proportionate amount of time for students to complete teacher-assigned extensions based on the small-group lesson focuses. In this way, the teacher can be confident in knowing that the students are practicing with materials at the appropriate independent level. Each component is discussed next, along with concrete examples for extension practice in each area.

Fluency

All elementary students need fluency practice, and some more so than others. Although students who lack fluency work on this during small-group time, additional fluency practice is necessary. For those students who are fluent readers, practicing independently outside of group is an effective activity. Fluency can only be developed through practice with text at the independent reading level. An independent reading level is best defined as a text that can be read with 98–100% accuracy (Felton, 1999). Fluency is developed as students read and reread text at this level for additional fluency practice. Figure 35 shows two students rereading a book that was read in small group.

Activities that students can do to increase fluency include the following:

- Reread a book with a partner that has been read previously in small group.
- Practice reading selected poems or rhymes.
- Reread a book to a buddy.
- Prepare a book to read to a lower-grade class.
- Practice with a Readers Theatre script.
- Sing karaoke.
- Record the readings of a book, listen to self-evaluate, and reread to improve.
- Practice reading a text piece and track fluency rates.

Word Study

Independent word study activities must be differentiated for the developmental levels of each student. This is assessed and addressed in the small-group models in Chapter 4. Students need independent practice to solidify this important word knowledge. Focus practice on the particular developmental stage that the students are currently studying.

FIGURE 35
Students Rereading to Improve Fluency

Activities that students in the alphabet stage can do to support increased letter recognition and producing the alphabet include the following:

- Match uppercase and lowercase magnetic letters.
- Locate specific letters in a magazine and cut and paste them. This gives students the opportunity to view letters in different fonts.
- Stamp the matching uppercase and lowercase letters.
- Play alphabet memory with a partner by matching uppercase and lowercase letter cards.
- Complete alphabet puzzles.

The following are activities that students can do to increase their identification of beginning and ending consonant sounds:

- Cut pictures from magazines that begin with the focus sounds.
- Sort picture cards by beginning or ending sounds.
- Write the beginning or ending sounds for picture cards.

- Draw pictures that have the focus beginning sounds.
- Play sound memory with a partner by matching picture cards with the beginning or ending sounds.

Activities that students can do to increase word family acquisition include the following:

- Complete word sorts based on word families.
- Complete word hunts to find words that belong to the focus family patterns.
- Write sentences with words.
- Use letter tiles to make words within the focus family.

The following are activities that support vowel pattern acquisition:

- Complete word sorts based on vowel patterns (see Figure 36).
- Complete word hunts in books to identify additional words with the focus vowel patterns.
- Play pattern memory with a partner by making matches based on words that have the same vowel patterns.

FIGURE 36
Students Working on a Word Sort to Support Vowel Pattern Acquisition

- Add suffixes to words that contain the focus vowel patterns (e.g., *-s, -es, -ed, -ing, -er, -est*).

To increase their knowledge of word study/syllabication and Greek and Latin word roots, students can create a notebook divided into word feature sections, such as compound words, contractions, Greek word roots, Latin word roots, and synonyms and antonyms. As word features are studied, they are recorded in the notebook along with meanings and drawing, as appropriate.

Vocabulary

Vocabulary development for beginning readers focuses on the acquisition of basic sight words. The need for students to recognize sight words automatically is a critical part of their reading development. Activities that students can do to increase their sight word recognition include the following:

- Flash sight words to a partner. Use a sand timer and record the number of sight words read in one minute.
- Using letter tiles, create and write focus sight words.
- Use a computer program that flashes sight words.
- Find sight words in magazines to cut and paste in a sight word collage.
- Play word memory with sight words by taking turns to make matches.

After students can automatically recognize 100 sight words, they then study vocabulary words in the context of literary or informational text read in small group. The following are activities that support further vocabulary development:

- Use each word in a sentence to tell something that happens in the story.
- Use each word in a text summary.
- In an individual dictionary, write each word on the correct alphabet page along with a sentence to show meaning. Include a sketch when appropriate.

Comprehension

Independent practice as students develop comprehension must be carefully planned to get the desired results. In the early stages of reading, this might include more drawing about the story than writing about the story. As students become capable of reading texts at levels that present more developed story lines and information, they then write about their reading to show their deep understanding of the text's message.

Activities that support comprehension development in beginning readers include the following:

- Draw pictures that represent the beginning, middle, and end of the story.
- Retell a story to a partner.

- Draw a picture to represent the main characters, setting, problem, and solution in a story.
- Draw pictures of the main ideas and supporting details in an informational text.

The following are activities that support comprehension development for later primary-grade readers:

- Use each story vocabulary word in a sentence that tells something that happens in the story.
- Choose an illustration in the story and write about what the illustrator is telling us in the picture.
- Use the words *first, then, next,* and *last* to write a paragraph that summarizes the story.
- Select the five most important events in the story and list them in order.
- With a partner, select the 10 most important sentences in the story.
- In an informational text, list the 10 most important things about the subject.
- Compare two characters in two different stories. Figure 37a is a first grader's comparison of a character in two different stories: *The Itsy Bitsy Spider* by Iza Trapani (1993) and *The Little Engine That Could* by Watty Piper (1991).
- After reading aloud *The Very Hungry Caterpillar* by Eric Carle (1987), students are asked to write in response to the question, "Why do you think the caterpillar ate so much food?" (see Figure 37b).

Activities that support comprehension development for intermediate-grade readers include the following:

- Rewrite or retell the story from the point of view of one of the characters.
- Write about the main character in the story. What character trait does he or she exhibit in the story? Give examples of how the character demonstrates the trait.
- Write a friendly letter to one of the characters in the story giving him or her advice about a problem in the story.
- Pretend that you are a newspaper reporter and write an article that answers the 5 Ws: who, what, when, where, and why.
- Write an acrostic poem. Figure 38 shows an acrostic poem by a fifth grader, who used a student interactive from ReadWriteThink.org after reading the book *Volcano: The Eruption and Healing of Mount St. Helens* by Patricia Lauber (1986). The student used this activity to summarize important facts learned from the text.

Self-Selected Independent Reading

Students who read independently become better readers, score higher on achievement tests in all subject areas, and have greater content knowledge than those who do not

(a) A First Grader's Comparison of a Character in Two Different Stories

(b) A Second Grader's Response to a Prompt About the Story

The Very Hungry Caterpillar

by Eríc Carle

Why do you think the caterpillar
ate so much food?

The caterplr ate so much because he was a baby caterplr
and babys are so hungry that they eay so much. They are
growng. Its good becuz it need enrgee to make a cocoon.
THat is hard werk!

Halie
Davon

(Krashen, 1993; Stanovich & Cunningham, 1993). Additionally, students who voluntarily read a substantial amount demonstrate a positive attitude toward reading (Long & Henderson, 1973).

Independent reading is the foundation of lifelong reading. However, independent reading should not be viewed as a time when students read and the teacher does

acrostic poems

VOLCANOES

V olcanoes are is a opening in the earth.

O ften explodes into the air.

L ayers are different parts of the earth.

C inder cone is a cone-shaped hill.

A volcano erupts in different ways.

N ot all volcanoes are dormant.

O ther volcanoes may give warnings sighns.

E xplosions blew the island in half.

S cientists sometimes study volcanoes.

Note. Acrostic created using the free online "Acrostic Poems" student interactive by ReadWriteThink.org, © International Reading Association/National Council of Teachers of English (see www.readwritethink.org/files/resources/interactives/acrostic).

something else. The teacher must plan an active role to support readers in building their reading independence. Independent reading time is the perfect opportunity to engage students in individual reading conferences. The success of independent reading is the end result of a well-orchestrated literacy curriculum and its delivery. With appropriately leveled text, students read confidently and are excited about reading. When students have a voice in their reading selection, they are motivated because they can read what interests them and begin to take ownership of their own learning. As students select their own books, they begin to view reading as a priority and a pleasurable activity.

A word of caution: There must be a solid structure in place so the selections are based on the students' reading levels. At the correct reading level means being able to read the text with 98–100% accuracy (Felton, 1999). This can be problematic for novice readers. The leveling of books is a very subjective process, so the teacher must be extremely knowledgeable of the books that students are selecting. In other words, if a student is reading a level D book, the teacher cannot assume that the student can read any level D book. Individual reading conferences provide the format for addressing this concern.

In one prominent independent reading program, students take a computerized test after reading each book. The comprehension assessed is at a very low level. Remain actively engaged in independent reading conferences to ensure that students are reading appropriate books with the appropriate understanding. Some reward-based independent reading programs that are geared to increase student motivation can sometimes actually have negative effects. This is especially true with struggling readers who feel very little reading success. Rather than exclude students from celebrations in which high-scoring readers are recognized, a universal celebration of reading is more motivating for all students. When students feel left out and punished for reading or not reading, the reading experience becomes tainted.

Considerations from teachers as they implement independent reading programs in the classroom include the following:

- Encourage students to read from a variety of genres.
- Build a classroom library with books on many levels, topics, and genres.
- Encourage students to set personal reading goals but not specific goals. Otherwise, a student's goal might only be to get to the end of the book.
- After reading a book, students should share their books either visually (e.g., creating a bookmark or collage) or by talking to another student or teacher about the book.

Most students are thrilled when they are given a choice of what they can read. Even the most reluctant readers find it refreshing and motivational. However, because students must make a selection that supports their reading level, the teacher needs an expansive classroom library. If students are to read a lot throughout the school day, they need a rich supply of books that they can actually read. Although this seems logical, it rarely exists. Although a plethora of materials, games, and workbooks are generally present, it is rare that a classroom or even a school has the book resources necessary to address the wide variety of reading levels and interests.

Research, Projects, and Presentations

If students are to be prepared for a future of higher education and the world of work, learning how to find needed information, conduct research, and assemble findings is important. These skills are introduced in the early primary grades. Moving forward, it will be difficult to provide the number of text resources that are necessary for students to engage in throughout this process, so many of the resources will have to be found online. By necessity, this process begins with the teacher modeling the research process during whole-group instruction. Although many students are quite competent in navigating the Internet, others do not have that advantage, so this modeling helps level the playing field.

If we are serious about preparing our students to meet the needs of an ever-expanding global society, we must consider the importance of project-based learning, including the development and delivery of presentations. For many of life's endeavors, whether planning for a trial, staging an art exhibit, or launching a satellite, an interdisciplinary team works together to solve a problem. In the classroom, a project-based approach gives students the opportunity to solve real-world problems or extend theme-based study, beginning in the early primary grades. Motivation is key: Projects offer students choice and voice, which personalizes their learning experiences.

Using technology as part of the research process and as a vehicle for presenting the information provides a wide range of interrelated literacy experiences. Technology allows students to communicate, collaborate, conduct research, analyze, create, and publish their own work for authentic audiences. Instead of writing book reports, for instance, students in a literacy project might produce audio reviews of books, post them on a blog, and invite responses from a partner class in another city or country. This venue motivates students who may not be successful in a more traditional classroom format.

Project-based learning applies across disciplines; it consistently emphasizes active, student-directed learning. Projects give students real-world contexts for learning, which creates a strong need to know. By design, projects are open ended so students must consider and evaluate multiple solutions and defend their choices. All of these activities engage students in high-order thinking skills.

The interest in project-based learning is part of an evolving definition of literacy. Learning to read is no longer enough. Today's student must be able to navigate and evaluate a vast amount of information, which requires fluency in technology along with the development of critical thinking skills. These projects offer students opportunities not only to make sense of this information but also to expand on it and share their contributions.

Finally, today's students will face complex challenges when they complete their formal education. Knowing how to solve problems, work collaboratively, and think innovatively are becoming essential skills, not only for future careers but also in tackling difficult issues in the local community and around the world. Thus, the role of teacher must move from expert to facilitator. Again, this takes time. One of the major advantages of project-based learning is that it makes school more like real life. In real life, we do not spend several hours at a time listening to authorities that know more than we do and who tell us exactly what to do and how to do it. We need to be able to ask questions of the person we are learning from. We need to be able to link what the person is telling us with what we already know. Furthermore, we need to be able to bring what we already know and relevant experiences that we have had to the topic. Figure 39 shows a group project completed by the Diddy Group, four third-grade boys who read the book *The Chocolate Touch* by Patrick Skene Catling (1979). Using templates from ReadWriteThink .org, the boys wrote a compare-and-contrast article about King Midas and John Midas.

Another example of a project in a primary-grade classroom centered on the question, "How can we recycle and reuse more in our school?" This second-grade class visited different parts of the school over a three-day period. Then, the teacher completed a shared writing to capture the students' thoughts about what they had observed. Finally, each student wrote a letter to the principal to try to persuade him to make some changes in how garbage was handled at the school.

An intermediate-grade class was studying landforms, and the teacher used the science unit as a platform for further investigation of a particular landform. The students

FIGURE 39
A Third-Grade Group's Compare-and-Contrast Article

Diddy News   What's the Difference   2012

What's In A Name
John Midas and King Midas

by: Noah, Ernest, Jakobi, and Savion

John Midas and King Midas

John Midas and King Midas are alike and different in several ways. One way that they are the same is that they both have the same last name. Also, they are both obsessed with things that they love. Finally, they both learn a lesson about their obsessions.

Not only are John Midas and King Midas alike, but they are also different. First, John Midas loved and was obsessed with chocolate, but King Midas was obsessed with gold. John is a little kid, but King Midas is an adult. John turned his mother into a chocolate statue, but King Midas turned his daughter into a golden statue. John hurt his family and friends, but King Midas just hurt his family. John's problem is that everything he puts into his mouth turns into chocolate, but King Midas's problem is that everything he touches turnes into gold.

As you can see, John Midas and King Midas are alike and different in many ways.

Note. Newsletter created using the free online "ReadWriteThink Printing Press" student interactive by ReadWriteThink.org, © International Reading Association/National Council of Teachers of English (see interactives.mped.org/ppress110.aspx). The ReadWriteThink.org "Compare & Contrast Map" student interactive helps students develop an outline for one of three types of comparison essays (see www.readwritethink.org/files/resources/interactives/compcontrast/map).

were asked to find information about the Grand Canyon. They then completed the "Grand Canyon Adventure" template created by the teacher. After students finished this research project, the teacher allowed them to select another landform and do more independent research.

Literacy Centers: A Cautionary Tale

In an attempt to actively engage students in meaningful literacy activities, literacy centers or workstations have been encouraged. When I think of the word *centers*, my mind conjures up a picture of a room full of small areas with cute activities that students rotate through when the bell rings. I also see teachers spending untold hours creating these centers. Be careful in how you develop and use center activities. One problem that teachers face with a specified center rotation is when some students finish faster than others. If you use centers, consider allowing students to move freely to other literacy activities as needed. Also, be thoughtful in the purpose for each center. Does each center address the developmental literacy levels of all the students?

Establish a self-selected book center and an area for reading so this option is always available as students finish assigned centers. A designated area where writing materials are stored is another worthy reason to have an established area. A listening center makes sense because it meets the literacy needs of a wide range of readers. Perhaps a mix of these kinds of centers along with extensions from small group is a good compromise. One model that has been successful for many teachers involves the students first completing small-group extensions and then moving to other centers that are appropriate for all students.

A rule of thumb: If it takes the teacher longer to create a center than it takes for the student to complete the activity, that particular center probably is not a good idea. The bottom line is that students need to be actively engaged in a variety of integrated reading and writing experiences that are both doable and meaningful. Use what you know about research and best practices along with what you know about your students to create the optimal use of this independent practice time.

Monitoring and Assessing Independent Activities

Students must recognize that independent literacy activities are important to you so they are also important to them. What is inspected gets respected. Determine a system for monitoring and assessing students as they engage in and complete these independent learning experiences.

For independent literacy activities, students should be assessed on effort and improvement rather than achievement. In this way, they can be rewarded for their individual efforts. This establishes a supportive, motivating environment, versus one where grades are awarded based primarily on achievement status. Grade-driven classrooms where the best performances get the best grades foster a classroom where no one works very hard. The more advanced students do not have to put out much effort to score well, and the lower achieving students soon realize that they will never perform or get good grades at the level of the higher achieving students.

Teachers must know each student thoroughly in order to effectively assign and assess his or her literacy learning. Teachers must also to be able to recognize growth and observe student effort. Rubrics provide the most appropriate assessment for these independent assignments. This allows for a shift in responsibility for earning grades to the students. Rubrics provide a no-excuse environment because the evaluation system is transparent from the beginning of the assignment. Although assessment is a necessity, it is in how this assessment is created and used that will best benefit and encourage literacy learning.

CHAPTER 6

An Overview of Literacy Assessments

I f we teach without appropriate assessment, it is like driving at night without head-lights. All across the nation, teachers assess for a multitude of purposes, stemming from federal, state, and district mandates. Unfortunately, the end result can be a blinding glare from countless headlights pointing in different directions. The glare from the confused and misinterpreted use of assessments confounds insights about children and their learning, as well as teaching. It is absolutely imperative that educators have a working knowledge of the foundational elements of reading to guide data-driven literacy decisions. These research-based elements that comprise the reading process make this knowledge even more vital to monitor acquisition and development as children grow as readers and writers.

What is tested has a strong influence on what is taught and how. On the surface, this makes perfect sense. However, the construction and administration of the assessment chosen and alignment with targeted skills can be problematic if interpreted in the wrong ways. As accountability and teacher quality is debated, high-stakes state assessments remain the primary driving force for the actions of teachers, administration, and district-level leaders. The overarching goal since the advent of No Child Left Behind has been to improve achievement levels for all students. Policymakers and educational leaders certainly need a standard barometer with which to gauge trends and overall educational needs. However, this goal can only be reached if the appropriate assessment is administered at the appropriate time, with appropriate expertise, and to the appropriate student. Researchers have warned policymakers that most statewide assessments fail to serve any of their purposes adequately (Hamilton, 2010). Accountability-focused assessments tend to be far less useful for guiding instruction than other data rendered by assessments that are more closely aligned with actual instruction. These important decisions must be made by the one who knows each student best: the teacher. An accomplished teacher who understands the underpinnings of literacy reaches deeper to identify reading and writing behaviors that are present or absent. Using a variety of assessments and observational data, carefully reflect and plan for the appropriate instruction that will drive literacy forward for all students.

At no time has the understanding of the many purposes and types of assessment been more important. As the Common Core standards infuse themselves across the country, educators are challenged to readdress beliefs and misconceptions about assessment and clarify the relationships between standards and curricula. To do that, it is imperative to examine the many forms that assessment takes, from statewide accountability tests, to benchmark tests, to teacher-created tests. The more relevant the information gleaned, the clearer the lens will be as decisions are made in the best interests of students.

Purposes for Formative and Summative Assessments

The majority of literacy assessments fit under two broad categories based on the purposes for the results: formative and summative.

Formative Assessment

Formative assessment is an ongoing process, not the end result of instruction that is reflected by a grade or score. The data provide feedback that is used to adjust teaching throughout the instructional sequence. The definition of *formative* reveals the appropriate use of formative assessment: "capable of giving form...[or] capable of alteration by growth and development" (*Merriam-Webster Dictionary*, 2012). The Latin word root *form* in the word *formative* reminds us that the teacher creates, shapes, or forms instruction based on data. Therefore the role of the teacher is active in this process not passive. The responsive nature of any formative assessment creates a cycle that transforms instruction as well as the learner. In other words, formative assessment revolves around how students learn and is embedded in the instructional process. Further, the adaptations that the teacher makes to instruction based on the results of a formative assessment take various shapes: a simple review of material, adjustments in lesson delivery, enhanced modality targets, or additional guided practice.

Formative assessment may be formal and/or standardized, using a diagnostic test with set directions and circumstances. Frequently, formative assessments are informal, using teacher-created performance tasks. These types of assessments qualify as "assessment FOR learning" rather than "assessment OF learning" (Stiggins, 2002). Stiggins makes this distinction and further states that this kind of assessment turns the formative classroom assessment process and its results into an instructional intervention that increases, not merely monitors, student learning.

Formative assessment focuses on classroom content rather than grades and test scores. These assessments evoke the following reflective questions of the teacher and, consequently, the student:

- What are my learning/teaching targets?
- Where are we now in this sequence of learning?
- What adjusted goals and actions will close whatever gaps remain?

Summative Assessment

Assessment *of* learning best describes summative assessment, a concept that contrasts with formative assessment, the process of decision-making as instruction unfolds. Summative assessment occurs after instruction and requires the assignment of a grade or score, as well as a judgment of the learning achieved.

The term *summative* derives from the Latin word *summa*, which explains our use of summative assessment further. It sums up the level of skill and renders a final product as it relates to a specific point in instruction. Summative assessments range from periodic checks of content mastery to year-end high-stakes state tests. A comprehensive

FIGURE 40
Assessment Trajectory

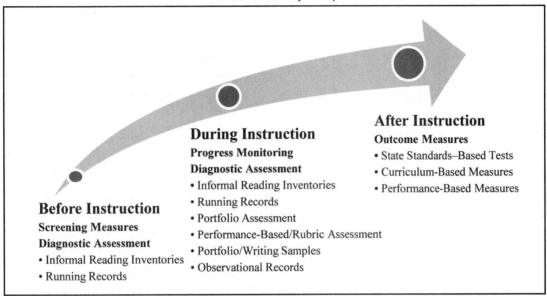

multiple-choice test at the conclusion of a unit of study may help the teacher judge the quality of instruction and the curriculum but is insufficient to determine gaps and learning needs for individual students. Without question, there is value in a statewide assessment framework that provides a portion of data derived from summative measures to be used for accountability. Comparisons between districts and schools help legislators and other educational leaders monitor and plan for curriculum improvement. In the 1990s, many states shifted to performance-based outcome measures in an effort to create tests that would measure a more complex integration of skills. In theory, the concept was a plausible solution to score inflation and create tests that measure standards more accurately. However, the cost of scoring these assessments was prohibitive, and the results were questioned because of scoring inconsistency. Was the past failure of performance-based assessment a result of misalignment of the assessment to standards, curricula, and instruction or flaws in the assessment itself? The former explanation is more likely. Compare the assessment examples on the trajectory in Figure 40 and consider short-term as well as long-term instructional goals.

Assessments Before Instruction

Screening Assessments

When students appear at the classroom door each fall, a screening measure provides an initial, albeit broad idea of reading ability. Screening instruments function under the premise that conditions of deficits can be predicted. Some can be given individually, whereas others are designed to be administered in a whole-group setting. These choices are dependent on the purposes of the teacher and the intended use of the results. A screener may be as simple as a graded word list to help the teacher choose manageable articles for a series of fifth-grade strategy lessons in informational text. In addition, screeners also enable the teacher to determine which students need further assessment and/or interventional support in reading. Screening tools save time when there is little historical data to confirm achievement in grade-based standards. A teacher also collects writing samples and uses evaluation rubrics to screen students for needs based on the developmental stages of writing.

By comparison, the concept of universal screening is a key element to the RTI process and ultimately the prevention of reading difficulties. Employment of the RTI model calls for all students to be screened to determine those who are at greatest levels of risk for failure. Universal screeners are designed to classify those at risk in an accurate, efficient, and valid way. Students who are found to have predictors that point to success in reading receive Tier 1 core curriculum instruction, determined by the district. Considering the future success of a kindergartener who has arrived in school lacking prerequisite skills such as phonemic awareness and sufficient oral language facility, there is no time to waste. No matter the grade, the teacher must identify at-risk students immediately and according to the RTI process, begin intensive Tier 2 interventions. This refers to additional reading instruction on top of what is gleaned in the classroom reading block. Strong foundational skills and the ability to access complex text independently remain paramount to overall academic achievement.

Universal screeners typically best identify those students who are at the very proficient or very deficient points in the reading spectrum. Students with average performance according to the predictors are much more difficult to pinpoint in comparison with others in the median range. A universal screener is insufficient to guide instructional planning and is used most frequently to help administrators and district leaders identify school and grade-level resource needs.

Diagnostic Assessments

A scenario of a common visit to the doctor best explains the process of diagnostic assessment in the area of literacy. A patient presents with complaints of a headache, and the nurse practitioner asks questions to obtain more information on medical and family history. This initial conversation serves as the screening instrument that calls attention to issues that impact care. When the doctor enters, he takes a blood pressure reading and finds that it is elevated above the normal ranges. He advises a reduction in caffeine and sodium and the addition of a regular exercise routine. The doctor schedules another appointment to monitor the results of his recommendations. What actions might the doctor take if after four months the patient's blood pressure has risen higher? Although the doctor initially intervened with a general strategy that could be successful for many people, he will need more diagnostic information to decide whether a blood pressure medicine will be sufficient to resolve the problem, or more invasive diagnostic tests are warranted to address underlying issues that limit function. In the meantime, he monitors progress as he addresses risk factors for further implications.

This medical analogy relates to the diagnosis of potential reading difficulties as well. Teachers provide instruction in a general curriculum that may be sufficient for grade-level readers to maintain growth. However, with at-risk students and those who need challenges, this plan proves ineffective to remediate gaps and/or enhance instruction for advanced learners. Diagnostic assessments, such as informal reading inventories (IRIs) and running records, go into much greater detail in each area of reading than the screening measures discussed earlier. The degree of deficiency in skill levels and discrete subskills are determined for differentiated instruction. Armed with diagnostic information, plan materials and strategies to meet the needs of all students.

IRIs

An IRI is a diagnostic assessment method that identifies gaps in development and zeroes in on instructional targets. IRIs render balanced information that can be used prior to instruction for initial screening, grouping for instruction, and choosing the most appropriate materials for reading. IRIs evolved from developmental reading research performed as early as Chall's work in 1983. Her stage model (Chall, 1983) underscores the substantive implications for differentiation of reading instruction. As Chall has noted, development at each stage is dependent on solid development at prior stages. The identification of levels of functioning through assessment guides planning of supportive instructional strategies. Students grow incrementally and strengthen their literacy base as they move through these predictable yet overlapping stages.

The following are examples of widely accepted and implemented IRIs:

- Assessments found in *Small-Group Reading Instruction: A Differentiated Teaching Model for Beginning and Struggling Readers* (Tyner, 2009): The stage-by-stage word study assessment included in this book is an example of an informal screening and diagnostic inventory that efficiently identifies levels of functioning in the production and use of phonics elements and reading in leveled text. These assessments are administered as a whole class or in small groups, as levels are filtered by the results. These word study assessments combine the administration of running records (discussed in the next section) and an assessment of sight word recognition and automaticity. The pre- and postassessment process included in this model is clearly actionable and monitors the mastery of skills and the coordination of skills within appropriately leveled text. These strategies for assessment and instruction have been successfully evidenced in research (Morris, Tyner, & Perney, 2000).

- Early Reading Screening Instrument (ERSI): The effectiveness and predictive validity of the ERSI has been verified by several research studies, such as those performed by Lombardino, Rivers, DeFilippo, Montgomery, and Sarisky (1992) and Perney, Morris, and Carter (1997). Critical early reading skills are assessed on an individual basis and can be readministered to determine gains for emergent and beginning readers. The ERSI is administered with individual students and assesses such beginning reading skills as concept of word, phonics, and basic sight word recognition.

- Developmental Reading Assessment (DRA): Commercially packaged diagnostic assessments, such as the DRA, identify what researchers consider the key characteristics and behaviors of readers. Researchers such as Clay (1993) have defined these integral components from an emergent literacy perspective rather than the former perspective of reading readiness. DRA results yield accuracy percentages and placement in an appropriate text level through running records. This diagnostic tool has a valuable place for instructional decision making when tempered by observational information and other available data (Beaver & Carter, 2005).

- Qualitative Reading Inventory (QRI): Reading inventories are available that provide both qualitative and quantitative analysis of reading performance using word lists and literary and expository texts. One such example is the QRI, which assesses background knowledge for a particular topic as well as comprehension through both retellings and questioning. Although time intensive because of individual administration, the QRI supplies quantitative scores to establish independent, instructional, and frustration levels. An added component is attention to the impact of varying types of text on comprehension based on the reader's prior knowledge (Leslie & Caldwell, 2006).

Running Records

A component of diagnostic assessment that is included in some of the diagnostics mentioned in the previous section is the running record. Used as a part of a broader assessment tool or alone, the teacher chooses text that is approximated as the student's instructional level, adjusting to more difficult or simple text depending on accuracy. Reading behaviors are noted by cueing systems, such as meaning, structure, and visual information. Self-corrections are noted as well, with standard error rules for consistency. Progress is monitored most frequently at emergent stages and for at-risk students. A running record is real-time observational evidence that supports the teacher in professional development using the most valuable tool for learning: the student.

Assessments During Instruction

Progress Monitoring

Progress is monitored regularly to determine whether the intervention provided is moving the student in the right direction or adjustments should be made to instruction. Targeted skills are monitored and recorded as often as is prudent, depending on the nature of the skill. This consideration is crucial as teachers plan the frequency of monitoring for decision making related to possible adjustments in materials and strategies. Expectations for improvement must be realistic while analyzing the full range of skills that result in a balanced reader profile.

One example of the use of progress monitoring is in the RTI process as data points are aligned and tracked to the intervention applied and to the goals set. The weakness that is diagnosed will become the target for interventional instruction and, in turn, the data point that is recorded and monitored. In much the same way, proactive instructional literacy leaders progress monitor all students in a variety of ways to assure progress toward established literacy targets.

Diagnostic Assessments

Like the specific examples discussed earlier, diagnostic measures during instruction are designed to be repeated throughout the year as a means for progress monitoring. Choose a diagnostic assessment that targets deficit areas or determines current instructional levels for guided reading groups. Diagnostics serve as pre- and postassessments in setting, adjusting, or maintaining individual and group goals.

IRIs

An IRI is also useful in revealing far more than functioning reading levels for students. In many instances, the teacher can gain powerful insights on the metacognitive processes of the student. The ability to think about one's own thinking during reading is a crucial goal. Independent readers develop as metacognitive strategy use is recognized as the key to comprehension. Additionally, an IRI brings to light the student's strengths and weaknesses in genre, background knowledge, and use of text features.

Running Records

Running records also provide evidence of the coordination of emerging and developing reading behaviors using any text type or genre. Types of miscues and confusion of semantic, syntactic, or visual cues give a clear picture of the silent actions of the reader as he or she processes language. Use this miscue analysis to plan lessons focused on skills and strategy and to clarify misconceptions. Johnston (2000) has delved into the importance of the teacher's reflection on a child's approximations:

> Running records of oral reading are basically a vehicle for error analysis—the imaginative challenge of figuring out the logic of error. Like oral reading, errors have had a bad rap. For teachers, the most useful aspect of errors is that people do not make them randomly. There is always a reason for them. If you can figure out the reason, then you know where to best use your instructional expertise and how to avoid confusing the student. (p. 1)

Portfolio Assessment

A portfolio is a collection of purposefully selected artifacts that showcase successes and achievements of the individual student. An important component is the involvement of the student in selecting the work samples or products. A portfolio broadens the scope of assessment by taking into account a range of skills or concepts that the student has achieved according to known criteria.

The portfolio contains both historical assessment data and varied diagnostic data. As one school labels them, portfolios are "success binders" that chronologically document achievement in an essential curriculum and skills. More than just a method of storing data, the portfolio contains performance-based learning opportunities that go well past skill and drill activities. In terms of literacy, writing in response to text evidences metacognition and is a valuable addition to the portfolio. Work samples become the basis for conversations between the teacher and the student to plan instructional goals for improvement.

Student conferencing and reflection on literacy growth involve the learner and encourage long- and short-term goal setting. Act as a consultant in the choice of representations of achievement and defer final selection to the student whenever feasible. The student may choose any of the following to include: journals, learning logs, mind maps, notes, quizzes, interest inventories, or peer reviews. Include your own observational/anecdotal records and review the portfolio regularly with the student.

A basis for developing alternative grading is possible through portfolio assessment because the student can compare and analyze his or her own growth rather than focus on peer competition. Parent conferences are clarified and facilitated by a discussion of portfolio contents instead of percentages from a test. Authentic work samples and inventories are passed along through the grades to streamline transitions. Portfolio assessment is a change in paradigm for many educators, but it effectively supplements more traditional grading methods.

Reading and writing are two connected links in the literacy chain. The observation of writing development points to foundational skills of reading as well. Proficiency in phoneme-level skills, concepts of word, left to right progression, sequencing of events, main idea and supporting details, and appropriate use of encoding are all evidenced by written communication. To provide the most accurate snapshot of literacy development, provide a variety of opportunities for students to write across content areas and in response to literature and expository text. The portfolio and accompanying rubrics become a base on which to balance assessment and next steps for instruction. Writing samples yield evidence of coordinated skills application and drive enhancement of skills or remediation.

Performance-Based/Rubric Assessment

Assessments that are embedded in instruction display the student's ability to integrate information and respond independently. A simple instructional task is an essential formative assessment that is qualified by a specific rubric, discriminating between levels of competence. A rubric is a scoring guide that evaluates performance on a full range of criteria rather than generating a single score. Rubrics can be holistic or analytic in their design and focus on measuring performance, behavior, or quality of work. They can be a simple checklist with steps to a process, used observationally by the teacher or to guide students through a task. Checklists make guidelines and expectations clear.

Rubrics with rating scales also clarify expectations, but they go a step further. Rating scales measure performance outcomes more specifically and include levels of competency. Given the means for qualitative judgment in advance, the student becomes an empowered, involved, and invested learner. Students and parents alike receive tangible information that clarifies goals toward improvement.

Differentiation is facilitated by the use of rubrics because of the accommodation afforded by the range of quality levels. Formative assessment with an experienced observational eye improves the teacher's ability to make wise decisions for instructional time, materials, and next steps. The continuing feedback loop that leads toward proficiency is the most obvious advantage of the use of rubric assessment. Classroom assessments match original instructional goals and drive tenaciously toward those goals.

Observational Records

Many skills in the area of literacy can only be assessed by observation. Levels of social development and oral language are seldom assessed accurately through other means. Many cues to instructional implications can only be imparted through observation of student conversations. Concept awareness, use of sentence structure, and vocabulary functioning are highlighted through informal classroom opportunities. Effective teachers are adept at picking up on students' behavioral signals and adapting instruction accordingly.

To take this ability to the next level, create a record-keeping system that targets particular skills and literacy behaviors. These observational records, commonly called anecdotal notes, can be purposely categorized for incidental examination throughout the day. As a reminder, teachers sometimes designate a time to walk around the room and observe student interaction, and others jot notes as observations are made during instruction. Teachers find it beneficial to post a category of special interest as a reminder to tune in to evidence of a particular reading, writing, or communicative trait. Experience in quickly noting relevant information streamlines this process and prevents any disruption to instruction or the routines of the class. The most effective teachers are avid student watchers and appreciate the value of considering a broad scope of demonstrated language ability in planning for reading and writing growth.

Assessment After Instruction: Outcome Measures

State Standards-Based Tests

The development of state standards has evolved since the 1960s with the recognition by policymakers that U.S. students have not kept pace globally. The federal government flooded billions of dollars into state budgets for school improvement with limited results. In 1994, the Improving America's Schools Act and Title I of the Elementary and Secondary Education Act called for state content standards, as well as state assessment systems to hold districts accountable for the accomplishment of those standards. More recently, the federal government enacted No Child Left Behind legislation in a stronger attempt to mandate a state system for reporting, standards alignment, and accountability (U.S. Department of Education, 2002). This standards reform movement requires standards-based assessment rather than norm-referenced tests. In other words, rather than grounding scores on norms that compare student to student, standards-based tests are based on criteria that reveal what students are expected to know and be able to do.

To be an effective and valid outcome measure, criteria must represent an attainable goal for all students and have the capability to show growth from year to year. Standards for these outcome measures must be carefully aligned with the curriculum, instruction, and assessment to accurately evidence achievement. District and state leaders use the results of these standards-based measures to follow growth trends, identify curricular needs, and specify areas of need for professional development. End-of-year assessments are also used at the school level as contributing data for retention and placement decisions. State and federal policymakers use data from outcome measures to evaluate the breadth of the curriculum, student achievement, allocation of resources, and the assessment itself. The careful alignment of accountability systems with curriculum and instruction is essential for school improvement in the United States.

Curriculum-Based Measures

Referred to as a general outcomes measure, these assessments are used to measure basic skills or content knowledge. These measures are simply constructed and brief, indicating progress on a particular standardized benchmark. Sometimes derived from a component of the core language arts materials, curriculum-based measures have become important to the data collection process of RTI. A student's proficiency toward grade-level expectations is measured and compared with expected performance relative to the time of year. Not to be confused with unit tests that correspond to core materials, the use of these measures serve to monitor progress in achievement of grade-level standards and help plan a trajectory of growth that culminates with the end-of-year state standards assessment.

Performance-Based Measures

This method of assessment emphasizes the application and integration of skills in an authentic literacy task. A student's performance demonstrates knowledge, understanding, and skills, as well as the process by which the answer or product was obtained. Performance-based tasks require coordination of all of the language arts processes, providing a broader picture of the student's ability to connect, reason, infer, and respond to reading. One drawback that has arisen from the use of performance-based tasks in the context of state accountability systems is the expense of scoring and the possible subjectivity of the assessor. In terms of matching assessment with standards, an integrated literacy approach to assessment is preferable in furnishing proof of higher order thinking and problem-solving skills.

An Essential Understanding of the Relationship Between Assessment and Instruction

Table 2 organizes the appropriate purpose and use of the four types of assessments classified under the broad categories of formative and summative assessments: screening, diagnostic assessment, progress monitoring, and outcome measures. The purposes highlight the necessity and far-reaching effects of the use of formative assessment. Teachers identify and shape learning *while* students are learning.

TABLE 2
Formative Versus Summative Assessment

	Formative Assessment			Summative Assessment
What	Screening	Diagnostic assessments	Progress monitoring	Outcome measures
When	Before instruction	Before and during instruction	During instruction	After instruction
Who	All students	Some students	Some students	All students
Why	• To identify potential at-risk readers and determine general ranges of proficiency	• To determine weak skills, gaps, and placement in small groups • To plan and provide strategies at Tier 2 and Tier 3 levels of intervention	• To revisit the plan for differentiated instruction • To adjust interventional strategies	• To identify the curriculum needs and quality of instruction • To evaluate trends and the professional development needs of teachers • To measure progress in meeting established benchmarks

An understanding of the role of assessment demands recognition of the powerful impact of formative data on instruction. The very nature of formative assessment propels daily decision making on the part of the teacher and provides specific feedback to the student that is necessary for improvement. Many teachers readily embrace the idea of formative assessment in relationship to math concepts and skills. Teachers are aware that they must understand the student's problem-solving approach to discern conceptual difficulties. An example in the realm of literacy is a writing response assignment after a shared informational reading. A brief teacher/student conference allows the student to reread and discuss his or her response. The conversation uncovers misconceptions in background knowledge that are vital for understanding the passage. Strategic questioning, as well as attention to text features and text evidence, fills in valuable information that generates new ideas and learning by the reader. The writing response is revised by the student and shared with the class as a noteworthy example of the importance of schemata to comprehension. Active learning, feedback, and constant reshaping of thinking are vital to literacy development as well.

Meta-analysis has shown appreciable gains when formative assessment is implemented across all boundaries of skill types, content, knowledge, and levels of education. As Marzano (2006) noted,

> Recall the finding from Black and Wiliams's (1998) synthesis of more than 250 studies that formative assessments, as opposed to summative ones, produce the more powerful effect on student learning. In his review of the research, Terrance Crooks (1988) reports that effect sizes for summative assessments are consistently lower than effect sizes for formative assessments. In short, it is formative assessment that has a strong research base supporting its impact on learning. (p. 9)

A focus on what is being learned is the hallmark of formative assessment, rather than a score based on performance on a given day at the end of the unit or year. Simply stated, formative assessments guide the teacher and fully involve the student in the process of literacy development. The full potential of a responsive teacher and active learner is realized. The following vignettes describe the assessment processes used by a teacher with a first-grade student, and an intermediate-grade teacher with a fifth-grade student. Note how each teacher uses various data points to guide literacy instruction.

A Primary-Grade Assessment Scenario: Lucas

Lucas enters first grade with a gift from his kindergarten teacher. He was exposed to developmentally appropriate experiences and emergent-leveled books the year before. He enjoys participating in shared reading and writing opportunities and is excited by the prospect of growing in independence. Lucas's first-grade teacher, Ms. Walker, checks his reading portfolio and discovers that he mastered beginning reader stage 2—initial consonant sounds, blends, and digraphs in the word study assessment in *Small-Group Reading Instruction: A Differentiated Teaching Model for Beginning and Struggling Readers* (Tyner, 2009). At the end of his kindergarten year, he read level C readers with 94% accuracy. Ms. Walker is anxious to determine his current level and begin differentiated instruction in small groups.

She begins by administering a simplified running record (see Figure 41a) of level D and E texts, which are reading levels typical of a beginning first-grade reader, and finds the best starting place for the guided reading component of her small-group routine. The Reading Review is stored in Lucas's portfolio to begin a first-grade collection that displays his beginning reading traits. A close look at miscues from the running record shows confusion in graphophonic cues, or visual information. Lucas made an attempt at many words based solely on configuration. With 91% accuracy, Lucas's instructional level is D: the point at which he can grow as a reader with teacher support.

Ms. Walker's next step is the administration of the spelling inventory for stage 3A, an assessment of one-syllable short vowel words inclusive of blends and digraphs typical of the fledgling reading stage. Along with a quick sight word assessment (Figure 41b), word study performance confirms that Lucas should be placed in the fledgling stage for instruction in small group (see Figure 41c). (All three of these assessments can be found in Tyner, 2009.)

Teacher Reflection

Ms. Walker places Lucas in a fledgling group and again notices his habit of guessing based on visual cues as he whisper reads. For example, he pronounces *fall* for *flat* and continues to read with few self-corrections. Picture clues are often ignored and frequent hesitations result in poor fluency and comprehension of story details upon retell. Wondering if stronger picture support would encourage improved monitoring, Ms. Walker considers informational text that focuses on animals for her guided reading because Lucas is fascinated by animals.

For word study, she plans to reinforce phonics through sorting and categorization of patterns in words. Lucas needs to notice chunks within words and look past the beginning sound and the basic visual shape of words. She notices that he is easily engaged by the use of manipulatives. The hands-on word scramble activity from the small-group model is a good choice so Lucas can make and compare words based on targeted features.

Instruction Planning and Decision Making

In Figure 42a, the word scramble activity is shown as a formative assessment with a corresponding rubric to guide the teacher in providing corrective feedback based on student performance of the task. Ms. Walker uses the formative task to observe, monitor, and guide correction of miscues. Dry-erase boards are used for independent spelling of words to solidify

FIGURE 41
A Student's Assessments at the Beginning of First Grade

(a) Reading

Reading Review

Name _Lucas_   Date _9-6-11_

Recorder _Walker_   Classroom Teacher _Walker - 1st grade_

Highest Level at 93–97% Accuracy

Instructional Level _Level D   91% Accuracy_

Fluency Rate _21 wcpm_

Page	Title Total Words 65	Errors Per Page
	Too Much Work Level E	
3		0
4	but/puts/T hunt/hunting/T cat/coat/T	3
5		1
6	body/T pouches/paws/T creep/T fell/flat/T	3
7	strips/stripes/T	1
8	He/His/T body/T	2
9	flew/flies/T	1
10	thing/thinks/T walk/work/T	2
	Total Errors	13

ACCURACY FORMULA

$\frac{\text{Running Words - Errors}}{\text{Running Words}} \times 100 =$ ___80___ % accuracy

Reading Fluency Rate

Number of words read correctly in one minute = fluency rate _15 wcpm_

(b) Sight Words

Sight Word Assessment

#	word		#	word		#	word		#	word	
1	the	✓	31	go	✓	61	here	her	91	by	be
2	a	✓	32	was	✓	62	your	✓	92	how	✓
3	and	✓	33	like	✓	63	an	✓	93	house	—
4	to	✓	34	what	—	64	back	✓	94	dad	did
5	I	✓	35	not	✓	65	mom	✓	95	or	—
6	in	✓	36	do	✓	66	dog	✓	96	two	✓
7	is	✓	37	then	✓	67	very	✓	97	red	read
8	on	✓	38	this	✓	68	did	✓	98	am	—
9	you	✓	39	no	✓	69	her	✓	99	over	—
10	it	✓	40	too	✓	70	from	✓	100	saw	—

#	word		#	word		#	word	
11	of	✓	41	she	✓	71	had	✓
12	said	✓	42	went	✓	72	got	✓
13	can	✓	43	see	✓	73	put	but
14	for	from	44	will	✓	74	came	✓
15	my	✓	45	so	✓	75	just	✓
16	but	✓	46	some	✓	76	cat	✓
17	all	✓	47	down	✓	77	them	✓
18	we	✓	48	little	✓	78	tree	three
19	are	✓	49	come	✓	79	where	—
20	up	✓	50	get	✓	80	away	—

✓ Correct

— no response

#	word		#	word		#	word	
21	at	✓	51	be	✓	81	time	—
22	with	when	52	now	no	82	as	✓
23	me	✓	53	when	✓	83	water	—
24	they	✓	54	there	—	84	home	how
25	have	✓	55	into	✓	85	made	mad
26	he	✓	56	day	✓	86	long	—
27	out	✓	57	look	✓	87	has	✓
28	that	✓	58	eat	✓	88	help	—
29	one	✓	59	make	✓	89	good	goes
30	big	✓	60	his	✓	90	going	✓

Student _Lucas_   Date _9-6-11_   Number correct _75_

(c) Spelling

Lucas

9-12-11

-9

55%

Stage 3A Word Families

1. wet
2. seck   sick
3. duck
4. bick   back
5. sit
6. jig
7. tin
8. ven   van
9. spot
10. drop
11. mop   mob
12. sook   sock
13. sut   shut
14. plug
15. bell
16. map
17. batt   bat
18. sed   shed
19. win   when
20. sun

FIGURE 42
A First Grader's Reassessment

(a) Word Scramble Assessment

Formative Task: Word Scramble, Fledgling Stage 3A

Resource: *Small-Group Instruction Reading Instruction: A Differentiated Model for Beginning and Struggling Readers*
CCSS: *RF.K.2d Isolate and pronounce the initial, medial vowel, and final sounds in three-phoneme words.*
Activity: This task is one of several word study options for the Fledgling reader to help in making connections between patterns and solidifying word knowledge. The activity involves students making words with the short vowel "e" family. The teacher gives directions to guide the process and observes development of sequencing of letter/sound correspondence.
Student Materials: Letter Cards or Tiles for the student: e, d, h, p, r, s, t, l
Teacher Directions:
1. Make the word pet.
2. Change one letter to spell let.
3. Change one letter to spell led.
4. Add one letter to spell sled.
5. Change one letter to spell shed.
6. Drop two letters, and add one letter to spell red.
7. Drop one letter, and add two letters to spell rest.
8. Change one letter to spell pest.

Rubric: Word Scramble, E Family Fledgling Stage 3A

Level 1 Description of Student Performance: Student is unable to make any of the words independently.	
If the student…..	Then the teacher…
Consistently substitutes the final sound for the initial sound or omits a letter in the word……..	• Checks understanding of left to right progression with Elkonin box with an arrow drawn below the box. Demonstrate how to make the words in order of the sounds heard. • Checks concept "beginning and end" with a model of a lunch line. • Models "stretching" sounds slowly and punches out the initial sound to reinforce auditory processing. Student echos.
Level 2 Description of Student Performance: Student makes 50% (4) of the words independently. Student needs prompting on the other 50%	
If the student….	Then the teacher….
Omits the "l" in sled, the "t" in rest or the "t" in pest….	Uses the Elkonin box with 4 positions to demonstrate the 4 discrete sounds in the words. Repeats the word, stretch the word, and has the student echo. Proceeds with review of digraph /sh/ review from Stage 2B. If blends are confused, digraphs should also be readdressed. Repeats the word, stretches the word, counts phonemes, and has the student echo.
Level 3 Description of Student Performance: Student makes 75% (6) of the words independently. Student hesitates and needs limited prompting.	
If the student…..	Then the teacher….
Hesitates or makes an error on the use of the digraph /sh/ or one of the words with blends (sled, rest, pest)…	Reviews the digraph /sh/ with other examples of words with /sh/. Reviews a lesson from Stage 2B with all digraphs and sort to classify. Repeats the word, stretches the word, counts phonemes, and has the student echo.
Level 4 Description of Student Performance: Student makes 100% of the words independently and automatically.	
If the student…..	Then the teacher….
Makes no errors and is quick in responding and pronouncing the new word…	Progresses to the next short vowel family, then mixes another short vowel to the activity to provide opportunity for discrimination of the medial sound.

(c) The Student's Reading Assessment Profile

Student Reading Assessment Profile Sheet

Student: Lucas

Word Study	Mastered/Date	Reading Level	Mastered/Date
K Stage 1 Alphabet Production	☑ 10/12/10 95%	Level A	☐
K Stage 2A Initial Consonant Sounds	☑ 1/6/11 100%	Level B	☐
K Stage 2B Initial Consonant Digraphs/Blends	☑ 2/17/11 65% 4/15/11 90%	Level C	☐
1st Stage 3A Word Families	☑ 9/12/11 50% 11/21/11 95%	Level D	☑ 9/2/11
Stage 3B Short Vowels	☐	Level E	☑ 9/30/11
		Level F	☑ 10/21/11
		Level G	☑ 11/17/11
		Level H	☐
Stage 4 Vowel Patterns 1	☐	Level I	☐
		Level J	☐
		Level K	☐
Stage 5A Vowel Patterns 2	☐	Level L	☐
		Level M	☐
		Level N	☐
Stage 5B Common Word Features	☐	Level O	☐
		Level P	☐
		Level Q+	☐

(b) A First Grader's Stage 3A Spelling Inventory

Lucas   11-21-11

1st 55%   ☺
2nd 80%
3rd

Stage 3A Word Families   -4 80%

1. wet
2. sick
3. duck
4. back
5. sit
6. jig
7. tin
8. ven   Van   *Missed on both Assessments*
9. spot
10. drop
11. nop   mob   *Missed on both Assessments — got b and p confused*
12. sock
13. sut   shut   *Missed on both Assessments*
14. plug
15. bell
16. map
17. got
18. shed
19. wen   when   *Missed on both Assessments*
20. sun

independent skill. Because Lucas is overly dependent on visual cues, she limits isolated sight word practice to a few minutes each day and encourages recognition in context. As he builds incrementally to level G text, Ms. Walker prompts his use of picture clues and uses a variety of passage reading options to build phrasing and fluency at text level. Frequent modeling of expected reading behaviors and guided support improve Lucas's ability to monitor his own reading and comprehension. He rereads and retells each story with a partner and responds to the text in writing after the teacher-directed small-group lesson.

After completing the word study scope and sequence for fledgling stage in word families, Ms. Walker reassesses Lucas's group with the stage 3A spelling inventory (see Figure 42b). He scores 80% and is ready to begin the transitional stage. Steady progress continues through kindergarten and first grade, as shown by the reading assessment profile (see Figure 42c). Lucas is well on his way to grade-level expectations by the end of his first-grade year.

An Intermediate-Grade Assessment Scenario: Clay

In conversation with his teacher, Mrs. Jones, Clay discusses a typical range of literacy habits and interests for a fifth-grade boy. He describes himself as an "OK" reader but does not enjoy writing because he has been predominantly required to do what most teachers call on-demand prompt writing. To delve deeper into Clay's literacy skills, Mrs. Jones administers diagnostic assessments and builds his reading portfolio. She gathers a wide variety of information to determine his instructional level and observe his use of cueing systems. An additional purpose is her analysis of his efficiency with metacognitive strategies and strengths that are dependent on genre.

In reviewing the previous year's state assessment results, Mrs. Jones notices that Clay's score in reading dropped from third to fourth grade. Particular difficulty is identified in standards related to inferencing and summarizing. From fourth-grade data, she finds that Clay tested in the maturing stage according to word study assessments found in *Small-Group Reading Instruction: Differentiated Teaching Models for Intermediate Readers, Grades 3–8* (Tyner & Green, 2012; see Figure 43a). For a more current idea of Clay's decoding ability, she administers Words Their Way, a similar word study inventory, and analyzes errors that correspond to word study stages (see Figure 43b). The triangulation of available data eliminates the need for a miscue analysis because he shows evidence of a firm foundation in phonetic patterns. Mrs. Jones moves along to explore other elements of reading.

She uses fluency materials from her core program to check Clay's accuracy, rate, and prosody. He reads 131 words correct per minute, close to the 75th percentile in the fall of fifth grade according to Hasbrouck and Tindal's (2006) study of oral reading fluency norms.

The QRI is next in diagnostic assessment for decision making. The graded word lists serve as a screening and placement tool that facilitates the diagnostic process. Clay reads the fifth-grade word list with sufficient accuracy to indicate that fifth-grade text would be an appropriate instructional level for him. The QRI provides brief concept questioning before each passage is read to determine the familiarity of the topic or concept. Clay's first passage is "Laser Light," a topic that the concept questions reveal is unfamiliar to him. He can relate an experience when he played laser tag and knows that lasers are "something about light," which uncovers a weak conceptual base from which to draw. Comprehension on retell is insufficient with explicit and implicit questions. The QRI includes an opportunity for the student to employ a look-back strategy and attempt to improve comprehension. Even with look-backs, Clay scores at a frustration level. As Mrs. Jones repeats the process with an unfamiliar literary passage, she notes

FIGURE 43
A Student's Word Study Assessments

(a) A Fourth Grader's Word Study Assessment

Clay   9-7-11

1. Bed
2. Skip
3. When
4. lump
5. float
6. tran
7. place
8. drive
9. bright
10. Shopping
11. Spoil
12. sereving
13. Chewed
14. Carrey's
15. marched
16. Shower
17. battel
18. flavor
19. ripen
20. coller
21. pleger
22. fourchewnot
23. Confindent
24. silviesed
25. opisition

(b) The Student's Words Their Way Assessment in Fifth Grade

Words Their Way Elementary Spelling Inventory Feature Guide

Student **Clay**   Teacher **Mrs. Jones**   Grade **5**   Date **9-7-11**

Words Spelled Correctly: **15** /25   Feature Points: **48** /62   Total **63** /87   Spelling Stage **Middle Syllables + Affixes**

Stages and gradations →	Emergent Late	Early	Letter Name Middle	Late	Within Word Pattern Early	Middle	Late	Syllables and Affixes Early	Middle	Late	Derivational Relations Early	Middle	Feature Points	Words Spelled Correctly
Features → ↓Words	Consonants Begin.	Final	Short Vowels	Digraphs	Blends	Long Vowels	Other Vowels	Inflected Endings	Syllable Junctures	Unaccented Final Syllables	Harder Suffixes	Bases or Roots		
1. bed	b ✔	d ✔	e ✔										3	1
2. ship		p ✔	i ✔	sh ✔									3	1
3. when			e ✔	wh ✔									2	1
4. lump	l ✔		u ✔		mp ✔								3	1
5. float		t ✔			fl ✔	oa ✔							3	1
6. train		n ✔			tr ✔	ai ✔							3	1
7. place					pl ✔	a-e ✔							2	1
8. drive	v ✔				dr ✔	i-e ✔							3	1
9. bright					br ✔	igh							1	0
10. shopping			o ✔	sh ✔				pping ✔					3	1
11. spoil					sp ✔		oi ✔						2	1
12. serving							er ✔	ving ✔					2	0
13. chewed				ch ✔			ew ✔	ed ✔					3	1
14. carries							ar ✔	ies	rr ✔				2	0
15. marched				ch ✔			ar ✔	ed ✔					3	1
16. shower				sh ✔			ow ✔			er ✔			3	1
17. bottle									tt ✔	le			1	0
18. favor									v ✔	or ✔			2	1
19. ripen									p ✔	en ✔			2	1
20. cellar									ll ✔	ar			1	0
21. pleasure											ure	pleas	0	0
22. fortunate							or				ate	fortun	0	0
23. confident											ent	confid	0	0
24. civilize											ize	civil	0	0
25. opposition											tion ✔	pos	1	0
Totals	7 /7	5 /6	6 /6	7 /7	4 /5	6 /7	4 /5	5 /5	3 /5	1 /5	0 /5		48 /62	15 /25

118

little difference. A third passage is entitled "The Octopus," a familiar topic. Clay scores 100% on implicit and explicit comprehension questions after look-backs.

Teacher Reflection

Mrs. Jones identifies a trend in Clay's summative assessment from the previous year that she does not want to continue as she examines state assessment data as an initial screener for her class. Unless Clay has prior knowledge of a topic, he is unable to monitor his comprehension effectively. He tells her, "It just takes too long to reread, and when the story is boring, I go fast to get done." Anything with which he lacks knowledge and strategies to chunk text, stop and summarize, and engage fully in the reading is "boring" to him. By fifth grade, half of the texts that students are typically presented on the year-end assessment are nonfiction. This explains the dip in Clay's fourth-grade scores, since nonfiction text is predominant and is likely to be more unfamiliar to him than literature. Mrs. Jones immediately sees that she should ramp up her think-aloud strategies during whole-group instruction and avoid giving away all the background knowledge before the students begin reading. As teachers analyze assessment data, the reflective process triggers a next step in instruction for all students. This incidental but important self-evaluation by the teacher serves to refine practice and evoke the most appropriate responses to student learning.

Instructional Planning and Decision Making

After identifying groups with similar needs, Mrs. Jones pulls a group to focus on their text monitoring three times weekly. She first uses a familiar science article to introduce the students to a comprehension instructional sequence. The familiar text supports the students in learning and practicing the routine. She previews the most important vocabulary necessary for understanding and then models text monitoring strategies as a shared reading experience to engage, provide purpose, and check metacognition. A graphic organizer is used, with support by the teacher and in student pairs, to sum up the generalizations and questions posed after reading. An independent writing response extends concepts and encourages the students to notice intertextuality and connections to their own lives.

After several weeks of small-group work using the monitoring strategies mentioned, Mrs. Jones reassesses Clay using the QRI and sees improvement. Curriculum-based measures also show improvement, and regular conferences with him reveal his ongoing application of the strategies in independent reading. All assessment materials are collected in Clay's reading portfolio, along with artifacts that document his journey toward comprehension skills and strategies that are consistently effective no matter what text he encounters.

Classroom Connections and Cautions

Assessment and Grading

Historically, the primary purpose of grading fulfills the expectation that parents remain informed of their children's progress. Grades are recorded and reported, comparing a student's progress with that of his or her peers. Grades additionally play an integral part in decision making for retention and remediation.

However, teachers typically tend to grade far too much; grading is assessment. Educators can control the issue of excessive assessment in the classroom in a tangible way. One of the complaints most frequently expressed by teachers is that there are too many assessments and too little time. Yet, excessive time spent in collecting papers to grade and scoring them serves little purpose. Teachers' efforts are best directed toward using all that is known about students to guide instruction in a rigorous and focused way. Unfortunately, many schools lose one-fifth of available instructional time by designating Fridays as test days. Most of these graded assignments confirm the same information time and time again. Although teachers are required to report to parents based on grade-level standards, the teachers frequently know the results of these curriculum-based measures beforehand. Curriculum-based assessment in reading discerns students who are moving toward the grade-level target, but it cannot be allowed to monopolize classroom time.

Time—the one commodity that is hardest to preserve—can be saved by a common-sense approach to grading and reporting to parents. Grade-level discussions and consensus among teachers and administrators determine the number and types of grades that provide a realistic picture of progress. Most current grading practices are vestiges of education as it presented itself in the past. With planning and professional collaboration, evaluation and reporting to parents becomes a combination of observational data, rubric use, and skill grades that can be properly quantified. A balance between discrete skills and elements of reading, evidence of comprehension strategy use, and holistic evaluation of overall reading proficiency is optimal. Meaningful grades are based on the skills that were actually taught and represent growth that is attainable. Further, as the CCSS are implemented and curricular expectations rise to meet those standards, grading procedures are necessarily adjusted through extended professional conversations. Parents, as partners in education, are an integral part of this discussion.

Another purpose for grading is the determination of classroom placement and retention for the coming year. Unit assessments based on core curricular materials are collected to confirm specific problem areas. These measures reveal trends and progress based on grade-level performance but seldom pinpoint specific prerequisite or deficit literacy skills. The measures are insufficient when used alone for high-stakes decision making that affects time for remediation or possible retention. Behavioral and developmental scales, in addition to the teacher's observational records, provide qualitative data that identify students who will benefit from more time to grow. When a single end-of-year assessment decides the fate of a student, the score is unlikely to represent true skill use on a daily basis in a natural and relaxed setting. Teachers and parents feel pressure and test anxiety, as do students, and the stakes are far too high to result in a truly reliable assessment environment. Nevertheless, statewide tests are valuable for limited purposes and remain inevitable. For the view of balanced literacy achievement for each student to be clear and unobstructed, results are triangulated with other pertinent data. As teachers and administrators make important decisions for interventions, placement, and possible retention, they recognize that manipulation of an entire year in the life of a child cannot be taken lightly. The decision to retain a student accompanies the strongest data that indicate that the benefits far outweigh any potential negative impact in the future.

Implications for the Assessment of Writing

Writing naturally lends itself to the use of portfolios and rubrics to qualify expectations and judge products objectively. Considering the developmental nature of writing, maintain observational checklists to guide individual writing conferences with students. Modeled minilessons and shared writing experiences evolve from generalizations made during teacher/student writing conferences. Skills are extended through discussion and the use of mentor texts to compare and contrast processes and craft. A vital factor in writing assessment is the teacher's ability to prompt the student in narrowing the focus for the determination of points for revision. Writing products may be assessed holistically or by specific targeted traits, using rubrics. Writing rubrics describe preponderant traits encompassing levels of development or skill attainment. These samples become a part of the writing portfolio to demonstrate growth and showcase the accomplishments of the writer. No matter the method of assessment, the student's self-reflection is irreplaceable as he or she grows as a writer.

An example of a writing rubric that specifies one element of the craft of writing is shown in Figure 44a. This rubric clarifies the teacher's expectations for first graders in responding to a story, comparing character traits within two texts, and forming an opinion based on text evidence. The student sample in Figure 44b shows a first grader's grasp of writing in response to text in a focused and well-organized manner in the beginning stages of literacy.

Using Balanced Assessment
for Differentiated Instruction

A mark of dynamic literacy instruction is equilibrium among all aspects of the curriculum, instruction, and assessment. The component of developmentally appropriate literacy learning demanding the most carefully crafted balance is differentiated instruction. Student achievement is affected by decisions for appropriate instructional-leveled text, teacher planning, use of time, and choices for assessment. The balanced alignment of instruction and assessment and the resulting treatment of formative and summative assessments are additional used but confused issues.

Classroom time is too valuable to spend on anything less than productive activities. Classroom-embedded formative assessment and diagnostics target the most vital skills for students at their level of development. Not only is the area of weakness determined but also the degree to which the weakness is impacting literacy functioning as a whole. Identify grade-level indicators to use as data points while tracking a student's growth as compared with grade-level peers. The frequency of grade-level comparisons is a point of contention in many districts when repeated assessments that glean no additional information bind classroom teaching time. A marked distinction to the use of grade-level indicators is progress monitoring of individual skills that measure acceleration by struggling students. These indicators reveal the most salient points to track as at-risk students continue in the tiers of instruction. Along with growth trends and

FIGURE 44
Using Writing Rubrics in First Grade

(a) Sample Writing Rubric for First Grade

Forming Opinions and Supporting With Text Evidence		
Level	**Description**	**Looks Like**
1	Unobservable	• Limited relevant ideas, no opinion, no reason, or no text evidence • No closure or organization to response
2	Emerging	• One relevant detail or reason but no text evidence • Minimal repetition and development of idea
3	Developing	• Opinion that is evidenced by text with more than one detail for support • Some extraneous details and/or limited organization
4	Proficient	• Clear opinion stated with example from text for support • Sequential organization and sense of closure to response

(b) A First Grader's Written Response

Frog and Toad

Frog and toad are alike in many ways. They are both kind. They like to help others. Having fun is also how they are the same. I think all friends should be like frog and Toad.

valuable observational and anecdotal records, consider the time consistently devoted to differentiation, instructional format, size of the small groups, and intervention materials. Formative assessment and instruction support and inform each other and can flow seamlessly throughout the school day.

The classroom teacher plays the most important role in making relevant choices for assessment and the instructional strategies that follow. The ongoing cycle of assessment, analysis, planning, and teaching maintains the structure in the teacher's instruction. One diagnostic assessment may progress monitor long-term goals, such as increasing comprehension of well-chosen leveled text. Another diagnostic or subtest effectively monitors short-term goals, such as improving phrasing and intonation, strengthening the automatic production of consonant-vowel-consonant words, or segmenting words by onset and rime. The most significant information is derived from formative assessments and decisions that guide teachers on a day-to-day basis (Chappuis, 2005).

In some schools, group placement decisions are based on one testing experience, with an assessor that may not be the student's teacher. This arrangement negates the teacher's indispensable knowledge of the student's day-to-day performance. The observational data collected by the teacher is a vital supplement to other results. For example, the use of the DRA without important teacher observations might profile a beginning reader as a level 4 instead of a level 8 because of incorrect responses to a few comprehension questions. The very nature of simple emergent text, with its supportive patterning, decreases the ability to use comprehension as a highly weighted factor in grouping for differentiation. Developmental milestones are notable considerations for group placement. In the assessments within *Small-Group Reading Instruction: A Differentiated Teaching Model for Beginning and Struggling Readers* (Tyner, 2009), attention is given to balancing placement for readers, whether they are below, on, or above grade-level expectations. Decisions for differentiation are made according to varied elements, such as sight word automaticity, appropriate fluency and phrasing, proficiency in monitoring strategies within leveled text, and production of word study elements. All of these elements orchestrate in the mind of the reader and lead to transfer within text.

Teaching and assessment that match the instructional goal is another concern that affects differentiation. A case in point is the following comment made by a frustrated kindergarten teacher: "My student knows these sight words on flash cards, yet he just can't recognize them in text. There has to be something wrong with his memory. I think we should initiate the RTI process." A reflective conversation follows with these questions:

- Was small-group time focused on isolated sight word practice?

- Was small-group time spent reading connected text that included the sight words?

- Were other important skills, such as tracking, concept of word, phonemic awareness, and phonics, considered for a true picture *before* decisions for intervention?

This teacher must understand the connection between the instructional strategy used (flash cards with sight words in isolation) and the desired outcome (reading sight words fluently in connected text). Although flashing sight words in isolation might be a stepping-stone to the learning goal, it is only when the student takes this skill to the real reading process that it meaningfully addresses the goal. The teacher, therefore, must consider whether the instruction is leading to the desired outcome. The effective teacher balances what is taught with what will be assessed and considers the end result of the assessment of isolated skills: independent application within connected text. Too much concentration on an assessment method that emphasizes only one reading component skews the teacher's perception of the student's potential and the teacher's conclusions for instructional action.

Another unproductive practice is the sole use of summative assessments for rigid placement purposes and retention decisions. An overall picture of student progress is best derived from the triangulation of several data points. This data may reveal weakness in tested skills but lack the specificity in assessing the degree to which vocabulary, content integration, and literacy processes factor into the results. The results of summative assessment may overlap into screening for the following school year but are not to be used alone, lacking additional data that reveal areas of instructional need. More important, there lies an important distinction, for example, between the ability to apply comprehension standards and the ability to read the text with the fluency and efficiency that allow for the evidence of that standard. If the issue of reading efficiency versus comprehension standard attainment is left unaddressed, each test becomes an evaluation of ineffective decoding and disfluency. The student repeatedly fails until he or she becomes disengaged and disillusioned with the prospect of improvement. However, if intensive and systematic interventions that address developmental needs accompany grade-level instruction, reading proficiency and text understanding can eventually meet the rigor of grade-level demands. Meanwhile, progress monitoring and formative tasks evaluate the success of instructional choices and adjustments.

The Effects and Future of High-Stakes Assessment

Policymakers and other officials place multiple demands on large-scale testing systems in hopes of serving a variety of purposes at once. High-stakes assessments in literacy are currently being administered and used for a variety of purposes, including providing information to determine nationwide trends and school/district needs, monitoring district/school/teacher performance, or a combination of the two.

Unfortunately, tests are seldom used solely for the purpose for which they are designed. Educational stakeholders, including parents, must be educated and informed. A test that identifies strengths and weaknesses in literacy skills cannot and should not be used to make decisions for student retention or teacher bonuses. If students receive an equitable and appropriate instructional program, it must be planned and implemented without the bias and stress of competition and artificial test preparation. We must be clear about the purpose for assessment and monitor the actual results as they relate to those purposes at state, district, and school levels. An accomplished teacher finds informal assessments that are embedded in authentic reading and writing tasks the most useful for making meaningful instructional decisions. These informed decisions best support students in their literacy growth.

Perhaps the biggest concern with universal high-stakes testing stems from the time devoted to preparing and practicing for the test rather than teaching. Trends in recent years show that teachers and other staff reallocate time and resources toward tested content. School funding and the very survival of a school may all but depend on how students perform on a given assessment over a limited number of days. A common knee-jerk reaction has been to single out particular students and particular grade levels to pump with additional resources, sometimes at the expense of balanced instruction for other students. At the classroom level, this type of response encourages a single-minded concentration on the subject area that is tested in that grade level, instead of balancing literacy strategies and integrating content areas.

It is obvious that the time and attention focused on test taking has decreased the rigor of what is taught and learned in the classroom. Simply put, it consumes time that teachers need to spend teaching. For example, time focused on short reading passages, generally seen in high-stakes assessments with primarily literal, closed-ended comprehension questions, limits the time spent on novels or writing extended responses to reading. Most questions in test preparation materials are in a multiple-choice format, which encourages the stressed teacher to use this format in the classroom for practice to save time. With its inherent lack of feedback and relevance to students, isolated test prep materials waste time, as well as money. This time and money could be better spent on a variety of authentic text materials.

Score inflation is another unintended but negative result of accountability-focused assessment. Teachers adapt their instruction and teaching time for test preparation. Because of this disproportional concentration on artificial passages and isolated comprehension skills, scores on high-stakes tests show greater gains than are evidenced by informal assessments of general reading growth and other teacher-selected measures.

The future of assessment and its appropriate alignment with curriculum and instruction will determine the future of school improvement in the United States. Assessment *for* learning is central to accomplished educational practice and should be a primary professional development goal at each school site. Teachers must have the skills to observe student behavior, analyze and interpret those observations, and provide specific feedback needed for improvement. In refining their professional skills, teachers model for their students the ability to become reflective and self-monitoring learners. For policymakers, assessment *of* learning will continue to be a topic of professional discussions in the quest to improve literacy and build college and career readiness within the next generation.

CHAPTER 7

Assembling the Literacy Pieces in the Primary-Grade Classroom

The primary-grade classroom is one of great diversity and curiosity. These young learners represent a wide variety of diverse backgrounds, and most primary-grade students have a keen curiosity about the world and are therefore eager to learn. Orchestrating a classroom inclusive of the critical pieces of literacy instruction is key to the success of the students both now and to their future education endeavors. In the first-grade scenario presented in this chapter, the teacher carefully analyzes the individual needs of her students and plans a thematic unit of study that meets the first-grade standards as well as the needs of her students. The theme is addressed in whole group through interactive read-alouds and shared reading. Additionally, modeled and shared writing create the venues for written responses to the text read in whole group. The theme extends to small-group instruction as students read appropriately leveled text.

This chapter first overviews the students in Ms. Smith's first-grade class and her daily classroom schedule. Next, there is an in-depth discussion of the development of a comprehensive theme and the pieces that must be included. Following, a first-grade theme-based unit identifying standards, student activities, assessments, and appropriate materials are presented. Finally, a reproducible weekly planner is presented along with an in-depth look at a typical day as it unfolds in this classroom.

Ms. Smith's First-Grade Class

With 21 students in her class, Ms. Smith accommodates a wide range of literacy needs. The following are identified exceptionalities among her students: two students receive speech and language services, two are English language learners, and one is supported through ESE (exceptional student education) because of his diagnosis of Asperger's syndrome. Four students receive additional intervention support from a Title I teacher who pushes into the classroom during the reading block to prevent interruption to daily instructional routines.

Because cohesive and planned thematic study results in the most lasting conceptual growth, Ms. Smith collaborates with special-area teachers to coordinate instruction around the current theme. As a result, the art teacher and music teacher observe that students are more receptive and successful in their creative activities when common knowledge and motivation have been previously established. The media specialist is able to plan the most appropriate texts to highlight in her read-alouds and shelf displays.

This team approach is beneficial to students' learning and streamlines the planning process for all teachers involved. Special-area instruction is provided on a rotation basis and is shown in Ms. Smith's schedule.

Daily Schedule

7:45–8:00	Unpacking, attendance, and morning greeting
8:00–8:45	Whole-group integrated language arts
8:45–10:15	Small-group differentiated reading
10:15–11:15	Math
11:15–11:45	Lunch
11:45–12:30	Specials (computer lab, PE, music, art, or media center)
12:30–1:00	Content area focus
1:00–1:45	Whole-group integrated language arts (continued)
1:45–2:15	Reading/writing conferences
2:15–2:30	Shared reading: poetry
2:30–3:00	Recapping the day, packing up, and review of homework assignments

The following section details the planning of a theme-based unit. Planning for theme-based instruction requires careful thought and preparation: Standards must be identified, resources selected, and appropriate assessments determined.

Developing a Theme-Based Unit

A reproducible for planning a theme-based unit is provided in the Appendix. The planner begins with an overview of the unit of study, which includes a description of the theme and connections to grade-level standards both in language arts and any content areas that might be related. Relevance and interest level of the specific age group should also be included.

Pose one or more essential questions that focus and correlate the study. The essential question(s) gives substance and reason for the particular unit of study. By the end of the unit, students should be able to answer or at least address the question(s) in a meaningful way. An essential question(s) presents the big ideas of the unit of study that are framed as questions and examined throughout the study. That is, how is the study relevant to the whole of learning? This question could certainly have more than one answer and requires higher order thinking skills to come up with an appropriate answer.

Next, determine the grade-level standards in language arts that will be the focus of learning in the unit. Although many standards might apply, the selections are those that most closely align to the topic and specific tasks that students will engage in throughout the unit. Additionally, identify content area standards that are appropriate to the theme.

Specify student learning objectives or goals in the next part of the plan. These goals document what students will learn as a result of the study. Not to be confused with the actual standards, these are the stepping-stones in both content and skills that are necessary for students to reach the standards. Unpacking the standards in a meaningful way for students is instrumental to reach the final standard goal. These learning goals are critical while planning for instruction as well as assessment.

Carefully select text pieces for text complexity and relevance to the unit. A wide range of genres are necessary to build foundations for both discussion and text-based written responses. Group texts according to the progression of the study as well as specified topics within the theme structure. Many appropriate text pieces could be used, but teachers often select too many, which makes it impossible to study any one text very closely. It is hard to anticipate the time frame needed for a particular text, so prioritizing the text order is appropriate. In this way, backup texts are ready for when the students progress more quickly than expected.

Include sample activities and assessments in the plan as appropriate examples for both the students' age group and the unit. Write these examples for specific text pieces as well as standards. Although a suggested list is given in the next section, it should be amended to meet the needs of the students. This is by no means an exhaustive list; it simply demonstrates how specific content can be used to help students learn skills that are necessary to meet the focus standards. Along with this, identify sample formative and summative assessments for the unit. This is an important step in planning a theme-based unit because they are designed to generate evidence of student understanding and give guidance in adapting the plan to best meet the identified needs of students.

Sample lesson plans for interactive read-alouds, shared reading, and modeled and shared writing were presented earlier in this book. Additionally, differentiated lesson plan models for small-group reading instruction have also been shared, along with appropriate independent activities.

The following pages provide a detailed theme-based plan for a first-grade unit of study of animal habitats. As you review the plan, pay special attention to how Ms. Smith integrates instructional activities to make the most of the learning time.

First-Grade Unit of Study: "Animal Habitats"

Figure 45 shows Ms. Smith's planned unit. The discussion in this section expands on her plan.

Overview

Ms. Smith's thematic unit is planned for the second semester and spans four weeks. Her students will explore animal habitats in divergent environments through integrated literacy activities. Based on a variety of text genres, the students will discover the many ways that animals adapt to their environments for survival. The first week begins with a familiar focus on woodland animals to build background and academic vocabulary for the unit concepts. Ocean habitats and other unique animal characteristics that ensure adaptation expand the study in the second week of the unit. Through the use of complex informational texts and related literary genres, the students continue to compare and contrast animal behaviors, traits, and needs as the third week shifts to the study of Arctic animals. The fourth, culminating week of this thematic unit focuses on animals of the African jungle. The topic of adaptation and habitat is broadened to include specific interaction among animals, humans, and the environment. The concept of interdependence is introduced as students categorize and classify the information gleaned from research, read-alouds, shared reading, and writing response activities. Foundational reading skills are infused throughout the study as Ms. Smith scaffolds during shared reading and provides differentiated guided practice in small groups with related instructional-leveled text.

Language Arts Focus Standards

These focus standards are taken from the Common Core Standards for English Language Arts for first grade (NGA Center & CCSSO, 2010b).

RL.1.9: Compare and contrast the adventures and experiences of characters in stories. (p. 11)

RIT.1.7: Use the illustrations and details in a text to describe its key ideas. (p. 13)

RIT.1.9: Identify basic similarities in and differences between two texts on the same topic (e.g., in illustrations, descriptions, or procedures). (p. 13)

RFS.1.3: Know and apply grade-level phonics and word analysis skills in decoding words. (p. 16)

RFS.1.4: Read with sufficient accuracy and fluency to support comprehension. (p. 16)

W.1.2: Write informative/explanatory texts in which they name a topic, supply some facts about the topic, and provide some sense of closure. (p. 19)

W.1.7: Participate in shared research and writing projects. (p. 19)

SL.1.1: Participate in collaborative conversations with diverse partners about *grade 1 topics and texts* with peers and adults in small and larger groups. (p. 23)

L.1.4: Determine or clarify the meaning of unknown and multiple-meaning words and phrases based on *grade 1 reading and content*, choosing flexibly from an array of strategies. (p. 27)

Science Focus Standards

Taken from Florida's Next Generation Sunshine State Standards (Florida Department of Education, 2010), these benchmarks are comparable to those specific to other states. Overarching goals for first grade include life science, the practice of science, and interdependence.

SC.1.N.1.1: Raise questions about the natural world, investigate them in teams through free exploration, and generate appropriate explanations based on those explorations. *Cognitive Complexity:* High

FIGURE 45
Sample First-Grade Theme-Based Unit Plan

Theme:	Animal Habitats	**Overview:** Four-week study of animals and habitats: (1) woodland animals, (2) ocean animals, (3) Arctic animals, (4) jungle animals. Unit includes science and language arts standards.
Essential Question(s)		• How do animals adapt to and interact with their environments? • What unique traits and characteristics allow for adaptation and survival in each habitat? • How do animals compare and relate to one another?
Focus Standards	Language Arts:	RL.1.9, RT.1.7, RT.1.9, RFS.1.3, RFS.1.4, W.1.2, W.1.7, SL.1.1, L.1.4
	Content Areas:	Science: SC.1.N.1.1, SC.1.N.1.2, SC.1.N.1.3, SC.1.L.17.1
Student Objectives/ Learning Goals	Week 1:	• Recognize ways that woodland animals adapt to their environment. • Use vocabulary orally and in writing to describe the habitat of woodland animals. • Compare and contrast literary animals and real animals (frog and toad).
	Week 2:	• Identify text features and their importance. • Recognize ways that ocean animals adapt to their environment. • Complete a written report that includes an opening, three facts, and a closing.
	Week 3:	• Retell stories including important details. • Compare and contrast two arctic animals (ways they adapt). • Compare and contrast information in two texts about polar animals. How is the information presented?
	Week 4:	• Recognize rhyme, rhythm, and alliteration in poetry. • Collect information through group research. • Describe ways that arctic animals adapt to their environment.
Student Activities	Week 1:	• Begin learning log for the four-week study. Add vocabulary/important information each week: woodland animals. • Begin connection chains. • Venn diagram: Frogs and toads (literary and real)
	Week 2:	• Ocean animal reports: online research • Add to learning log (ocean animals).
	Week 3:	• Digital newspaper project • Make animal puppets; use for retelling stories. • Venn diagram to compare/contrast two arctic animals (ways they adapt)
	Week 4:	• Write an informational summary: "How Jungle Animals Adapt." • Group project: Create habitat and label parts. Write a group report that tells how the animals adapt in the environment created. • Complete journals. • Present project to the class.
Formative and Summative Assessments		• Rubric assessment for writing tasks and projects • Running records using related instructional-leveled text • Student self-evaluation of team performance and individual contribution (based on qualitative features on a rubric provided in advance) • Teacher observations

130

Week and Theme	Literary Text		Informational Text		Websites	Media
	Interactive Read-Alouds	Shared Reading	Interactive Read-Alouds	Shared Reading		
1: Woodland animals	• Hello, Red Fox by Eric Carle • Knuffle Bunny: A Cautionary Tale by Mo Willems • The Mitten by Jan Brett • Owl Moon by Jane Yolen • Roger and the Fox by Lavinia R. Davis • The Story of Jumping Mouse by John Steptoe	• All the World by Liz Garton Scanlon • Bear Party by William Pène du Bois • Frog and Toad Are Friends by Arnold Lobel • "Mary Had a Little Frog" by Bruce Lansky • Possum Come a-Knockin' by Nancy Van Laan	• Crinkleroot's Guide to Knowing Animal Habitats by Jim Arnosky • Squirrels by Emily Rose Townsend • Temperate Forest Mammals by Elaine Landau	• Biggest, Strongest, Fastest by Steve Jenkins • What Do You Do When Something Wants to Eat You? by Steve Jenkins • What Do You Do With a Tail Like This? by Steve Jenkins • Who Lives Here? Forest Animals by Deborah Hodge	• National Geographic: Habitats (environment.nationalgeographic.com/environment/habitats) • Reading A–Z (www.readinga-z.com) • ReadWriteThink (www.readwritethink.org)	• Smithsonian: Animal Photo Galleries (nationalzoo.si.edu/Animals/PhotoGallery/default.cfm)
2: Ocean animals	• Big Al by Andrew Clements • Fish Is Fish by Leo Lionni • A House for Hermit Crab by Eric Carle • If All the Seas Were One Sea by Janina Domanska • Swimmy by Leo Lionni	• One Fish, Two Fish, Red Fish, Blue Fish by Dr. Seuss • The Rainbow Fish by Marcus Pfister	• Beluga Whales by Ann O. Squire • Sea Creatures by Chris Madsen • Sea Horses by Elaine Landau • A Whale of a Tale! All About Porpoises, Dolphins, and Whales by Bonnie Worth • Winter's Tail: How One Little Dolphin Learned to Swim Again by Juliana Hatkoff, Isabella Hatkoff, and Craig Hatkoff	• Humpback Whale by Lloyd G. Douglas • Hungry, Hungry Sharks by Joanna Cole • "Shark" (sciencepoems.net/sciencepoems/shark.aspx) • Sharks! by Anne Schreiber • Whales by Laura Marsh	• Aaron Shepard's RT Page (Readers Theatre Scripts: www.aaronshep.com/rt/index.html) • eNature.com (www.enature.com/home) • KidsBiology.com (www.kidsbiology.com/animals-for-children.php) • National Geographic Kids (kids.nationalgeographic.com/kids)	• Storyline Online: "The Rainbow Fish" by Marcus Pfister (www.storylineonline.net) • "Winter's Tail" (virtual field trip to Clearwater Marine Aquarium, Florida; www.scholastic.com/winterstail)
3: Arctic animals	• And Tango Makes Three by Justin Richardson and Peter Parnell • The Polar Bear Son: An Inuit Tale by Lydia Dabcovich • Tooth Trouble by Jane Clarke	• "Little Polar Bear" by Kevin Mooney • Polar Bear, Polar Bear, What Do You Hear? by Bill Martin Jr.	• The Arctic Habitat by Molly Aloian and Bobbie Kalman • Arctic Hares by Therese Shea • The Big Caribou Herd: Life in the Arctic National Wildlife Refuge by Bruce Hiscock • Who Grows Up in the Snow? A Book About Polar Animals and Their Offspring by Theresa Longenecker	• Amazing Arctic Animals by Jackie Glassman • In Arctic Waters by Laura Crawford • Living in the Arctic by Allan Fowler • Penguins! by Anne Schreiber • Polar Animals by Wade Cooper	• Giggle Poetry: Animal Poems (www.gigglepoetry.com/poemcategory.aspx?poemcategoryID=11&CategoryName=Animal Poems) • Mr. R's World of Math and Science: Science Poems: Animals (sciencepoems.net/index.html#animals)	• Storyline Online: "The Polar Express" by Chris Van Allsburg (www.storylineonline.net)
4: Jungle animals	• Giraffes Can't Dance by Giles Andreae • Verdi by Janelle Cannon	• "Boa Constrictor" by Shel Silverstein • "The Elephant" (www.preschoolrainbow.org/animal-rhymes.htm) • Five Little Monkeys by Juliet Kepes • "Jumping Monkey" by Kaitlyn Guenther • "Monkey Me" by CJ Heck	• Koko's Kitten by Dr. Francine Patterson • Me . . . Jane by Patrick McDonnell • The Watcher: Jane Goodall's Life with the Chimps by Jeanette Winter	• Baby Animals: Tigers by Kate Petty • "Cheetah" (sciencepoems.net/sciencepoems/cheetah.aspx) • Chimpanzees by Sarah Albee • Giraffes by Valerie Bodden • Wild Wild World: Crocodilians by Tanya Lee Stone	• National Geographic Kids: Mammals: King of the Jungle? (video nationalgeographic.com/video/kids/animals-pets-kids/mammals-kids/porcupine-lions-kids)	• Storyline Online: "Private I. Guana" by Nina Laden (www.storylineonline.net) • Storyline Online: "To Be a Drum" by Evelyn Coleman (www.storylineonline.net)

Academic/ Content Area Vocabulary		
Week 1:	behavior, characteristics, environment, forest, habitat, habits, informational text, woodlands	
Week 2:	bold print, caption, chart, fantasy, ocean, photograph, realistic	
Week 3:	Arctic, communicate, compare, contrast, traits	
Week 4:	Africa, biography, environmentalist, rain forest, relationships	

SC.1.N.1.2: Using the five senses as tools, make careful observations, describe objects in terms of number, shape, texture, size, weight, color, and motion, and compare their observations with others. *Cognitive Complexity:* Moderate

SC.1.N.1.3: Keep records as appropriate—such as pictorial and written records—of investigations conducted. *Cognitive Complexity:* Moderate (Grade 1 section)

SC.1.L.17.1: Through observation, recognize that all plants and animals, including humans, need the basic necessities of air, water, food, and space. *Cognitive Complexity:* Low

Suggested Student Objectives/Learning Goals

- Identify the text features in informational texts. Recognize the native habitat for targeted animal groups.

- Participate actively in shared reading, modeled writing, and interactive read-alouds, responding verbally to the teacher and classmates.

- Identify rhyme, rhythm, and alliteration in poetry and finger plays.

- Read with appropriate automaticity and phrasing in instructional-leveled text.

- Build stamina in independent reading.

- Create explanatory writing to compare ideas and connect two texts.

- Write in response to a topic with supporting details and a sense of closure.

- Include theme vocabulary in oral extension activities and writing responses.

- Recognize ways that animals adapt to their environment.

- Generate questions about animal traits and habitats and collect information through team research.

Sample Activities

- Students listen to informational interactive read-alouds and write or draw new learnings on sticky notes. They think-pair-share and strengthen and rewrite facts. Next, they classify animal and habitat characteristics on a large posterboard with predetermined headings. Facts are confirmed with teacher guidance, and students add them to connection chains each week to reinforce and expand concepts. Facts are written on paper strips and added to the appropriate chain in order to categorize.

- Students engage in interactive read-alouds. Afterward, with teacher prompting and support, students compare and contrast an imaginary animal from a literary read-aloud and an animal from an informational text. They use a graphic organizer to create a visual support that demonstrates similarities and differences. Finally, students draw an illustration that shows likenesses and differences and respond in writing to contrast another animal pair from the text.

- Using shared reading text resources, play Say Something to monitor comprehension and chunk text into manageable units. Students sit knee to knee and take turns whisper reading the text to one another. The reader stops when the teacher announces, "Say something!" looks up from the text, and briefly summarizes what he or she just read. The game continues until the text is completed. A teacher-modeled written summary is facilitated by the use of this strategy.

- After modeling a vocabulary map with unfamiliar vocabulary, students create "It Is/It's Not" cards to match new vocabulary words. On one side of an index card, the student draws a picture or scenario that represents the meaning of the word. On the reverse side, the student draws a nonexample representation of the appropriate use of the word in the context in which it was read. Pairs sort the examples from the nonexamples and match the examples to the terms.

- Students create a habitat from found natural elements, then brainstorm adjectives that describe the habitat and discuss with partners. Students write about the traits that make the habitat unique and include details and a sense of closure to the writing.

- Students conduct a text treasure hunt, searching for common text features in nonfiction selections that have been read. Examples of text features to list for the hunt include captions, photographs, maps, bold print, and charts.

- Students complete open and closed sorts with related vocabulary words. They explain the rationale of the open sort as meaning, syntactic function, or phonics element. Partners play Concentration with double sets of the words.

- Students maintain a learning log of observations and new learning from the unit.

- Students create a digital newsletter to report on important animal traits and/or an online graphic organizer from ReadWriteThink to compare and contrast.

- Students use highlighter tape to flag evidence in the text in response to teacher questions.

- Partners use animal puppets to retell the interactive read-aloud.

- Students reread shared reading resources to build fluency and automaticity. Then, partners tape repeated readings to improve phrasing and intonation.

- After teacher support and shared reading using a Readers Theatre online resource, students prepare an original Readers Theatre script based on a literary or informational text and perform for classmates.

Tools for Planning Weekly Lessons

This section discusses the specific planning tools that are needed to effectively plan for the delivery of the theme-based instruction on a weekly basis. Note the two types of plans and the purposes for each. Also, focus on the instructional time blocks that allow for integrated theme-based instruction.

Weekly Planning Overview

Those who have long struggled with getting everything on one weekly plan will appreciate the need for both a weekly overview and specific daily lesson plans.

A reproducible weekly planning overview is located in the Appendix. This sheet is where you would detail the materials and instructional focuses for the week. By design, it is not a day-by-day plan; rather, it shows teachers the information and materials necessary to effectively plan for the week. The texts, assessments, and vocabulary listed on the unit plan (see Figure 45) are plugged into the weekly planning overview.

Suggested Student Objectives/Learning Goals for Week 4

- Describe how unusual text features contribute to information and message.
- Compare and contrast texts and events verbally and with simple details in writing.
- Create a timeline of Jane Goodall's life.
- Continue diary entries in response to group characterization discussions.
- Use examples and nonexamples to represent meanings of new vocabulary.
- Complete a learning log, incorporating learning from previous weeks.
- Recognize the native habitat for animals of Africa and communicate simple details about how their needs are met in that region.
- Name ways that animals adapt to their environment.
- Generate questions about animals of Africa and collect information through individual and team research.
- Create a newsletter, graphic organizer, and connection chain to classify and organize information.

Weekly Lesson Planner

Figure 46 is a weekly lesson planner that provides a day-by-day schedule for Ms. Smith's instruction (see the Appendix for a reproducible). The weekly lesson planner provides the scope and sequence necessary to guide instruction on a daily basis as the week unfolds. Notice that a large part of the day is devoted to teaching integrated language arts. Ideally, large blocks of time are for this kind of instruction. However, in reality, the time is most likely broken into parts. This kind of planning allows for the flexibility needed when special activities interrupt the flow of the lesson. Simply pick up where the lesson left off when the students return to class so the lessons can flow based on the students' needs. The lesson planning for small-group instruction is completed separately along with the independent extensions from small group. (All of these reproducibles are in the Appendix.)

Daily Instruction

The narrative that follows gives day-to-day insight into the instructional sequence that is appropriate for thematic unit study with differentiated reading instruction for the last

FIGURE 46
Sample First-Grade Weekly Lesson Planner

Weekly Lesson Planner		Week of May 7, 2012	
Integrated Language Arts	Math	Content Area Science/ Social Studies	Independent Practice Assessment
Monday IRA Me...Jane MW • "I wonder" statements • Chart questions (ongoing) SW Create a timeline of Jane Goodall's life.		Observation Walk: Record data through pictures and labels like Jane. SR Chimpanzees	Complete learning log entries; "I wonder" statements and questions Repeated reading of leveled text
Tuesday IRA The Watcher Use Venn diagram to compare to Monday's text. SR "Giraffe and a Half" SW Compare the fantasy giraffe.		Weigh, measure, and mount natural artifacts. Revisit the text for features that compare in Jane's style.	Use a graphic organizer to compare two texts or characters. Vocabulary map of new words
Wednesday IRA Verdi How do Verdi's changes protect him? What other animals use camouflage? MW Diary Entry: Personal Narrative TML Grammar: Tenses		Science Connection Chains: Arrange charted information in categories linked and hung together. (FA)	Diary Entry: Personal Narrative "How have you changed as you're growing, like Verdi?"
Thursday IRA KoKo's Kitten MW How are Jane and KoKo both conservationalists? SR "Five Little Monkeys"		Video Clip: National Geographic Kids (Lion and Porcupine) Turn Talk: How do animals and/or humans interact?	Use text evidence to explain how KoKo and Jane protected nature. (FA)
Friday SR "Boa Constrictor" TML Focus on /e/ /ee/ Perform as alternate reading TML Text Feature Treasure Hunt (SA)		IRA Wild Wild World: Crocodilians Repeat Observation Walk. Focus on ways to protect wildlife. Discuss and chart.	Create and perform a Reader's Theater that demonstrates ways to protect nature. (SA)

IRA: Integrated Read Aloud	MW: Modeled Writing	TML: Targeted Mini Lesson	V: Vocabulary
SR: Shared Reading	SW: Shared Writing	SA: Summative Assessment	
Small Group Reading: See Lesson plans		FA: Formative Assessment	

semester of first grade. The week described is the fourth week of this unit (see Figure 45) and extends concepts of animal habitats and adaptation to behavior and relationships with other animals and humans. The concept of conservation of the environment is an introductory but underlying topic to be explored.

Ms. Smith uses an interactive read-aloud or shared reading experience to begin her whole-group thematic instruction and purposefully chooses passage reading options and predictable routines that assure access to the text for all of her first graders. Because of the diverse language needs of her students, she provides strong vocabulary instruction and frequent opportunities for paired activities that encourage transfer of vocabulary into immediate use. This whole-group period supportively exposes all readers to complex text and modeling of comprehension skills and strategies. A modeled writing opportunity is typically part of the whole-group time and is related to the read-aloud or shared reading venue. This modeled writing is the basis for foundational grammar skills in the area of syntax and usage, as well as goals in the craft of writing.

Small-group differentiation is next in the daily schedule and is planned with the needs of each student in mind. Ms. Smith studies running records, placement inventories, and other available data to discern the most struggling readers. She sees her most fragile readers every day and rotates groups between the remaining instructional levels. The ESE and Title I teachers join the class during small-group instruction to give additional support. In a workshop format, students engage in writing extensions and paired or independent reading that corresponds to small-group leveled text. Others complete differentiated word study activities. Soft, instrumental music plays in the background as teacher-led groups take place each day. This plan is for Monday of week 4 of the unit on animal habitats.

8:00–8:45: Whole-Group Integrated Language Arts: Ms. Smith reviews the animal habitats studied thus far and provides time for the students to reread their learning log entries from the previous week with a partner. She introduces the African continent using a world map, after which the students brainstorm the animals that they think live in the jungle or rain forest. On a chart, Ms. Smith jots down the animals named to revisit the list when the animals are addressed throughout the week. She then introduces the jungle animals theme with an informational shared reading of *Chimpanzees* by Sarah Albee (2009). Because Ms. Smith has a single copy, she projects the book so the students can participate in the reading. Afterward, they add a new section and heading to their learning logs for the week's study.

Ms. Smith introduces the Jane Goodall lesson featuring the biographical narrative *Me...Jane* by Patrick McDonnell (2011). Before the read-aloud, she says, "Think about the text features we've noticed in our nonfiction texts. As I read the book, look for some unusual ways that this author shares information." After reading, she projects the pages with key text features (Jane's scientific drawings and logs from her childhood). Ms. Smith calls attention to new and unfamiliar vocabulary in context. Next, she asks the students to think-pair-share about how the unique illustrations add to the information provided in the text. After reading, Ms. Smith engages the students in a shared writing activity. As they review the text features in the book, she records the main ideas that the features depicted (see Figure 47).

Then, Ms. Smith models the writing of an "I wonder" statement and a question that remains about nature. After teacher modeling, the students generate and write questions about nature that come from what they see in the unusual text features, illustrating their wonderings in Jane Goodall's style (see Figure 48). Ms. Smith rounds the room and charts the questions to be addressed as additional informational texts are read throughout the week. Shared and interactive read-aloud selections and modeled writing activities are short but serve well in forming a solid base for the entire week's study of the practice of science, relationships among animals and humans, and environmental conservation.

8:45–10:15: Small-Group Differentiated Reading: Ms. Smith implements the model provided in *Small-Group Reading Instruction: A Differentiated Teaching Model for Beginning and Struggling Readers* (Tyner, 2009). The model is well balanced and provides for each stage in developmental reading growth. Her students' needs are met with differentiated word study activities and guided practice in appropriately leveled text. She chooses leveled readers to further reinforce the concepts studied in the unit. After the teacher-led group, the students work on independent and paired activities that

FIGURE 47
Sample First-Grade Lesson Plan

Planner for Modeled and Shared Writing

Text: "Me...Jane" by Patrick McDonnell   **Type:** Expository

Learning Goals: Language Arts (LA) or Content Area (CA)
- LA: Use illustrations to determine key ideas.
- LA: Participate in collaborative conversations about the topic and text.
- CA: Question the topic and text and investigate.

Written Comprehension Focus (if applicable): Finding main ideas in illustrations

Writing Format:

Writing Process/Traits: Convention, ideas, and content

Before Writing
- Project pages 8-9 of the book. Discuss ways that Jane recorded her information. How do her text features help us understand her message?

During Writing: Teaching Points
- Make a list of main ideas that Jane represented through her drawings.

After Writing
- Point out the significance of labeling.

Assessment: Create your own "I wonder" statement and use a picture and labeling to demonstrate your thinking. Teacher observation.

FIGURE 48
A First Grader's Written Response for an Activity After Reading

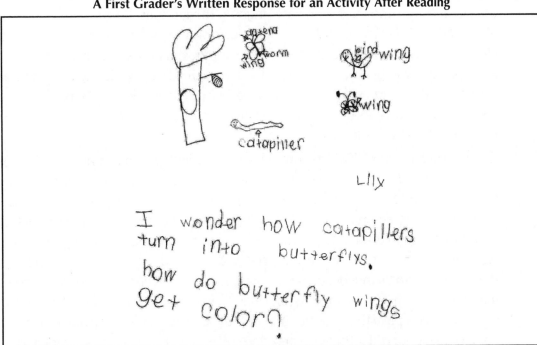

extend skills in writing explanatory text and narrative pieces, word study, and fluency building through poetry, Big Books, and leveled text. During this workshop time, the students also work on research projects that relate to the thematic study.

- Group A (30 minutes): This group of four students works in small group with Ms. Smith every day, as well as with the Title I teacher in a second group. These students struggle with gaps in phonemic awareness and sound manipulation that aid in word study and decoding within text. Even in the second semester of first grade, Ms. Smith incorporates additional sound stretching routines using manipulatives to make decoding and recoding more concrete. These students are reading well below grade level and are now reading *Grumpy Elephant* by Joy Cowley (1990), which is level 8 (see Figure 49a).

- Group B (30 minutes): These five students meet three times a week with Ms. Smith. Using the same small-group model and comparable instructional routines, word study and leveled text placement are near grade level for this group. The students still struggle with automaticity and coordinating the use of picture clues and cueing systems that help maintain fluency. A word study notebook provides a way to monitor successful completion of word study activities and are checked each time the group meets. Ms. Smith's ESE student functions well in this group with support from his ESE teacher. This group is reading *Hippo's Hiccups* by Amanda McKay (1998), which is level 12 (see Figure 49b).

- Group C (30 minutes): The six students in this group read grade-level text fluently. Efficient monitoring is an issue, and Ms. Smith devotes much of the group time to guided comprehension work with text. Because of their proficiency in decoding and fluency, these students only meet three times each week for small-group instruction. Writing extensions are ongoing throughout the week and brought to the individual teacher/student conferences for a "glow and grow," which is an element in the child's writing that is developing well and another that presents an opportunity to grow as an author. Intertextuality between leveled text genres is reinforced through extensions and group discussions. Figure 49c presents the lesson plan for this group, which is focusing on *Mr. Sun and Mr. Sea* by Andrea Butler (1994), which is level 16.

- Group D (30 minutes): This group is reading leveled text that is more typical of midyear second grade. These six students are ready for simple chapter books and meet with Ms. Smith twice a week. Through her modeling of group discussion routines based on reciprocal learning, the students run literature circles in a carpeted area to discuss their text and record their connections and questions. After administering spelling inventories and running records, Ms. Smith finds these students to be independent readers who need challenges in their reading to maintain growth. She follows an above-level word study sequence, allowing the students to complete the activities in pairs, and concentrates the group time most heavily on higher order thinking and close reading of the text. These students are

FIGURE 49
Sample Small-Group Reading Lesson Plans for First Grade

(a) Below Grade Level

Lesson Planner for Primary-Grade Small-Group Differentiated Instruction

Group: A

Fluency (Rereading)
Text: "In the Jungle" by Anne Miranda   Level: 8

Learning Goals

Word Study
- Digraphs: br, tr, cr
- Picture sort: Students write on dry-erase boards.
- Write sentence with students, then cut it up and have them put it back together: "The tractor went over the bridge."

Vocabulary:
- Sight words 50-75

Comprehension
Text: "Grumpy Elephant" by Joy Cowley   Level: 8

Before Reading: Background Knowledge, Vocabulary, Purpose
- Picture walk, point out word habitat

During Reading: Teaching Points
- How do we know that the elephant is grumpy?
- What do you think will make him happier?

After Reading: Comprehension Focus Activity
- Summarize.
- How was elephant's problem solved?
- Retell the story to your partner.

Outside-of-Group Extensions
- Reread the book with a partner.
- Cut up the sentence and draw an illustration: "The tractor went over the bridge."

Assessments
- Observations

(b) Near Grade Level

Lesson Planner for Primary-Grade Small-Group Differentiated Instruction

Group: B

Fluency (Rereading)
Text: "The Big Crocodile: A Song" by Ethel Crowninshield   Level: 12

Learning Goals

Word Study
- Short vowels: a, u, e
- Card sort
- Spell sort
- Sentence dictation

Vocabulary:
- Sight words 75-100

Comprehension
Text: "Hippo's Hiccups" by Amanda McKay   Level: 12

Before Reading: Background Knowledge, Vocabulary, Purpose
- Will this story be fiction or nonfiction? How do you know?
- How do you get rid of the hiccups?
- Predict: How will he get rid of his hiccups? Confirm while reading.

During Reading: Teaching Points
- Summarize and check predictions. Use text-based evidence.

After Reading: Comprehension Focus Activity
- Compare and contrast how hippo gets rid of his hiccups and how you get rid of the hiccups. (Record students' responses on a graphic organizer.)

Outside-of-Group Extensions
- Create a script for a puppet show.
- Sort words and glue them into word study notebook.
- Listening center: Listen to the nonfiction book about the hippopotamus.

Assessments
- Observe spell sort responses.
- Responses in word study notebooks
- Observations

(c) On Grade Level

Lesson Planner for Primary-Grade Small-Group Differentiated Instruction

Group: C

Fluency (Rereading)
Text: "Anansi's Narrow Waist" by Len Cabral   Level: 16

Learning Goals

Word Study
- Common u patterns: cute, hurt, blue
- Word ladders/sentence dictation

Vocabulary:
- Preview vocabulary before reading: legend, fable, Africa.

Comprehension
Text: "Mr. Sun and Mr. Sea" by Andrea Butler   Level: 16

Before Reading: Background Knowledge, Vocabulary, Purpose
- Discuss characteristics of fables.

During Reading: Teaching Points
- Use sticky notes to mark text evidence that the story is a fable.

After Reading: Comprehension Focus Activity
- How do Mr. Sun and Mr. Sea impact their environments?
- Chart human characteristics of the sun and the sea.
- Review text evidence that the story is a fable.

Outside-of-Group Extensions
- Word sort with a partner
- Create a fable about a chimpanzee. (Compile students' fables into a book using the template from ReadWriteThink.)

Assessments
- Observations
- Rubric for fable assignments

(d) Above Grade Level

Lesson Planner for Primary-Grade Small-Group Differentiated Instruction

Group: D

Fluency (Rereading)
Text: "Cheetah" (sciencepoems.net/sciencepoems/   Level: Poem
cheetah.aspx)

Learning Goals

Word Study
- Prefixes: re–, re–, un–
- Spell sort/sentence dictation

Vocabulary:
- Preview vocabulary before reading: Amazon, rain forest, understory, forest floor, canopy, continent

Comprehension
Text: "Afternoon on the Amazon" by Mary Pope Osborne   Level: 24

Before Reading: Background Knowledge, Vocabulary, Purpose
- Introduce and rate students' knowledge of the story vocabulary.

During Reading: Teaching Points
- Monitor targeted vocabulary with bookmarks.
- Follow the characters and their characteristics in the story.

After Reading: Comprehension Focus Activity
- Revisit and rate students' knowledge of the vocabulary.
- Self-assessments

Outside-of-Group Extensions
- Complete vocabulary maps and include definitions and illustrations.
- Research the jackdaw, an animal introduced in the story.

Assessments
- Observations
- Review students' vocabulary maps and research.

reading *Afternoon on the Amazon* by Mary Pope Osborne (1995), which is level 24 (see Figure 49d.)

Ms. Smith follows a rotating schedule to maintain consistency in providing for the diverse needs of her students. The following weekly schedule shows the time spent with group A (her most struggling readers) versus group D (her most independent and proficient readers). She reserves two extra group blocks (X) each week for reading or writing conferences with her Title I and ESE students, who are pulled out of class in the afternoon to receive additional intervention.

Monday: A, B, C

Tuesday: A, X, D

Wednesday: A, B, C

Thursday: A, X, D

Friday: A, B, C

The thematic unit is supported by the choice of leveled readers for each small group. Table 3 shows some text selections that address the theme but are written at various levels of text complexity. These texts are short, so numerous books may be read by these early readers throughout the week.

Research projects and writing extensions at workshop time revolve around small-group foundational skills or those targeted in whole-group integrated language arts instruction. (Refer back to the lesson plans in Figure 49 for more details on extensions and small-group instructional strategies.)

11:45–12:30: Specials: While the students are at the computer lab, Ms. Smith has planning time.

12:30–1:00: Content Area Focus: Ms. Smith provides each student with a clipboard to hold their learning log during a nature walk around school grounds. After a brief review of Jane Goodall's habits as a child, Ms. Smith reminds the students to observe and record like a scientist. They collect natural artifacts to draw and describe in detail. After online research, reading, and an additional observation trip around the school later in the week, learning logs are completed and evaluated using a rubric that qualifies performance.

1:00–1:45: Whole-Group Integrated Language Arts (continued): Ms. Smith models the creation of a sample timeline sequencing the events of a typical school day. Grammar skills related to past and present tenses are embedded and directly taught during this minilesson. Next, she reviews vocabulary from *Me...Jane*. Partners think-pair-share about the sequential events in Jane's early life that led her to her goal of becoming an environmentalist. The students begin pictorial timelines from their conversations and add written details. They each maintain a portfolio of their completed writing and another folder of writing that is under construction and will be finished during workshop time over the week.

1:45–2:15: Reading/Writing Conferences: Writing workshop time continues as Ms. Smith visits students for individual writing conferences. All components of literacy development are intertwined as each student reads his or her work. Ms. Smith shares

TABLE 3
Examples of Theme-Related Leveled Readers for Small-Group Instruction and Shared Reading

Fountas and Pinnell Levels	Early Intervention Levels	Books
C	3–4	• Artell, M. (1994). *Big long animal song*. Glenview, IL: Good Year. • Bueller, M. (1993). *An elephant's trunk*. Glenview, IL: Scott Foresman. • Hong, L.T. (1997). *Jungle spots*. Persippany, NJ: Celebration. • Vaughan, M. (1989). *Monkey's friends*. Auckland, New Zealand: Shortland. • Vaughan, M. (1997). *Whose tracks?* Persippany, NJ: Celebration.
D	5–6	• Iversen, S. (1996). *Baby elephant gets lost*. Bothell, WA: Wright Group. • Miranda, A. (1998). *The elephants have a house*. New York: Macmillan/McGraw-Hill. • Miranda, A. (1998). *In the jungle*. New York: Macmillan/McGraw-Hill. • Randell, B. (2006). *Baby hippo*. Austin, TX: Harcourt. • Vaughan, M. (1996). *Jungle parade: A signing game*. Glenview, IL: Good Year. • Zane, R.M. (1998). *Happy monkeys*. New York: McGraw-Hill.
E	7–8	• Boland, J. (1996). *The strongest animal*. Katonah, NY: R.C. Owen. • Cowley, J. (1990). *Grumpy elephant*. Bothell, WA: Wright Group. • Hamsa, B. (1985). *Animal babies*. New York: Scholastic. • Kenah, K. (2007). *Big beasts*. Columbus, OH: School Specialty.
F	9–10	• Iversen, S. (1997). *Baby elephant's sneeze*. Bothell, WA: Wright Group. • Phillips, J. (1986). *Tiger is a scaredy cat*. New York: Random House. • Randell, B. (2006). *The lion and the mouse*. Austin, TX: Harcourt. • Smith, A. (2004). *Tiger runs away*. Austin, TX: Harcourt.
G	11–12	• Aesop. (1966). *Two fables of Aesop*. Menomonie, WI: Vagabond. • Crawford, T. (1970). *Elephant in trouble*. Mahwah, NJ: Troll. • Crowninshield, E. (1993). *The big crocodile*. Glenview, IL: Scott Foresman. • Giles, J. (2001). *The donkey in the lion's skin: An Aesop's fable*. Orlando, FL: Rigby. • Kraus, R. (1995). *Leo the late bloomer*. New York: HarperCollins. • McKay, A. (1998). *Hippo's hiccups*. Hawthorn, VIC, Australia: Mimosa.
H–I	14–16	• Butler, A. (1994). *Mr. Sun and Mr. Sea*. Glenview, IL: Good Year. • Cabral, L. (1994). *Anansi's narrow waist*. Glenview, IL: Good Year. • Eggleton, J. (2004). *Piranhas*. Orlando, FL: Rigby. • Oram, H. (2004). *Why bears have short tails*. Orlando, FL: Rigby. • Randell, B. (2001). *Little Chimp and the termites*. Austin, TX: Harcourt. • Steck-Vaughn. (2002). *Frogs and toads*. Orlando, FL: Author.
J–K+	18–24	• Daniel, C. (2001). *Amazing birds of the rain forest*. Austin, TX: Steck-Vaughn. • Mike, J.M. (1997). *Chang and the tiger*. New York: Macmillan/McGraw-Hill. • Osborne, M.P. (1995). *Afternoon on the Amazon*. New York: Random House. • Stott-Thornton, J. (1994). *Monkey and fire*. Orlando, FL: Rigby.

a specific "glow and grow." Ms. Smith logs her writing conferences and observations, striving to meet with each student individually twice a week. The ESE and Title I students who leave the classroom for additional assistance have conference time reserved during the small-group rotation in the morning.

FIGURE 50
A First Grader's Wordle to Review a Literary Text and an Informational Text

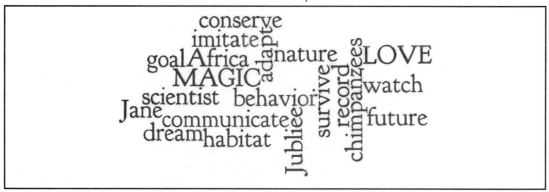

2:15–2:30: Shared Reading: Poetry: The day ends with a shared reading of Giles Andreae's (1999) *Giraffes Can't Dance*, a fantasy verse about a giraffe with a big goal: He wants to be able to dance. Ms. Smith relates his goals to that of Jane Goodall's to review and connect to one of the themes from the morning. Ms. Smith begins the lesson by doing a review of Jane Goodall with a Wordle (see Figure 50). Then, she reads the giraffe story once for recognition and appreciation of rhyme, rhythm, and alliteration, then a second time to allow students to supply the rhyming words. Ms. Smith plans interactive vocabulary strategies for the next morning, using the multimeaning words in the text. She compares the fantasy character with the giraffe in Shel Silverstein's (1964) *A Giraffe and a Half* through modeled writing on Tuesday.

Summary

Instructional planning and delivery are facilitated by the use of thematic units. Primary-grade students require the formation of connections within a variety of genres and instructional contexts to grow in conceptual knowledge. Maintaining a flow of instruction that is based on a common topic builds interest and results in improved engagement throughout the day. Ms. Smith scaffolds the literacy experiences so every learner is able to access the text and grapple with new ideas through writing extensions and meaningful conversations. Each week's study contributes to the objectives of the unit and supports students' higher order thinking through the use of complex text. Through interactive vocabulary instruction and comprehension strategies made visible through modeled and sharing reading and writing, these first graders explore the relationships between animals and humans, as well as the impact that each has on the environment. The students are redirected to the essential questions throughout the unit study as important connections and literacy skills are formed, revised, and consolidated. As with all good instruction, the formative assessments given during the unit guide Ms. Smith's critical day-to-day instructional decisions as well as her more long-term instructional adjustment. The culminating project at the end of the unit provides summative assessment information.

CHAPTER 8

Assembling the Literacy Pieces in the Intermediate-Grade Classroom

Assembling the critical pieces of literacy instruction in the intermediate-grade classroom is no easy task. Utilizing the instructional delivery venues discussed in previous chapters, the day is balanced between whole group, small group, and independent practice. Theme-based instruction allows the teacher to make the most of every minute of the instructional day. Students need time to read closely and critically in both literary and informational texts. In many instances, these content text types can be integrated effectively while addressing the language arts standards. In reality, the intermediate-grade standards may not always lend themselves to the integrated curriculum, but in most cases, they do. Text-dependent written responses, research, and presentations also require extended independent time. Theme-based instruction provides students with the opportunity to study a topic more deeply and make curricular connections that make sense. This chapter shows how an integrated theme is developed and implemented in an intermediate grade. Additionally, the direct classroom applications demonstrate how the essential pieces of the literacy jigsaw puzzle are assembled in the most effective ways to meet the needs of all students.

Sample lesson plans for interactive read-alouds, shared reading, and modeled and shared writing have been presented throughout this book. Additionally, differentiated lesson plan models for small-group reading instruction have been shared along with appropriate independent activities. After introducing you to a fourth-grade class with mixed abilities, this chapter details a sample unit of study in a fourth-grade integrated unit of study titled "Heroes: Read and Imaginary." (The planner used for developing theme-based units was discussed in Chapter 7; see the Appendix for the reproducible.) Then, a weekly planning overview is presented that establishes the language arts focuses, materials, activities, and assessments to be included for the week. This information is then broken down into a more specific weekly lesson planner for a particular week of study. Finally, a typical day in the classroom is detailed to demonstrate how the plan is implemented in a fourth-grade classroom.

Ms. Bolick's Fourth-Grade Class

Ms. Bolick teaches a fourth-grade class of 24 students. The readers in the classroom range from a late second-grade level to a high sixth-grade level. Two students receive special education services, and another receives English language support. Additionally, four students leave the classroom for reading intervention delivered by the Title I teacher.

During whole-group instruction, all students are present, so the instructional delivery must be appropriate for a wide range of learners; therefore, interactive read-alouds are an important delivery venue. Additionally, short shared reading pieces are supported with scaffold support. Small-group differentiated reading instruction occurs on a systematic basis, with the readers who struggle most being seen in small group more often. Extensions from small-group reading provide important independent practice.

Ms. Bolick works closely with the support teachers to coordinate instructional focuses. The special education teacher pushes into the classroom setting to provide those students with extra support while the classroom teacher works with other small groups. Ms. Bolick also works with the special-needs students in an appropriate small group with other students in her class who are functioning at the same instructional level.

Ms. Bolick feels that her students are more motivated and focused when she anchors the daily instruction around a central theme. The school media specialist stays informed about the areas of study in the classroom and supports students with research opportunities in their rotation to the media center. Even the music teacher includes some appropriate selections in her class that supports the theme. This team approach to integrated instruction maximizes student opportunities for connected learning. The following shows the daily schedule for Ms. Bolick's fourth-grade class:

Daily Schedule

7:45–8:00	Unpacking, attendance, and greeting
8:00–8:50	Whole-group integrated language arts
8:50–10:00	Small-group differentiated reading (includes 30-minute push-in for special education and pull-out for the English learner)
10:00–10:45	Specials (computer, PE, music, media center, etc.)
10:45–11:45	Whole-group integrated language arts (continued)
11:45–12:15	Lunch
12:15–12:45	Reading/writing conferences (Intervention students leave for 30 minutes.)
12:45–1:45	Math
1:45–2:30	Content area focus (Science and Social Studies)
2:30–2:45	Reading/writing conferences

Fourth-Grade Integrated Unit of Study: "Heroes: Real and Imaginary"

Figure 51 shows Ms. Bolick's planned unit. The discussion in this section expands on her plan.

Overview

Over the course of this four-week unit, the students will generate a definition of a hero as they read about brave and courageous fictional and real-life heroes. As the unit progresses, the students will continue to add and revise their thoughts about how a hero is best defined. The unit begins with the study of heroes of the American Revolution that supports fourth-grade social studies standards. Next, the focus turns to fictional literary heroes in tall tales, legends, and myths. Animal heroes, both real and imaginary, are the focus of the third week, which brings a different dimension to the study. Finally, the unit turns to modern and unsung heroes.

Classroom discussions now focus on how these everyday heroes, who often go unnoticed, have many of the same characteristics of other, well-known heroes. Throughout the study, the students make entries in their journals about the characteristics and circumstances of each hero discussed. The students also explore literary texts, informational texts, poetry, and songs as they relate to the characteristics of heroes and how those characteristics intersect.

Connections are also made to other literary heroes who were encountered in readings completed earlier in the year. The culminating project involves students choosing a hero for further research and study. Based on the character traits collected during this study, an argument is presented in a multimedia presentation to the class as to how this person or animal fits the definition of a hero.

Language Arts Focus Standards

These focus standards are taken from the Common Core State Standards for the English Language Arts for fourth grade (NGA Center & CCSSO, 2010b).

> RL.4.6: Compare and contrast the point of view from which different stories are narrated, including the difference between first- and third-person narrations. (p. 12)
>
> RIT.4.5: Describe the overall structure (e.g., chronology, comparison, cause/effect, problem/solution) of events, ideas, concepts, or information in a text or part of a text. (p. 14)
>
> RIT.4.8: Explain how an author uses reasons and evidence to support particular points in a text. (p. 14)
>
> RFS.4.4: Read with sufficient accuracy and fluency to support comprehension. (p. 17)
>
> W.4.1: Write opinion pieces on topics or texts, supporting a point of view with reasons and information. (p. 20)
>
> SL.4.2: Paraphrase portions of a text read aloud or information presented in diverse media and formats, including visually, quantitatively, and orally. (p. 24)
>
> SL.4.3: Identify the reasons and evidence a speaker provides to support particular points. (p. 24)
>
> SL.4.5: Add audio recordings and visual displays to presentations when appropriate to enhance the development of main ideas or themes. (p. 24)
>
> L.4.4: Determine or clarify the meaning of unknown and multiple-meaning words and phrases based on *grade 4 reading and content*, choosing flexibly from a range of strategies. (p. 29)

FIGURE 51
Sample Fourth-Grade Theme-Based Unit Plan

Theme:	Heroes: Real and Imaginary	**Overview:** Four-week integrated unit: (1) Revolutionary heroes, supports social studies standards; (2) animal heroes; (3) heroes in myths, legends, and tall tales; (4) famous and unsung heroes.
Essential Question(s)		• How is a hero defined in literary and informational text as well as in real life heroes? • What life lessons can we learn from these heroes?
Focus Standards	Language Arts:	RL4.6, RIT4.5, RIT4.8, RFS4.4, W4.1, SL4.2, SL4.3, SL4.5, SL4.4, SL4.5, SL4.6
	Content Areas:	Social Studies: SS4H4.d
Student Objectives/ Learning Goals	Week 1:	• Recognize famous Revolutionary heroes' contributions and characteristics. • Identify and create similes and metaphors. • Recognize first- and third-person accounts.
	Week 2:	• Compare print and film versions of Black Beauty. • Present an argument with evidence from text.
	Week 3:	• Compare and contrast literary and real-life characters. • Compare/contrast poetic techniques.
	Week 4:	• Use multimedia to develop a presentation. • Recognize characteristics of heroes.
Student Activities	Week 1:	• Create a biopoem about a hero. • Write a color poem using similes and metaphors. • Prepare and present a debate for/against the Revolutionary War. • Begin a Hero journal to record heroes and their characteristics.
	Week 2:	• Pick an animal hero and write an argument: Why is the animal a hero? (Animal Hall of Fame.) • Update journal and record observations of hero characteristics.
	Week 3:	• Write a tall tale. • Compare and contrast literary and real-life heroes. (Inspiration software) • Update journals.
	Week 4:	• Write an acrostic on hero characteristics. • Update journals. • Create a multimedia presentation and present it to the class (group project).
Formative and Summative Assessments		• Teacher observations of discussions and interactions among students • Rubric to evaluate the final unit presentations • Rubrics to assess writing assignments and oral presentations

146

Week and Theme	Literary Text		Informational Text		Websites	Media
	Interactive Read-Alouds	Shared Reading	Interactive Read-Alouds	Shared Reading		
1: Revolutionary heroes	• "Hero" sung by Mariah Carey • How Ben Franklin Stole the Lightning by Rosalyn Schanzer • Where Was Patrick Henry on the 29th of May? by Jean Fritz • And Then What Happened, Paul Revere? by Jean Fritz	• "George Washington" by Rosemary and Stephen Vincent Benét • "The Patriot's Courage" by Henry Abbey	• "Give Me Liberty or Give Me Death" by Patrick Henry • Poor Richard's Almanack by Benjamin Franklin	• "The Midnight Ride of Paul Revere" by Henry Wadsworth Longfellow		
2: Animal heroes	• Black Beauty: The Greatest Horse Story Ever Told by Anna Sewell	• The Beauty of the Beast: Poems From the Animal Kingdom by Jack Prelutsky	• Horse Heroes: True Stories of Amazing Horses by Kate Petty	• Marley: A Dog Like No Other by John Grogan • Wonder Dog by Melissa Fay Greene	• AnimalHero (www.animalhero.com)	• "The Story of Shanti: Laurel Seeks Animal Heroes in India" (animalhero.com/v_shanti.html) • "Interview: Flying Lily" (animalhero.com/v_kdka.html) • Because of Winn-Dixie directed by Wayne Wang (www.imdb.com/title/tt0317132/) • Black Beauty directed by Caroline Thompson (www.imdb.com/title/tt0109279/)
3: Heroes in myths, legends, and tall tales	• American Tall Tales by Adrien Stoutenberg • The Lost Hero by Rick Riordan • "Robin Hood and Little John" (www.blackcatpoems.com/a/robin_hood_and_little_john.html) • "Robin Hood and Maid Marian" (www.blackcatpoems.com/a/robin_hood_and_maid_marian.html)	• The Legend of Pecos Bill by Terry Small • John Henry: An American Legend by Ezra Jack Keats • The Adventures of Robin Hood by Roger Lancelyn Green			• Apples! Apples! (its.guilford.k12.nc.us/webquests/Apples/apples.htm)	• "The Man Who Could Out-Lumber Paul Bunyan" by Kay Houston • Robin Hood: Prince of Thieves directed by Kevin Reynolds (www.imdb.com/title/tt0102798/)
4: Famous and unsung heroes	• Tales of Famous Heroes by Peter and Connie Roop • "Standing Tall" by Jamie McKenzie		• Who Was Martin Luther King, Jr.? by Bonnie Bader • "The Ultimate Comeback Kid" by Mary Margaret • "Foster Parents Are the Unsung Heroes of Kids" by Shelley Duncan	• Jackie Robinson: Hero of Baseball by Carin T. Ford • Oprah Winfrey by Stephen Feinstein	• Bethany Hamilton (bethanyhamilton.com) • "Heroes Around Us" (www.readwritethink.org/classroom-resources/lesson-plans/heroes-around-174.html?tab=3) • "Is Superman Really All That Super? Critically Exploring Superheroes" (www.readwritethink.org/classroom-resources/lesson-plans/superman-really-that-super-990.html)	• Soul Surfer directed by Sean McNamara (www.imdb.com/title/tt1596343/)

Academic/Content Area Vocabulary		
Week 1:	acrostic, biography, character development, hero, heroine, heroism, lyrics, metaphor, perspective, point of view, primary sources, revolution, revolutionary, secondary sources, simile	
Week 2:	courageous, loyal, responsible, trustworthy	
Week 3:	humorous, legend, myth, tall tale	
Week 4:	conviction, focused, humanitarian, persistent, selfless, unsung hero	

L.4.5: Demonstrate understanding of figurative language, word relationships, and nuances in word meanings. (p. 29)

L.4.6. Acquire and use accurately grade-appropriate general academic and domain-specific words and phrases, including those that signal precise actions, emotions, or states of being…and that are basic to a particular topic. (p. 29)

Social Studies Focus Standards

The standard is taken from the fourth-grade Georgia Performance Standards for Social Studies (Georgia Department of Education, 2008), which are similar to those of other states. In some states, the focus is on state history, so biographies of famous hometown heroes are appropriate.

SS4H4.d: Describe key individuals in the American Revolution. (p. 2)

Suggested Student Objectives/Learning Goals

- Define the word *hero* both collectively and individually. Compare and contrast current heroes and heroes of the past.
- Support an argument with text-based evidence.
- Recognize heroes who contributed to history.
- Compare and contrast heroic characteristics of heroes in literary texts and real heroes.
- Discuss and interpret poetic techniques.
- Present a written argument based on text evidence.
- Present oral arguments that have substance and evidence to support a point of view.
- Identify similarities and differences in how literary and real characters are depicted.
- Compare print and film versions of stories.
- Explain the major differences between primary and secondary accounts of historical events.
- Recognize and use similes correctly to describe various heroes.
- Use technology to present information in an entertaining and meaningful way.

Sample Activities

- Conduct short research projects on real and literary heroes.
- Write an acrostic about a hero that includes his or her personal traits, achievement goals, and impact on others' lives.
- Use an expository prompt to write a paper.
- Shape a journal response into an informative/explanatory essay in several well-constructed paragraphs.

- Pick two tall tale characters and analyze how they are alike and different. Use Inspiration software (www.inspiration.com) to create a diagram showing your comparison.

- Complete a biopoem about one of the Revolutionary heroes.

- Research, design, and present a multimedia presentation about a self-selected hero. Persuade the audience that the person or animal that you selected is indeed a hero. Give evidence to support your argument.

- After reading several different stories, write your own tall tale and publish it using Word, HyperStudio, or PowerPoint.

- Create an Animal Heroes Hall of Fame. Working in a small group, research an animal recognized as a hero. Using an award certificate, summarize the animal's accomplishments and provide evidence for why the animal is a hero and should be considered for the hall of fame.

- Compare and contrast the film and print versions of *Black Beauty* by Anna Sewell. Include comparisons of characters, setting, descriptions, and dialogue.

Tools for Planning Weekly Lessons

The next section discusses the specific planning tools that are needed to effectively plan for the delivery of the theme-based instruction on a weekly basis. Note the two types of plans and the purposes for each. Also, focus on the instructional time blocks that allow for integrated theme-based instruction.

Weekly Planning Overview

The weekly planning overview (see Chapter 7 for further discussion and the Appendix for a reproducible) provides the foundation for integrated language arts instruction for the week. Keep in mind that this weekly overview, by design, is not a day-by-day plan but outlines at a glance the information and materials that are necessary to effectively plan for the week. The overview includes materials, student learning goals, activities, and assessments. The texts, assessments, and vocabulary listed on the unit plan (see Figure 51) are plugged into the weekly planning overview.

Suggested Student Objectives/Learning Goals for Week 1

- Differentiate between similes and metaphors.
- Identify characteristics of a hero.
- Identify evidence from the text to support/prove that an individual is a hero.
- Understand and use vocabulary that describes a particular hero.
- Identify the contributions of famous Revolutionary heroes.
- Determine essential information in the reading.

- Describe the differences between primary and secondary sources that give accounts of historical events.

Sample Activities for Week 1

- Create a biopoem for Paul Revere.
- Begin journal entries for heroes that include main ideas and supporting details.
- Contribute to the class biopoem about Patrick Henry.
- Complete small-group extensions (refer to Figure 53).
- Use similes and metaphors correctly to write a color poem.
- Participate in a debate for colonists who are for or against the war.

Assessments for Week 1

- Teacher observations
- Journal entries
- Writing rubric for the biopoem of Paul Revere

Weekly Lesson Planner

The weekly lesson planner provides both the focus and the scope and sequence that are necessary for effective instructional delivery as the week unfolds (see the Appendix for a reproducible). Notice that a large part of the day is devoted to the teaching of integrated language arts. Ideally, large blocks of time are available for this instruction. However, in reality, the time is most likely broken into parts. This kind of planning allows for flexibility as activities such as PE and arts class interrupt the flow of the lesson. In this planning guide, the teacher simply picks up where the lesson left off when the students return to class so the lessons can flow and integrate based on the students' needs. The lesson plans for small-group instruction are completed separately along with the extensions for independent practice. Figure 52 shows the weekly lesson planner for the following discussion.

Daily Instruction

The following narrative describes the first day of the unit of study and demonstrates the daily flow of instruction. This plan is for Monday of week 1 of the unit on heroes, real and imaginary.

8:00–8:50: Whole-Group Integrated Language Arts: To introduce the hero unit, Ms. Bolick begins by playing a recording of "Hero" sung by Mariah Carey. After listening to the song, the class discusses the lyrics. How is the hero defined? Ms. Bolick distributes the printed lyrics to the song for further investigation. The students reread the lyrics chorally. They are assigned to small groups to determine phrases from the song that describe a hero. Afterward, the class reconvenes to share their findings. The

Sample Fourth-Grade Weekly Lesson Planner

Week of: January 8–12	Integrated Language Arts	Math	Content Area Science/Social Studies	Independent Practice and Assessment
Monday	• Play "Hero" song, discuss lyrics, small groups • Pick words/phrases to describe hero. • Begin "Hero Characteristics" notebook. • Play Hero game (V), work with group, record character traits in notebook. • IRA: "Where Was Patrick Henry on the 29th of May?" • SW: Biopoem on Patrick Henry		• SR: "The Midnight Ride of Paul Revere" • Determine his hero characteristics and contributions.	• Complete Hero game. • Self-selected reading. • SGR: Extensions
Tuesday	• SR: Reread lyrics for "Hero" (fluency). • IRA: "And Then What Happened, Paul Revere?" • "Give Me Liberty or Give Me Death" • SW: Compare and contrast two accounts using primary and secondary sources. • Record in notebooks. • Establish debate teams.		• Prepare debate: For or against the Revolutionary War (Patrick Henry or opposition).	• SGR: Extensions • Self-selected reading. • Work on hero notebook.
Wednesday	• IRA: "Poor Richard's Almanack" • Discuss purposes. • Discuss quotes and what they mean. • Is he a hero? Record notes.		• Present the debates. • Principal will determine winner based on evidence.	• SGR: Extensions • Self-selected reading. • Write to explain quotes from "Poor Richard's Almanack."
Thursday	• IRA: "And Then What Happened, Paul Revere?" • Compare and contrast primary and secondary sources. • SR: "The Patriot's Courage," determine characteristics		• Write similes and metaphors for three Revolutionary heroes.	• FA: Write a biopoem for the hero from small-group books. • SGR: Extensions
Friday	• TM: Similes and metaphors • Introduce project on heroes and rubric. • Students select a hero. • SR (reread): "The Patriot's Courage" by Henry Abbey (fluency)		• FA: Choose one Revolutionary hero we read about and write an essay. • Give evidence from the social studies textbook that he/she is a hero.	• Begin hero project. • SA: SGR extensions

Note. FA = formative assessment. IRA = I read aloud. MW = modeled writing. SA = summative assessment. SGR = small-group reading (see lesson plans). SR = shared reading. SW = shared writing. TM = targeted minilesson. V = vocabulary.

students begin a hero journal to note personal characteristics of heroes as well as phrases that relate to particular characters throughout the unit of study.

Ms. Bolick asks the students to complete the Hero game with a small group while she pulls individual groups for small-group reading instruction. In this game, the students must match the characteristics that define a hero with the correct definitions. When there is some overlap in the definitions, the students must be ready to provide an argument to support their decisions. When the group reaches consensus on each trait, the students are directed to read their self-selected books. The purple group, however, has been asked to read the first chapter in their new book that will be discussed in small group the next day. These fluent readers are capable of completing much of their reading outside of group.

8:50–10:00: Small-Group Differentiated Reading: Ms. Bolick chooses books for each of the four groups that are examples of heroes for use during the small-group time. The books are at the appropriate levels of reading difficulty so that with her support, the students should be able to successfully navigate the text. Although each group is reading a different text, the written response assignments are similar. This allows each group to report to their classmates on the particular hero they read about. It is the third quarter of the school year, and two of the groups are reading below grade level and two above grade level. Time allocations for the groups are based on need.

- Green Group (30 minutes): These six students are functioning significantly below grade level and therefore need to be seen more frequently and for a longer period of time in small group than the other three groups. The last five minutes of the lesson are devoted to individual reading/writing conferences. Each student is assigned a day to stay after group for the conference. All but one of these students attends intervention outside of the classroom during the scheduled conference time. The group's book selection is *Susan B. Anthony* by Don McLeese (2002), which is level L (see Figure 53a).

- Blue Group (20 minutes): This group is reading below grade level and is seen more frequently than the two groups who are reading above grade level. These students are seen every day. Ms. Bolick requires them to complete rereadings outside of group to develop needed fluency. This week the group is reading *George Washington and the American Revolution* by Joanne Wachter, which is level M (see Figure 53b).

- Yellow Group (20 minutes): This group is reading above grade level and is seen alternately with the purple group. Ms. Bolick assigns in-depth written responses to challenge these accomplished readers. Their lesson this week centers on the book *Molly Pitcher* by Frances E. Ruffin (2002), which is level R (see Figure 53c).

- Purple Group (20 minutes): These students are reading significantly above grade level and are seen in small group every other day. Much of their reading is completed outside of group. Small-group time is spent on in-depth comprehension conversations and specified word study. The group begins reading their book, *Patrick Henry: Voice of the Revolution* by Amy Kukla and Jon Kukla (level U),

FIGURE 53
Sample Small-Group Reading Lesson Plans for Fourth Grade

(a) Well Below Grade Level
Lesson Planner for Intermediate-Grade Small-Group Differentiated Instruction

Group: Green

Fluency (Rereading, optional)

Learning Goals
- Identify factors that influenced her life choices.
- Identify contributions of Susan B. Anthony.
- Determine the character traits that make her a hero and give evidence for each trait.

Word Study
- Similes and metaphors

Comprehension

Text: "Susan B. Anthony" by Don McLeese   **Level:** L

Before Reading: Background Knowledge, Vocabulary, Purpose
- Discuss the status of women at the time.
- Vocabulary intro: Quaker, civil right, social barriers, diligence, tolerance
- Purpose: To identify reasons why Susan B. Anthony might be called a hero

During Reading: Teaching Points
- What happened to Susan B. Anthony that gave her "revolutionary" ideas?
- What did others think about her actions? Why?
- What contributions did she make to society?
- How did she demonstrate diligence and tolerance?

After Reading: Comprehension Focus Activity
- Characterization: What are the character traits that identify Susan B. Anthony as a hero? What evidence do you have from the book to support this?
- Do all people view her as a hero? Why or why not

Outside-of-Group Extensions
- Reread parts of the text to build fluency.
- Create a biopoem about Susan B. Anthony.
- Write two similes and two metaphors to describe Susan B. Anthony.

Assessments
- Observations in small groups
- Assessment of biopoems with rubric
- Assessment of similes and metaphors

(b) Below Grade Level
Lesson Planner for Intermediate-Grade Small-Group Differentiated Instruction

Group: Blue

Fluency (Rereading, optional)

Learning Goals
- Identify ways that George Washington showed integrity.
- Identify character traits and text evidence that make him a hero.
- Use similes and metaphors to describe George Washington.

Word Study
- Similes and metaphors

Comprehension

Text: "George Washington and the American Revolution" by Joanne Wachter   **Level:** M

Before Reading: Background Knowledge, Vocabulary, Purpose
- Discuss information from social studies about George Washington.
- Discuss the time period in which he lived.
- Vocabulary intro: integrity, responsibility, respect, patriotism, sacrifice
- Purpose: To determine the character traits and actions of George Washington that make him a hero

During Reading: Teaching Points
- How did George Washington make the best of his mistakes?
- What factors inspired him?
- Find examples from the text that show that George Washington had integrity.

After Reading: Comprehension Focus Activity
- What evidence from the text shows that George Washington was honest, sacrificial, and courageous?
- Create a simile and a metaphor to describe George Washington.

Outside-of-Group Extensions
- Reread parts of the text to build fluency.
- Write a biopoem about George Washington.
- Write journal entries for selected heroes.

Assessments
- Observations in small groups
- Rubric to assess biopoems
- Review similes and metaphors.

(c) Above Grade Level
Lesson Planner for Intermediate-Grade Small-Group Differentiated Instruction

Group: Yellow

Fluency (Rereading, optional)

Learning Goals
- Identify contributions of Molly Pitcher.
- Write a persuasion essay based on evidence from the text.
- Use similes and metaphors to describe Molly Pitcher.

Word Study
- Similes and metaphors

Comprehension

Text: "Molly Pitcher" by Frances E. Ruffin   **Level:** R

Before Reading: Background Knowledge, Vocabulary, Purpose
- Have we read about any women who played a part in the American Revolution?
- How was the role of women different then than it is now?

During Reading: Teaching Points
- What evidence do we have that she is a fictitious character?
- Why would someone make up a character like Molly Pitcher?
- Why could she be considered an unlikely hero?

After Reading: Comprehension Focus Activity
- Discuss the contributions that this character made to the Revolution and the Women's Movement.

Outside-of-Group Extensions
- Write an "unlikely hero" essay that presents an argument for why Susan B. Anthony should or should not be considered a hero.
- Extend reading from small groups.
- Write journal entries about selected heroes.

Assessments
- Observations during small-group discussions
- Rubric to score essays

(d) Well Above Grade Level
Lesson Planner for Intermediate-Grade Small-Group Differentiated Instruction

Group: Purple

Fluency (Rereading, optional)

Learning Goals
- Recognize and use similes and metaphors.
- Identify characteristic that identify Patrick Henry as a hero.
- Identify contributions of Patrick Henry to the American Revolution.

Word Study
- Similes and metaphors

Comprehension

Text: "Patrick Henry: Voice of the Revolution" by Amy Kukla and Jon Kukla   **Level:** U

Before Reading: Background Knowledge, Vocabulary, Purpose
- Discuss information read in the social studies book.
- Vocabulary intro: integrity
- Purpose: To identify characteristic that qualify Patrick Henry as a hero

During Reading: Teaching Points
- How did Patrick Henry show integrity and be true to himself?
- In what ways did he impact society?

After Reading: Comprehension Focus Activity
- Compare and contrast Patrick Henry's and Paul Revere's contributions to the American Revolution.
- Identify the character traits that qualify Patrick Henry as a hero.

Outside-of-Group Extensions
- Students read their group book on days that they don't attend small group.
- Make journal entries in hero notebook.
- Write similes and metaphors to describe Patrick Henry.
- Write a compare and contrast essay about Patrick Henry and Paul Revere.

Assessments
- Observations during small-group discussions
- Writing rubric to assess essays

during Monday's small-group time and discusses it in group on Tuesday (see Figure 53d).

Ms. Bolick develops a rotating schedule for meeting with her small groups. The green group struggles with reading the most, and the purple group is the highest achieving group of readers. The following is the weekly schedule:

Monday: Blue, Green, Yellow

Tuesday: Blue, Green, Purple

Wednesday: Blue, Green, Yellow

Thursday: Blue, Green, Purple

Friday: Blue, Green, Yellow

The green group is seen every day for 30 minutes, whereas the other groups only meet for 20 minutes. The green and blue groups meet daily, the yellow group meets three times a week, and the purple group meets twice a week. The majority of the outside-of-group independent work centers around extension activities that are based on the small-group lessons. Ms. Bolick feels that her students need ample time for reading and writing in response to appropriate text difficulty. Additionally, the students complete research and projects with other groups of students. (See Chapter 4 for detailed information on planning and implementing small-group differentiated reading instruction.)

10:00–10:45: Specials: While the students are in PE, Ms. Bolick has planning time.

10:45–11:45: Whole-Group Integrated Language Arts (continued): The class reviews the Hero vocabulary game, and Ms. Bolick asks them to staple the sheet in their notebooks for reference during the unit.

She then turns the discussion to heroes of the Revolutionary War. She chooses to do an interactive read-aloud of *Where Was Patrick Henry on the 29th of May?* by Jean Fritz (1997; see Figure 54). During the reading, Ms. Bolick poses questions for partners to discuss. The students are also asked to question the text. As the story is read, they take notes, including quotations, that provide evidence to persuade someone that Patrick Henry is indeed a hero. Ms. Bolick realizes that she will need to model the processes of creating a biopoem about Patrick Henry that reflects this information. Later, the students use this same format to summarize information about another hero (see Figure 55).

12:15–12:45: Reading/Writing Conferences: Ms. Bolick meets with three students during this time frame. Today she asks each of these students to bring the self-selected book that he or she is currently reading. The conference allows Ms. Bolick to check on appropriate book choice and provides for discussion about the book's content. She makes note of the book choice and where in the book the student has completed reading. In this way, she can monitor the amount of text being read independently. Today Ms. Bolick asks each student to identify an exciting part of the book and read it to her. Based on the reading, Ms. Bolick poses thoughtful questions to determine the student's level of understanding. (See Chapter 5 for more detail on implementing reading and writing conferences.)

FIGURE 54
Sample Fourth-Grade Lesson Plan

Planner for Interactive Read-Alouds and Shared Reading

Text: "Where Was Patrick Henry on the 29th of May?" by Jean Fritz   **Type:** Historical fiction

Learning Goals: Language Arts (LA) or Content Area (CA)
- CA: Identify the impact of Patrick Henry on the Revolutionary War.
- LA: Identify character traits of Patrick Henry.
- LA: Find evidence from the text that he was a hero.
- LA: With evidence from the text, persuade an audience to be for or against the war.

Before Reading

Build Background Knowledge: Review the causes of the Revolutionary War.

Introduce Story Vocabulary: intro: integrity, scholar, liberty

Set the Purpose: To determine whether Patrick Henry was a hero

During Reading: Teaching Points
- How did Patrick Henry's actions affect the Revolutionary War?
- How did the people respond to his message?
- What character traits did Patrick Henry exhibit?
- What evidence from the text shows each of those traits?

After Reading

Comprehension Focus: Give evidence from the text about each of Patrick Henry's character traits.

Vocabulary Review: Use each word in a sentence that tells something about Patrick Henry.

Written Response: Biopoem about Patrick Henry (modeled writing)

Assessment: Teacher observation/rubric for poem.

1:45–2:30: Content Area Focus: Ms. Bolick chooses to continue the focus of Revolutionary heroes during the social study block (see Figure 56). Today the students are discussing the role of Paul Revere in the Revolutionary War. Then, they complete a shared reading of the poem "The Midnight Ride of Paul Revere" by Henry Wadsworth Longfellow (2002). The lesson wraps up as students identify the heroic characteristics of Paul Revere and evidence of each characteristic from the text.

2:30–2:45: Reading/Writing Conferences: Knowing that these intermediate-grade students are capable of packing up for the day and checking homework assignments on the board, Ms. Bolick uses part of this time to meet with one or two students. She also notes that six of her students ride home on the last bus, so they make great candidates for this time slot.

FIGURE 55
Fourth-Grade Modeled Writing of a Biopoem

(a) Sample Lesson Plan

Planner for Modeled and Shared Writing

Text: "Where Was Patrick Henry on the 29th of May?" by Jean Fritz   **Type:** Biopoem

Learning Goals: Language Arts (LA) or Content Area (CA)

- Identify character traits of Patrick Henry from the text.
- Summarize text information in the biopoem template.

Written Comprehension Focus (if applicable):
- Main ideas and supporting details

Writing Format: Poem

Writing Process/Traits:
- Word choices

Before Writing
- Review hero characteristics from the Hero game.

During Writing: Teaching Points
- Use think-aloud strategies to construct the poem.

After Writing
- Read the poem together.

Assessment: Teacher observation.

(b) Completed Biopoem

Hero Bio Poem

First name Patrick

Who is passionate, couragrous, focused.

(3 hero characteristics)

Who fears: England, Vetos, King of England

Who needs: to speak, to fight to be free

Who feels: desperate, frightened, angry

Who would like to see: liberty

Resident of Virginia

Last name Henry

FIGURE 56
Sample Fourth-Grade Lesson Plan for the Content Area Block

Planner for Interactive Read-Alouds and Shared Reading

Text: "The Midnight Ride of Paul Revere" by Henry Wadsworth Longfellow   **Type:** Poem (narrative)

Learning Goals: Language Arts (LA) or Content Area (CA)
- Read with the speed, accuracy, and expression necessary to understand the text.
- Identify poetic elements of rhyme and rhythm.
- Identify heroic characteristics evidenced in the poem.
- Identify factual information in the poem.
- Identify words using context clues.

Before Reading

Build Background Knowledge:
- Review last week's lesson on Paul Revere.
- How did people receive information during that time period?
- Discuss the time when the poem was written.

Introduce Story Vocabulary:
- phantom, defiance, impetuous, belfry

Set the Purpose:
- To determine whether the poem gives factual information of the real event

During Reading: Teaching Points
- What task does Paul Revere need to complete?
- How would he signal the people?
- Do you recognize any information that we didn't read in our social studies book?
- Why do you think Longfellow wrote the poem?
- How can we figure out this word? What clues do we have?

After Reading

Comprehension Focus:
- What happens when people write about events that they don't observe? Why?
- How does this compare with the pieces we read this morning?

Vocabulary Review:
- What part of the story does each word refer to?

Written Response:
- Tomorrow: Reread the poem. Divide into groups and find evidence that is factual and made up.
- Wednesday: Divide up the poem. Have different groups of students prepare to read their assigned parts to the class.

Assessment: Teacher observation.

Summary

A carefully planned unit provides a solid foundation to build effective instruction. Here the development of the heroes theme is the glue that holds the curriculum together. Ms. Bolick uses not only grade-level standards as a basis for instruction but also her students' interest and instructional reading levels. Text pieces from a variety of genres include song lyrics, poetry, newspaper articles, websites, and literary and informational book selections. The essential questions provide an opportunity for students to think about the characteristics of the heroes and apply the lessons learned to the way they live their lives. This four-week unit of instruction connects student learning opportunities through a variety of instructional venues that provide meaningful instruction for all students.

CONCLUDING REFLECTIONS

Teaching literacy effectively is indeed a jigsaw puzzle: All pieces must fit together succinctly to bring together the full power of a quality literacy experience. Missing pieces can make the difference between the success or failure of students. This literacy foundation prepares students for whatever they choose to do or become. Each student is important: Each is poised to make significant contributions to both family and society.

Without question, a knowledgeable literacy teacher is the most important piece of the puzzle. The teacher is responsible not only for assembling the puzzle pieces but also for delivering the instruction embedded in each piece. No longer is it enough to teach the prescribed literacy curriculum. Teachers must be armed with the knowledge of standards, research, and best practices to provide for the developmental literacy needs of each learner.

Teachers step into classrooms daily and are presented with new opportunities and new challenges, as seen in the faces of each unique student. Each school day must be carefully crafted, using every minute in the instructional day in a powerful way to promote high literacy levels. Our goal is to invest in every piece of the puzzle, making each one the most powerful it can be for each student.

Time, and how we use that time in the classroom, is essential to making this goal a reality. The length of the school day is not increasing to meet an ever-increasing scope of standards, and in some cases, time is even decreasing because of budget cuts. The time needed to effectively deliver the curriculum and for students to engage in literacy learning is limited at best. Therefore, how we plan and deliver literacy instruction must be efficient and effective. Careful planning and orchestration of time contributes to students' literacy success.

Clearly, delivering the curriculum in an integrated fashion is an efficient use of time and meaningful to students. Also, consider the teaching venues and their value as they are used in whole-group, small-group, and independent learning opportunities. Striking a balance with these instructional settings and delivery venues to meet student needs is critical.

Teaching is not for the faint of heart. Never before has teaching been more demanding or more rewarding. For instance, the very definition of what it takes to be literate is changing daily with the contributions of technology and an ever-expanding global economy. The goal is to produce students who thrive and strive to be lifelong learners: students who enjoy collaboration and problem solving, students who respect the uniqueness of each individual in the classroom, and students who want bright futures and productive lives. Students who sit in our classrooms every day rely on us to make their education count. Yes, our students come with baggage—academic, physical, and emotional—and some contend with huge environmental challenges, such as poverty, homelessness, and extreme hunger. As much as we would like to change the home environment for many of these students, it is simply not possible. Instead, focusing on solid literacy instruction, bell to bell, greatly increases the possibility that these students will indeed have a brighter future. Students spend much of their waking lives in our classrooms, which presents a golden opportunity to change the direction of individual lives and society as a whole. For many children, the key to unlocking their futures starts with a quality education, and a quality education is grounded in solid literacy skills. My hope is that you will find the guidance needed to successfully teach students, using the information in this book as a starting point.

Never before has the saying "work smarter not harder" been more true. Most teachers are working very hard and rarely reap the fruits of their labors. This book is intended to assist teachers in planning more efficiently and powerfully. Teachers come to school each day to succeed with their students, not fail. Thoughtful planning of each of the critical puzzle pieces is the starting point. Much of this book describes the importance of planning and provides planning models for various settings. These models are not meant to be an additional burden but a helpful tool. My deep desire is to assist teachers with concrete, research-based practices and models to utilize as they address the literacy needs of all students.

There is no greater gift to share with a child than the literate world. To see a child's eyes light up at the first realization that he or she can indeed read is a magical moment. Teaching a child to read is a privilege. It is indeed the most humbling of teaching experiences and one of the most pleasurable. I hope that the resources in this book help lead you and your students to that magical moment of literacy achievement that leads to lifelong learning.

Reproducibles

Planner for Interactive Read-Alouds and Shared Reading

Text: **Type:**

Learning Goals: Language Arts (LA) or Content Area (CA)

Before Reading

Build Background Knowledge:

Introduce Story Vocabulary:

Set the Purpose:

During Reading: Teaching Points

After Reading

Comprehension Focus:

Vocabulary Review:

Written Response:

Assessment

Planner for Modeled and Shared Writing

Text: **Type:**

Learning Goals: Language Arts (LA) or Content Area (CA)

Written Comprehension Focus (if applicable):

Writing Format:

Writing Process/Traits:

Before Writing

During Writing: Teaching Points

After Writing

Assessment:

Planner for a Targeted Skill Minilesson

Learning Goals

Build/Access Background Knowledge

Model: Teaching Points

Guided Practice

Independent Practice

Assessment

Lesson Planner for Primary-Grade Small-Group Differentiated Instruction

Group:

Fluency (Rereading)
Text: **Level:**

Learning Goals

Word Study

Vocabulary:

Comprehension
Text: **Level:**

Before Reading: Background Knowledge, Vocabulary, Purpose

During Reading: Teaching Points

After Reading: Comprehension Focus Activity

Outside-of-Group Extensions

Assessments

Lesson Planner for Intermediate-Grade Small-Group Differentiated Instruction

Group:

Fluency (Rereading, optional)

Learning Goals

Word Study

Comprehension
Text: **Level:**

Before Reading: Background Knowledge, Vocabulary, Purpose

During Reading: Teaching Points

After Reading: Comprehension Focus Activity

Outside-of-Group Extensions

Assessments

Reading Conference Log

Student: _____

Currently Reading: _____

Date: _____

Check the items below as they are observed.

Fluency: ___ Adequate   ___ Needs improvement

Strategies Used: ___ Sounds out words   ___ Context clues   ___ Uses picture clues
___ Self-corrects

Comprehension: ___ Excellent   ___ Good   ___ Fair   ___ Poor

Book Choice: ___ Too easy   ___ Just right   ___ Too hard

Notes:

Goals for Next Conference:

Reading Conference Log

Student: _____

Currently Reading: _____

Date: _____

Check the items below as they are observed.

Fluency: ___ Adequate   ___ Needs improvement

Strategies Used: ___ Sounds out words   ___ Context clues   ___ Uses picture clues
___ Self-corrects

Comprehension: ___ Excellent   ___ Good   ___ Fair   ___ Poor

Book Choice: ___ Too easy   ___ Just right   ___ Too hard

Notes:

Goals for Next Conference:

Writing Conference Record

Name: _____ Date: _____

Writing Piece for Conference: _____

Focuses for Conference

_____

Goals for Next Conference

_____

Writing Conference Record

Name: _____ Date: _____

Writing Piece for Conference: _____

Focuses for Conference

_____

Goals for Next Conference

_____

Writing Conference Record

Name: _____ Date: _____

Writing Piece for Conference: _____

Focuses for Conference

_____

Goals for Next Conference

_____

Theme-Based Unit Planner

	Overview:			
Theme:				
Essential Question(s):				
Focus Standards	**Language Arts:**			
	Content Areas:			
Student Objectives/ Learning Goals	**Week 1:**			
	Week 2:			
	Week 3:			
	Week 4:			
Student Activities:	**Week 1:**			
	Week 2:			
	Week 3:			
	Week 4:			
Formative and Summative Assessments:				

(continued)

Theme-Based Unit Planner *(continued)*

Week and Theme	Literary Text		Informational Text			
	Interactive Read-Alouds	Shared Reading	Interactive Read-Alouds	Shared Reading	Websites	Media

Academic/ Content Area Vocabulary	Week 1:
	Week 2:
	Week 3
	Week 4:

The Literacy Jigsaw Puzzle: Assembling the Critical Pieces of Literacy Instruction by Beverly Tyner.
© 2012 International Reading Association. May be copied for classroom use.

Weekly Lesson Planner

Week of:	Integrated Language Arts	Math	Content Area Science/ Social Studies	Independent Practice Assessment
Monday				
Tuesday				
Wednesday				
Thursday				
Friday				

Note. FA = formative assessment. IRA = I read aloud. MW = modeled writing. SA = summative assessment. SGR = small-group reading (see lesson plans). SR = shared reading. SW = shared writing. TM = targeted minilesson. V = vocabulary.

Weekly Planning Overview

Week of   Week #

Unit Theme:

Literary Text
   Interactive Read-Alouds   Websites

   Shared Reading   Media

Informational Text
   Interactive Read-Alouds   Websites

   Shared Reading   Media

Writing
   Modeled/Shared Writing:

   Text-Based (if applicable):

   Other:

   Written Comprehension Focuses:

   Weekly Writing Focuses:

Academic/Content Vocabulary

Suggested Student Objectives/Learning Goals

Sample Activities

Formative and Summative Assessments

REFERENCES

Allington, R.L., & Woodside-Jiron, H. (1998). Decodable text in beginning reading: Are mandates and policy based on research? *ERS Spectrum, 16*(2), 3–11.

Batsche, G., Elliott, J., Graden, J.L., Grimes, J., Kovaleski, J.F., Prasse, D., et al. (2005). *Response to Intervention: Policy considerations and implementation.* Alexandria, VA: National Association of State Directors of Special Education.

Bean, T. (1997). Preservice teachers' selection and use of content area literacy strategies. *Journal of Educational Research, 90*(3), 154–163.

Beaver, J., & Carter, M. (2005). *Developmental reading assessment* (2nd ed.). New York: Pearson.

Beck, I.L., & McKeown, M.G. (2001). Text talk: Capturing the benefits of read-aloud experiences for young children. *The Reading Teacher, 55*(1), 10–20.

Bell, L.C., & Perfetti, C.A. (1994). Reading skill: Some adult comparisons. *Journal of Educational Psychology, 86*(2), 244–255. doi:10.1037/0022-0663.86.2.244

Bess, J.L. (Ed.). (1997). *Teaching well and liking it: Motivating faculty to teach effectively.* Baltimore: Johns Hopkins University Press.

Blachowicz, C.L.Z., & Fisher, P. (2004). Vocabulary lessons. *Educational Leadership, 61*(6), 66–69.

Blachowicz, C.L.Z., & Fisher, P.J. (2006). *Teaching vocabulary in all classrooms* (3rd ed.). Upper Saddle River, NJ: Prentice-Hall.

Blachowicz, C.L.Z., & Fisher, P.J. (2009). *Teaching vocabulary in all classrooms* (4th ed.). Boston: Allyn & Bacon.

Bodrova, E., Leong, D.J., & Semenov, D. (1998). *100 most frequent words in books for beginning readers.* Denver, CO: McREL. Retrieved May 22, 2012, from www.mcrel.org/PDF/Literacy/4006CM_100words.pdf

Bransford, J.D., Brown, A.L., & Cocking, R.R. (Eds.). (1999). *How people learn: Brain, mind, experience, and school.* Washington, DC: National Academy Press.

Caine, R.N., & Caine, G. (1994). *Making connections: Teaching and the human brain* (Rev. ed.). Menlo Park, CA: Addison-Wesley.

Chall, J.S. (1983). *Stages of reading development.* New York: McGraw-Hill.

Chappuis, S. (2005). Is formative assessment losing its meaning? *Education Week, 24*(44), 38.

Clay, M.M. (1993). *An observation survey of early literacy achievement.* Portsmouth, NH: Heinemann.

Culham, R. (2003). *6+1 traits of writing: The complete guide grades 3 and up.* New York: Scholastic.

Cunningham, P.M. (2007). Best practices in teaching phonological awareness and phonics. In L.B. Gambrell, L.M. Morrow, & M. Pressley (Eds.), *Best practices in literacy instruction* (3rd ed., pp. 159–177). New York: Guilford.

diSessa, A. (2000). *Changing minds: Computers, learning, and literacy.* Cambridge, MA: MIT Press.

Ehri, L.C., & Nunes, S.R. (2002). The role of phonemic awareness in learning to read. In A.E. Farstrup & S.J. Samuels (Eds.), *What research has to say about reading instruction* (3rd ed., pp. 110–139). Newark, DE: International Reading Association.

Ehri, L.C., Nunes, S.R., Stahl, S.A., & Willows, D.M. (2001). Systematic phonics instruction helps students learn to read: Evidence from the National Reading Panel's meta-analysis. *Review of Educational Research, 71*(3), 393–447. doi:10.3102/00346543071003393

Felton, R. (1999). *Developing automaticity and fluency.* Retrieved June 3, 2012, from www.ncsip.org/reading/Developing-Automaticity-and-Fluency.pdf

Florida Department of Education. (2010). *Next Generation Sunshine State Standards: Science standards.* Tallahassee: Author. Retrieved June 8, 2012, from www.floridastandards.org/ReportViewer39443.aspx

Forehand, M. (2010). Bloom's taxonomy. In M. Orey (Ed.), *Emerging perspectives on learning, teaching, and technology* (pp. 41–47). Zurich, Switzerland: Global Text Project.

Gambrell, L.B., Malloy, J.A., & Mazzoni, S.A. (2011). Evidence-based best practices in comprehensive literacy instruction. In L.M. Morrow & L.B. Gambrell, L.B. (Eds.). *Best practices in literacy instruction* (4th ed., pp. 11–36). New York: Guilford.

Georgia Department of Education. (2008). *Social studies grade 4 standards.* Retrieved June 9, 2012, from www.georgiastandards.org/Standards/Pages/BrowseStandards/SocialStudiesStandardsK-5.aspx

Hamilton, L.S. (2010). Testing what has been taught: Helpful, high-quality assessments start with a strong curriculum. *American Educator, 34*(4), 47–52.

Hart, L.A. (1983). *Human brain and human learning.* New York: Longman.

Hasbrouck, J., & Tindal, G.A. (2006). Oral reading fluency norms: A valuable assessment tool for reading teachers. *The Reading Teacher, 59*(7), 636–644. doi:10.1598/RT.59.7.3

Johnston, P.H. (2000). *Running records: A self-tutoring guide.* York, ME: Stenhouse.

Kovalik, S.J., (with Olsen, K.D.). (1994). *Integrated thematic instruction: The model* (3rd ed.). Kent, WA: Susan Kovalik & Associates.

Krashen, S. (1993). *The power of reading: Insights from the research.* Englewood, CO: Libraries Unlimited.

Leslie, L., & Caldwell, J. (2006). *Qualitative reading inventory* (4th ed.). Boston: Allyn & Bacon.

Lombardino, L., Rivers, K., DeFilippo, F., Montgomery, A., & Sarisky, C. (1992, November). *Kindergarten children's performance on reading readiness measures: A normative study.* Paper presented at the annual meeting of the American Speech-Language-Hearing Association, San Antonio, TX.

Long, B.H., & Henderson, E.H. (1973). Children's use of time: Some personal and social correlates. *The Elementary School Journal, 73*(4), 193–199.

Marzano, R.J. (2006). *Classroom assessment and grading that work.* Alexandria, VA: Association for Supervision and Curriculum Development.

Maxwell, L.A. (2011, November 4). What teachers can learn from English-language learners [Web log post]. Retrieved June 11, 2012, from blogs.edweek.org/edweek/learning-the-language/2011/11/

McKeon, D. (2005). *Research talking points on English language learners.* Washington, DC: National Education Association. Retrieved June 11, 2012, from https://www.nea.org/home/13598.htm

Merriam-Webster Dictionary. (2012). Formative. Retrieved June 5, 2012, from www.merriam-webster .com/dictionary/formative

Meyer, M.S., & Felton, R.H. (1999). Repeated reading to enhance fluency: Old approaches and new directions. *Annals of Dyslexia, 49*(1), 283–306. doi:10.1007/s11881-999-0027-8

Morris, D., Tyner, B., & Perney, J. (2000). Early Steps: Replicating the effects of a first-grade reading intervention program. *Journal of Educational Psychology, 92*(4), 681–693. doi:10.1037/ 0022-0663.92.4.681

Morrow, L.M., & Gambrell, L.B. (Eds.). (2011). *Best practices in literacy instruction* (4th ed.). New York: Guilford.

National Center for Education Statistics. (2011). *The Nation's Report Card: Reading 2011: National Assessment of Educational Progress at grades 4 and 8* (NCES 2012-457). Washington, DC: National Center for Education Statistics, Institute of Education Sciences, U.S. Department of Education. Retrieved June 10, 2012, from nces.ed.gov/nationsreportcard/pubs/main2011/2012457.asp

National Governors Association Center for Best Practices & Council of Chief State School Officers. (2010a). *Application to students with disabilities.* Washington, DC: Authors.

National Governors Association Center for Best Practices & Council of Chief State School Officers. (2010b). *Common Core State Standards for English language arts and literacy in history/social studies, science, and technical subjects.* Washington, DC: Authors.

National Institute of Child Health and Human Development. (2000). *Report of the National Reading Panel. Teaching children to read: An evidence-based assessment of the scientific research literature on reading and its implications for reading instruction* (NIH Publication No. 00-4769). Washington, DC: U.S. Government Printing Office.

Pearson, P.D., & Gallagher, M.C. (1983). The instruction of reading comprehension. *Contemporary Educational Psychology, 8*(3), 317–344.

Perney, J., Morris, D., & Carter, S. (1997). Factorial and predictive validity of first graders' scores on the Early Reading Screening Instrument. *Psychological Reports, 81*(1), 207–210. doi:10.2466/ pr0.1997.81.1.207

Pressley, M. (n.d.). *Balanced elementary literacy instruction in the United States: A personal perspective.* Retrieved June 10, 2012, from enumeracy.com/files/pressley_balanced.pdf

Proctor, C.P., Dalton, B., & Grisham, D.L. (2007). Scaffolding English language learners and struggling readers in a universal literacy environment with embedded strategy instruction and vocabulary support. *Journal of Literacy Research, 39*(1), 71–93.

Rasinski, T.V. (2010). *The fluent reader: Oral and silent reading strategies for building fluency, word recognition and comprehension* (2nd ed.). New York: Scholastic.

Routman, R. (2002). *Reading essentials: The specifics you need to teach reading well*. Portsmouth, NH: Heinemann.

Skinner, E., Kindermann, T., Furrer, C., & Marchand, G. (2008). Engagement and disaffection in the classroom: Part of a larger motivational dynamic? *Journal of Educational Psychology, 100*(4), 765–781.

Snow, C.E., Burns, M.S., & Griffin, P. (Eds.). (1998). *Preventing reading difficulties in young children*. Washington, DC: National Academy Press.

Stanovich, K.E., & Cunningham, A.E. (1993). Where does knowledge come from? Specific associations between print exposure and information acquisition. *Journal of Educational Psychology, 85*(2), 211–229.

Stiggins, R.J. (2002). Assessment crisis: The absence of assessment *FOR* learning. *Phi Delta Kappan, 83*(10), 758–765.

Tomlinson, C.A. (2001). *How to differentiate instruction in mixed-ability classrooms* (2nd ed.). Alexandria, VA: Association for Supervision and Curriculum Development.

Tomlinson, C.A. (2003). *Fulfilling the promise of the differentiated classroom: Strategies and tools for responsive teaching*. Alexandria, VA: Association for Supervision and Curriculum Development.

Trelease, J. (2006). *The read-aloud handbook* (6th ed.). New York: Penguin.

Turner, J.C. (1995). The influence of classroom contexts on young children's motivation for literacy. *Reading Research Quarterly, 30*(3), 410–441.

Tyner, B. (2009). *Small-group reading instruction: A differentiated teaching model for beginning and struggling readers* (2nd ed.). Newark, DE: International Reading Association.

Tyner, B.B., & Green, S.E. (2012). *Small-group reading instruction: Differentiated teaching models for intermediate readers, grades 3–8* (2nd ed.). Newark, DE: International Reading Association.

U.S. Department of Education. (2002). *No Child Left Behind: A desktop reference*. Washington, DC: Office of Elementary and Secondary Education, U.S. Department of Education. Retrieved February 2, 2012, from www2.ed.gov/admins/lead/account/nclbreference/reference.pdf

Vygotsky, L.S. (1978). *Mind in society: The development of higher psychological processes* (M. Cole, V. John-Steiner, S. Scribner, & E. Souberman, Eds. & Trans.). Cambridge, MA: Harvard University Press.

Wentzel, K.R., & Wigfield, A. (Eds.). (2009). *Handbook of motivation at school*. New York: Routledge.

Whitehurst, G.J. (2002, October). *Evidence-based education (EBE)*. Handout distributed at the Student Achievement and School Accountability Conference, Washington, DC. Retrieved June 10, 2012, from www2.ed.gov/nclb/methods/whatworks/eb/edlite-index.html

Zhou, M., Ma, W.J., & Deci, E.L. (2009). The importance of autonomy for rural Chinese children's motivation for learning. *Learning and Individual Differences, 19*(4), 492–498.

Children's Literature Cited

Aesop. (1966). *Two fables of Aesop*. Menomonie, WI: Vagabond.

Albee, S. (2009). *Chimpanzees*. New York: Gareth Stevens.

Andreae, G. (1999). *Giraffes can't dance*. New York: Scholastic.

Artell, M. (1994). *Big long animal song*. Glenview, IL: Good Year.

Bagert, B. (1993). Caterpillars. In *Chicken socks: And other contagious poems* (p. 16). Honesdale, PA: Boyds Mills.

Bloom, B. (1999). *Wolf!* New York: Orchard.

Boland, J. (1996). *The strongest animal*. Katonah, NY: R.C. Owen.

Bueller, M. (1993). *An elephant's trunk*. Glenview, IL: Scott Foresman.

Burton, M., French, C., & Jones, T. (2011). *How do animals stay alive?* Pelham, NY: Benchmark.

Butler, A. (1994). *Mr. Sun and Mr. Sea*. Glenview, IL: Good Year.

Cabral, L. (1994). *Anansi's narrow waist*. Glenview, IL: Good Year.

Carle, E. (1987). *The very hungry caterpillar*. New York: Philomel.

Catling, P.S. (1979). *The chocolate touch*. New York: HarperTrophy.

Cowley, J. (1990). *Grumpy elephant*. Bothell, WA: Wright Group.

Crawford, T. (1970). *Elephant in trouble*. Mahwah, NJ: Troll.

Cronin, D. (2000). *Click, clack, moo: Cows that type*. New York: Simon & Schuster Books for Young Readers.

Crowninshield, E. (1993). *The big crocodile*. Glenview, IL: Scott Foresman.

Dahl, R. (1982). Little Red Riding Hood and the wolf. In *Roald Dahl's revolting rhymes* (pp. 36–40). New York: Puffin.

Daniel, C. (2001). *Amazing birds of the rain forest.* Austin, TX: Steck-Vaughn.

Eggleton, J. (2004). *Piranhas.* Orlando, FL: Rigby.

Fritz, J. (1997). *Where was Patrick Henry on the 29th of May?* New York: Puffin.

Giles, J. (2001). *The donkey in the lion's skin: An Aesop's fable.* Orlando, FL: Rigby.

Hamsa, B. (1985). *Animal babies.* New York: Scholastic.

Hong, L.T. (1997). *Jungle spots.* Persippany, NJ: Celebration.

Iversen, S. (1996). *Baby elephant gets lost.* Bothell, WA: Wright Group.

Iversen, S. (1997). *Baby elephant's sneeze.* Bothell, WA: Wright Group.

Kenah, K. (2007). *Big beasts.* Columbus, OH: School Specialty.

Kraus, R. (1995). *Leo the late bloomer.* New York: HarperCollins.

Lauber, P. (1986). *Volcano: The eruption and healing of Mount St. Helens.* New York: Bradbury.

Lobel, A. (1970). *Frog and Toad are friends.* New York: HarperTrophy.

Lobel, A. (1980). The bad kangaroo. In *Fables* (p. 28). New York: HarperTrophy.

Longfellow, H.W. (2002). *The midnight ride of Paul Revere.* Des Moines, IA: National Geographic Children's.

McDonnell, P. (2011). *Me…Jane.* New York: Little, Brown.

McKay, A. (1998). *Hippo's hiccups.* Hawthorn, VIC, Australia: Mimosa.

McLeese, D. (2002). *Susan B. Anthony.* Vero Beach, FL: Rourke.

Mike, J.M. (1997). *Chang and the tiger.* New York: Macmillan/McGraw-Hill.

Miranda, A. (1998). *The elephants have a house.* New York: Macmillan/McGraw-Hill.

Miranda, A. (1998). *In the jungle.* New York: Macmillan/McGraw-Hill.

Oram, H. (2004). *Why bears have short tails.* Oxford, UK: Rigby.

Osborne, M.P. (1995). *Afternoon on the Amazon.* New York: Random House.

Park, B. (1993). *Junie B. Jones and a little monkey business.* New York: Random House.

Paterson, K. (1977). *Bridge to Terabithia.* New York: HarperCollins.

Phillips, J. (1986). *Tiger is a scaredy cat.* New York: Random House.

Piper, W. (1991). *The little engine that could.* New York: Platt & Munk.

Randell, B. (2001). *Little Chimp and the termites.* Austin, TX: Harcourt.

Randell, B. (2006). *Baby hippo.* Austin, TX: Harcourt.

Randell, B. (2006). *The lion and the mouse.* Austin, TX: Harcourt.

Ransom, C. (2003). *Liberty Street.* New York: Walker.

Rosen, M. (2009). *We're going on a bear hunt.* New York: Margaret K. McElderry.

Ruffin, F.E. (2002). *Molly Pitcher.* New York: PowerKids.

Sharmat, M. (1980). *Gregory, the terrible eater.* New York: Scholastic.

Silverstein, S. (1964). *A giraffe and a half.* New York: HarperCollins.

Smith, A. (2004). *Tiger runs away.* Austin, TX: Harcourt.

Steck-Vaughn. (2002). *Frogs and toads.* Orlando, FL: Author.

Stott-Thornton, J. (1994). *Monkey and fire.* Orlando, FL: Rigby.

Trapani, I. (1993). *The itsy bitsy spider.* Watertown, MA: Charlesbridge.

Trumbauer, L. (2003). *Insect families.* Woodridge, IL: Shutterbug.

Vaughan, M. (1989). *Monkey's friends.* Auckland, New Zealand: Shortland.

Vaughan, M. (1996). *Jungle parade: A signing game.* Glenview, IL: Good Year.

Vaughan, M. (1997). *Whose tracks?* Persippany, NJ: Celebration.

Waldman, N. (2001). *They came from the Bronx: How the buffalo were saved from extinction.* Honesdale, PA: Boyds Mills.

Zane, R.M. (1998). *Happy monkeys.* New York: McGraw-Hill.

INDEX

Note. Page numbers followed by *f* and *t* indicate figures and tables, respectively.